ADVANCE PRAISE FOR

EARTH, ANIMAL, AND DISABILITY LIBERATION

"*Earth, Animal, and Disability Liberation: The Rise of the Eco-Ability Movement* is a trenchant analysis of normalcy, ableism, and civilization in the manner of eco-feminism, critical studies of eco-racism, and eco-colonialism. For anyone looking for an intelligent and coherent discussion of the emerging field of study, this book will be an exciting, and surprising, experience."

—Susan Thomas, Associate Professor of Gender and Women's Studies and Political Science, Hollins University, Virginia

"Nocella, Bentley, and Duncan finally bring three of the largest marginalized communities in the world to the center and stress their value philosophically, holistically, and socially. This volume is sure to break new ground in the field of critical animal studies, environmental education, and disability studies. Truly one of the most radical cutting-edge social justice books to come out in recent years!"

—Renee L. Wonser, Center for Global Environmental Education, Hamline University

"This ambitious and important book should be read, studied, debated, and referenced for years to come. The idea of eco-ability is a path-breaking and controversial concept that encourages a critical engagement with ecology, technology, and the myriad borders that contain and define so many of us within and across species. This book represents a clarion call for new ways of imagining and practicing mutually respectful relationships with all forms of life."

—David Naguib Pellow, Don Martindale Professor of Sociology, University of Minnesota, and co-author of *The Slums of Aspen: Immigrants vs. the Environment in America's Eden*

"Provocative and multi-disciplinary, *Earth, Animal, and Disability Liberation* is necessary justice reading for organizers and educators. Centering an intersectional analysis, this project brings us closer to understanding new relationships between disability and animal rights. Contributions push readers to think differently about 'normal,' the body, and most centrally, provide readers with radical visions for change."

—Erica R. Meiners, Professor of Education and Gender and Women's Studies at Northeastern Illinois University, and author of *Flaunt It! Queers Organizing for Public Education and Justice* and *Right to Be Hostile: Schools, Prisons, and the Making of Public Enemies*

EARTH, ANIMAL, AND DISABILITY LIBERATION

This book is part of the Peter Lang Education list.
Every volume is peer reviewed and meets
the highest quality standards for content and production.

PETER LANG
New York • Washington, D.C./Baltimore • Bern
Frankfurt • Berlin • Brussels • Vienna • Oxford

EARTH, ANIMAL, AND DISABILITY LIBERATION

the rise of the eco-ability movement

EDITED BY ANTHONY J. NOCELLA II
JUDY K.C. BENTLEY
JANET M. DUNCAN

PETER LANG
New York • Washington, D.C./Baltimore • Bern
Frankfurt • Berlin • Brussels • Vienna • Oxford

Library of Congress Cataloging-in-Publication Data

Earth, animal, and disability liberation: the rise of the eco-ability movement / edited by Anthony J. Nocella II, Judy K.C. Bentley, Janet M. Duncan.
p. cm.
Includes bibliographical references and index.
1. Sociology of disability. 2. People with disabilities. 3. Environmental sociology.
4. Environmentalism. 5. Animal welfare.
I. Nocella, Anthony J. II. Bentley, Judy K. C. III. Duncan, Janet M.
HV1568.E27 304.2—dc23 2012032446
ISBN 978-1-4331-1507-3 (hardcover)
ISBN 978-1-4331-1506-6 (paperback)
ISBN 978-1-4539-0876-1 (e-book)

Bibliographic information published by **Die Deutsche Nationalbibliothek.**
Die Deutsche Nationalbibliothek lists this publication in the "Deutsche Nationalbibliografie"; detailed bibliographic data is available on the Internet at http://dnb.d-nb.de/.

The paper in this book meets the guidelines for permanence and durability of the Committee on Production Guidelines for Book Longevity of the Council of Library Resources.

29 Broadway, 18th floor, New York, NY 10006
www.peterlang.com

Printed in the United States of America

This book is dedicated to all life that has been murdered, tortured, exploited, in the name of being different from the norm, nonhuman, and wild—and to those who fight against constructed normalcy, speciesism, and ecological destruction.

Contents

Acknowledgments

Acknowledgments are so important because it is impossible to be here or do anything on this planet without the support of others. We—Anthony, Judy, and Janet—would like to thank first and foremost Connie, Justin, and everyone at Peter Lang, especially Chris Myers, Bernadette Shade, and Stephen Mazur. We would also like to thank Julie Andrzejewski for writing a wonderful foreword to the book, and all the contributors of the book, Robin M. Smith, Jack P. Manno, Amber George, Sarat Colling, A. J. Withers, Bill Lindquist, Anna Grimm, Alessandro Arrigoni, Deanna Adams, Kimberly Socha, Lynn Anderson, Vicki Wilkins, Laurie Penney-McGee, Carrie Griffin Basas, Norm Phelps, and David Nibert, for if they were not involved, this book would not be possible. We would also like to thank, in no particular order, Zack Furness, Leslie James Pickering, Corey Lewis, Diane R. Wiener, Susan Thomas, Renee L. Wonser, David Pellow, Erica Meiners, John Alessio, and Jason Del Gandio, who have supported this book by reviewing it. We would finally like to thank our families and our many friends, colleagues, universities, centers, institutes, and organizations.

Judy K. C. Bentley: I would like to thank all the human and nonhuman animals it has been my great honor and privilege to know and live among, and in particular my son, Toby; my coeditors and colleagues, Anthony and Janet; a dog named Clyde; and my students at SUNY Cortland, all of whom give me faith and inspiration in the future of eco-ability, education, and social justice.

JANET DUNCAN: I would like to thank my friend and mentor, Peter Knoblock, and my dear friends, Sue and Bob Lehr. At SUNY Cortland, colleagues in the Foundations and Social Advocacy Department, the Inclusive Recreation Resource Center, and the Institute for Disability Studies were invaluable in providing critical analysis when needed. The student organizations, Cortland Animal Allies, and Meeting Advocacy with Disability, under the leadership of Ashley Mosgrove, were instrumental in helping others think about these issues on campus. The people in my personal life who kept the momentum going for the project, and who inspire me daily, are my husband, Robert Alexander, son Evan, and Wally. A special thanks to my father-in-law, Dr. Maurice Alexander, who was one of the original ecologists at SUNY ESF, "back in the day," before it was cool and mainstream.

ANTHONY J. NOCELLA II: I would first like to thank my family, who always say they come last in every acknowledgment of mine. Next I would like to thank Janet and Judy for being amazing friends and coeditors of this great, important, critical book. I would also like to thank my advisors, Peter Castro, Richard Loder, Micere Mugo, Tucker Culbertson, Piers Beirne, Kishi Ducre, Barbara Applebaum, and Dalia Rodriguez at Syracuse University. I would also like to thank all of my friends and colleagues at SUNY Cortland and Le Moyne College for their support and care. I would like to thank everyone with Save the Kids in and outside the walls of detention facilities; everyone with the Institute for Critical Animal Studies, especially the board members, Susan Thomas, Carolyn Drew, Sarat Colling, Amber Gilewski, Stephanie Jenkins, Helena Pedersen, Les Mitchell, Colin Salter, Vasile Stanescu, Nicola Taylor, Richard Twine, Richard White, Felipe Andrusco, Kimberly Socha, and Dylan Powell; everyone with the Central New York Peace Studies Consortium, the *Peace Studies Journal,* the *Journal for Critical Animal Studies*, the *Journal for Critical Urban Education*, the Center for Excellence in Urban Teaching, the Institute for Hip Hop Knowledge, Hillbrook Youth Detention Facility, Hamline University, and of course the Hamline School of Education. Finally, my friends, in no particular order, Ernesto Aguilar, Josh Baker, Mecke Nagel, Donald Easton-Brooks, Matt Hernandez, Lara Drew, Laura Shields, Jay Grims, Alma Williams, Kevin Beacham, Naomi Taylor, Jean Strait, Rachel Endo, Frank Hernandez, Tessa Tiogress, Moses Jame, Stephanie Robinson, Taylor Andrew, Peter McLaren, Brian Trautman, Liat Ben-Moshe, Don Sawyer, Daniel Hodge, James Czarniak, Jackie Denero, Catherine Garrone, and Hasan Stephens. I would like to especially remember and thank my late best friend and roommate loved by many, Kevin Pieluszczak.

Foreword

Julie Andrzejewski

Every day alternative, nonprofit press sites post urgent warnings from reputable and documentable sources about worsening conditions of various ecologies of the earth: the acidification of the oceans, the release of methane by the melting of permafrost, the massive vortices of plastic garbage expanding in many oceans, contaminated food created by genetically engineered plants, the toxic and radioactive legacy of contemporary warfare, and the list goes on. Similarly, every day alternative publications bring news of increasing inequalities, social injustices, and violence experienced by many of the world's communities and peoples: aggressive wars of domination and exploitation, extreme poverty and desperation, global food and water shortages, systematic life advantages or disadvantages based on physical, cultural, or behavioral characteristics, and more. Much more irregularly, such sites expose systemic atrocities against other animals and life forms: the violence and abuse of factory farming, the emptying of the oceans by massive trawlers, the shocking and rapid mass extinction of species.

Very few of these crucial pieces of information are published in the corporate-owned press, where owners and directors are busy protecting the profits of the wealthy and their corporations. Because acts of censorship and heavily funded propaganda campaigns deny or raise doubts about such alarming developments, the damaging but profitable policies creating these conditions continue unchallenged by the mainstream, uninformed public. Even fewer articles and publications attempt to critically analyze how these trends, events, and policies are integrally related by underlying agendas and actions of the economic and political elites.

Fortunately, some activists and scholars are forging ahead to study, investigate, and act on the junctures of justice for humans, other animals, and the earth. Working at the frontiers of what at first may appear to be disparate movements of social and environmental justice, the authors of *Earth, Animal and Disability Liberation: The Emergence of the Eco-Ability Movement* spotlight the root causes of contemporary global subjugation and exploitation. The authors critically dissect disciplinary hegemonies that have created "versions of the truth" used to manufacture social conformity to constructed ideologies of what is "normal" and "natural."

These pages unveil previously unexamined facets of the life- and earth-threatening consequences of the insidious activities of advanced industrial capitalism and the links between the commoditization and domination of people with disabilities, nonhuman animals, and non-sentient life. In *Earth, Animal and Disability Liberation: The Emergence of the Eco-Ability Movement* the authors challenge layers of concealed "hierarchies of worth" in the human/other animal, ability/disability, "civilization"/nature, uniformity/diversity binaries. They expose and connect manipulative endeavors to dominate, control, and profit, such as the Project Fishbowl, behavior modification, eugenics, the promotion of "meat"-eating, counterinsurgency programs, vivisection, free-trade agreements, shock treatments, monocultures, and more. They demonstrate how the causes of these severe problems and the activism needed to reverse and alleviate them (where possible) are, in fact, not disparate but intimately and fundamentally joined.

Earth, Animal and Disability Liberation: The Emergence of the Eco-Ability Movement is the first book to excavate and scrutinize the intersections of these crucial issues, along with important connections to race, class, and gender. This ovular work will help forge the basis for innovative activism when nonelite humans take the initiative to generate profound changes in human thinking, institutions, actions, and lifestyles.

INTRODUCTION

The Rise of Eco-Ability

Anthony J. Nocella II, Judy K. C. Bentley, and Janet M. Duncan

A positive and proactive field of scholarship would truly embrace differing abilities and a theory of ability; hence the notion of developing ability studies and doing away with the concept of disability or dis-ability makes the most sense. To understand one's ability or dis-ability, we must also see the similarities and how the two are directly related. One has abilities because of one's particular physical and/or intellectual capabilities, technological assistance, or society's respect for a particular inclusion of a group. When a group is not accepted, or an individual is unable to utilize (access) something such as a computer, it is external factors in the environment that lead them to become "disabled." Where ecology meets ability, human and nonhuman animals and nature are seen as truly diverse and interdependent—not equal, but different—in the most liberating sense of the word.

Ecology Meets Ability

Eco-ability interrogates normalcy, ableism, and civilization, in the manner of eco-feminism (Gaard, 1993), critical scholarship on eco-racism (Bullard, 1993), and eco-colonialism (Best & Nocella, 2006), which are social manifestations of oppression and domination, rooted in patriarchy, racism, and colonization. Similar to the field of eco-feminism that rose out of the feminist and deep ecology movements in the early 1970s and critiqued patriarchal domination of nature, nonhuman animals, and women (Warren & Erkal, 1997), *eco-ability* arose out of the animal advocacy, environmental, and disability rights movements, to challenge domination of normalcy, competition, and individualism. Eco-ability challenges ableism and normalcy within the environmental movement. Eco-ability advocates for a new understanding of nature as diverse and interdependent, with each part, regardless of size, function, or impact, having a valued role to play. Life is not about the *survival of the fittest*, as if one were the only resident of an island, or a social Darwinian notion of competition, where there is a winner and a loser. Rather, we must recognize how the bio-community promotes a win-win situation instead of the win-lose relationship with other species. In contrast, humans have for centuries disregarded nature as a force to honor, support, and value, resulting in the destruction of countless species and biomes. Eco-ability is derived from the concept that the survival of humans, nonhuman animals, and the biosphere as interdependent forces is of greater importance.

When a natural disaster or massive oil spill by a corporation (such as British Petroleum) in the Gulf Coast off the United States wipes one species off this planet, that extinction and event affect us all. The theory of eco-ability employs the concept of the web of life, which stresses that all are unique with differing abilities (e.g., flying, walking, swimming, slithering, and jumping). Interrelationships, interconnectedness, and interdependence must be respected and valued. Respect means understanding and valuing the needs of another being or element because it liberates, frees, and completes one's self. Respect is greatly different from tolerance, or acceptance, which arise from places of domination. Tolerance is the act of not wanting someone in a specific place but managing to act in a way that does not physically force the person out of that place (by trying to fire them, beat them, or verbally insult them). Acceptance is too often an act of approving of someone's presence or existence, while having ownership and domination over the place.

In contrast, within an eco-ability perspective, respect is mutual for all parties involved, and not simply for the *Other* that is being referred to. We must respect all for their value toward the larger bio-community and strive for global inclusion. The term, *global inclusion* has taken on new meanings as part of a lexicon for global trade, international development, and, in many ways, is co-opted by transnational corporations as part of doing business. Here, global inclusion is a critical theory that is more of a process and a perspective than a state of being, one that is continuously challenging the notion of community and the barriers, borders, and boundaries we construct. These barriers, borders, and boundaries foster a devaluing and exclusionary relationship to others, found, for example, in the many urban parks, apartments, schools, and public transportation vehicles that do not allow dogs and other nonhuman animals. Hence, when we employ universal design toward a school, park, or company to challenge ableism and speciesism, we must welcome plants and nonhuman animals. The Center for Universal Design at North Carolina State University defines universal design as, "the idea that all new environments and products, to the greatest extent possible, should be usable by everyone regardless of their age, ability, or circumstance" (2010, para. 1).

The traditional field of special education developed in response to fixing, curing, and rehabilitating people with disabilities, at a time when little, if any, care was provided to people and their families. At the time, this "service" was helpful as a first stage toward tolerance in society. Still, this treatment was ableist in focus: if you can endure physical therapy you might be able to walk; if you practice penmanship long enough you can write; if you can learn self-help skills you might be able to live independently.

In the early 1970s Wolf Wolfensberger (1972) proposed a theory of "normalization," suggesting that people with disabilities should lead as normal a life as possible, with assistance from caregivers. This theory evolved, too, with a recognition that in order for people to lead normal lives, they also had to play socially valued roles in society. This thinking removed people with disabilities from a charity model toward an acceptance in society. With school mainstreaming efforts, followed by school integration of students with disabilities, and now inclusive education, the field of special education has evolved toward inclusive practices.

The field of disability studies developed from the sociological examination of people with disabilities in society, which had been based on the concept of deviance in sociological studies. Early on, Bogdan and Taylor (1987) challenged this notion of deviance, once accepted as a truth, and posited the corollary: people with disabilities are accepted in their communities, with many examples of love, compassion, and inclusion.

Still, the field of disability studies evolves, in keeping with academic fields such as critical theory, feminism, environmentalism, and animal rights. Scholarship in disability studies today focuses on the power relationships in society between and among people with disabilities, the struggles for acceptance, self-advocacy, and finding a place within society. As in all fields of study, there are several points of view and perspectives to appreciate. In this book, eco-ability stresses the socially valued roles people with disabilities play, and, further, that society needs to embrace difference in ability as a continuum of the human condition.

One of the few arguments made to discuss the complex connections between the two (ecology and people with disabilities) was during a panel Dr. Nocella co-organized with Dr. Judy K. C. Bentley at the Peace Studies Conference hosted by the Central New York Peace Studies Consortium in 2007, at SUNY Cortland. In one of the papers presented on the panel, "Disability Studies and the Social Construction of Environments," Dr. Robin M. Smith and Dr. Jack P. Manno stressed that disability, as well as the environment, is a social constructions developed through relationships, noting: "These relationships are institutional, cultural, and interpersonal social structures" (Smith & Manno, 2008, p. 2). They went on to write, citing Manno (2000):

> The social construct "environment" is defined through a web of socio-economic relationships that privileges commodities over relationships, where a tree is regarded far more as timber and paper pulp than as oxygen producer, shelter for beings, builder of soil or the many other roles it plays in a complex set of ecosystem relationships (Manno, 2000). (Smith & Manno, 2008, p. 3)

Rather than being recognized as members of a large and complex eco-community, domesticated animals such as cows, monkeys, and horses are viewed by human society as mere resources to be exploited for profit. This is promoted in the ideological interests of capital, according to which people are either producers or consumers.

Capitalists and Marxists view people with disabilities as limited consumers (as a purchasing power group) and producers, never able to be useful enough to be part of the serious means of production. On the contrary, people with disabilities are significant consumers of medicine, technology, and goods. Just as green anarchists view people with disabilities as a liability to a self-sustaining community, capitalists devalue the role of these individuals as consumers. While important in the relationship of consumer and producer, this notion also needs critique because much of the medicine produced is tested on nonhuman animals, and the production of it causes a great amount of pollution, not to mention pain. Further, the medicine that is produced often has adverse effects and is highly addictive, causing the user to become dependent.

Therefore, not only the disability community but much of the world that uses corporate-produced medicine should look for organic, natural alternatives, which are sometimes proven to be more effective and do not support the medical-industrial complex. The reason many of these natural medicines, such as herbs, are not promoted is because corporate medical doctors are: (a) not knowledgeable about or trained in natural medicines; thus, they claim they are not affective; (b) entangled in economic commitments or interests with Big Pharma, discrediting alternative medicine; and/or (c) susceptible to the social and peer pressures of supporting medical traditions, which include vivisection—the testing of nonhuman animals for medicine, cleaning products, and experimentation for comparative human surgery in medical schools.

Eco-ability argues for the respect of difference and diversity, challenging social constructions of what is considered normal and equal. Eco-ability also challenges labels and categories that divide and separate rather than unify and collaborate.

Eco-ability respects imperfection and the value of "flaws." Perfection suggests an imaginary ideal of flawlessness. But everyone can be perceived through the eco-ability lens as unique and valuable. Perfection and purity are ideals that "normalized" society believes it is necessary and possible to achieve. Perfection and purity are notions that the Nazis strived for but did not recognize. Rather, perfection and purity already exist, in diversity. Difference was, and is, the essential ingredient for human and global survival.

By erecting a standard of normalcy, society devalues diversity. While technology can be a wonderful tool, some technology destroys at the expense of difference, such as by making a paved path through a forest to accommodate everyone instead of making a wheelchair that is meant for off-road use or admitting that some people simply cannot go down that path. Not everyone can climb Mount Everest, but that does not mean we need to make a road to the top. While some environmentalists believe that society should destroy urban areas, and that technology is the cause of ecological destruction, others argue that going back to a primitive lifestyle would cause a mass amount of waste and wear on the ecological system. Eco-ability is not about going back and romanticizing the past but about building a sustainable future void of exploitation of all life and elements by systems of domination.

Inclusion means access and full participation with support, which might involve allowing others to have technological assistance, such as wheelchairs, glasses, or custom computer software. It is important to point out the difference between technological tools that allow one to be included, and technology that is globally destructive to the bio-community, such as bombs. This is not to say that computers, cell phones, and other forms of technology do not have destructive impacts. They do, and they should be challenged. But there is also a great deal of technology that can be phased out first before there is a full boycott on all electronic devices, even if we consider such a boycott helpful. This chapter is just posing dramatic contrasts; there is a much more nuanced argument to be made. Technology, broadly stated, has revolutionized the lives of people with disabilities through social media, communication, and accessibility. It diminishes the argument about wearing glasses versus making bombs.

Inclusion also means giving up power, and challenging all forms of domination, therefore resisting gatekeeper terms such as "accept," "tolerate," "allow," "approve," and "permit." The unchecked desire for technology is a slippery slope that can cause a destructive rippling effect, but we would argue that tools can be a very beneficial part of the bio-community today. For example, instead of flying to conferences in Europe or across the United States, one can use Skype on the Internet to provide presentations, which eliminates the travel carbon footprint. As we are caught in a life of hypocrisy with our use of and reliance on potentially destructive technologies, we must do our best to minimize the ecological impact we make. If we do utilize electronic devices, we must use them to make the world a better place. The most difficult part of figuring out this ethical equation is acknowledging that inclusion is determined by the dominator. The dominator is a sociopolitical, economic, and ecological gatekeeper, determining who is included and who is not.

This decision comes with great ignorance. For example, it is only recently that social justice movements have called for the inclusion of people of color, people with disabilities, women, children, and nonhuman animals. Social justice activists and the oppressed fight to remove barriers, borders, and boundaries that exclude those who are dominated, while dominators consciously and ignorantly support and construct oppressive tools of division. To deconstruct these exclusionary structures, institutions, systems, and tools we must critically examine, resist, dismantle, and transform the global community.

We must move forward rather than backward, utilizing renewable eco-technology and nonpolluting resources. Unfortunately, corporations and governments have promoted destructive technologies through "green-washing," while their domination is globalized through industrialization, institutionalization, civilization, and capitalism (Tokar, 1997). Eco-ability is against genetically modified organisms (GMOs) and other science, technologies, and theories that control and manipulate life, a stance that is shared with green anarchists (Best & Nocella, 2006). Eco-ability favors respect and inclusive change, rather than conservationism, which frames the ecosystem as resources and property. Eco-ability is rooted in anarchist principles that oppose competition, domination, and authoritarianism (Ben-Moshe, Hill, Nocella, & Templer, 2009). The development of sustainable technology and resources must be implemented from a nonhierarchical community in which everyone recognizes the interests of all—human and nonhuman—as a priority over personal profit.

Some technology has the potential, if used to advance peace, to give people opportunities to reduce fossil fuel use and clear-cutting. Technology can also aid a person to read a book, walk across the street, roll to class, and see birds in the air. Such progress toward human simplicity—a decrease in consumption and materialism—and global sustainability cannot be advanced through acts of domination such as testing on fellow humans, nonhuman species, or ecological communities. Eco-ability argues for social transformation away from acts of domination and towards compassion. There is no need to imprison fellow humans to teach a lesson, drop bombs on other countries for freedom, or put chemicals in the eyes of animals to protect humans from illness.

Vivisection, testing, experimentation, and dissection dominate, divide, and create a false construction of social and ecological individualism, emphasizing our nonhuman, nonanimal, and nonnatural identities. Assisting dis-ability through technology allows us to be self-reliant and reinforces that dis-ability is a valued quality, which should be respected and praised. This assistance stresses the ecological importance of interdependency on which the life system is based but which, throughout human history, we have been moving away from seemingly as fast as we can.

Synopsis of Book

Developing the intersectional theory of eco-ability was no easy task. The book began with a simple task of bringing animal advocacy together with disability rights and studies. But we found the goal of merging the two groups to be limiting and not articulating fully the perspective of what we were arguing for. It was then that we understood the need to include the ecological world in this dialogue, and it was then that the concept of eco-ability was born. This book was difficult to put together for two major reasons. First, it was difficult to find contributors for the book who made the connections of the three groups in their lives; and second, some people in the book, who in their lives connected the three groups together, never wrote about it. Once we found all the contributors, we felt confident that each contributor would approach this intersectional social justice topic differently, because no one had done it before. We found out that the authors did approach eco-ability from varied perspectives. The editors only asked the contributors to argue for the dismantling of systems of domination, discuss all three marginalized groups within the chapter, and support the understanding that all are interdependent, and that difference must be respected. It is difference that keeps the ecological, social, and political worlds balanced. Equality, sameness, normal, and average are measurements that promote social construction.

In Chapter One, Anthony J. Nocella II introduces the concept of eco-ability: the interrogation of normalcy, ableism, and civilization as a social manifestation of oppression and domination. Eco-ability advocates for understanding how nature is diverse and interdependent—not equal, but different.

In Chapter Two, Judy K. C. Bentley constructs a Foucauldian genealogy of toxicity, exposing the intersectionality of ableism, speciesism, and Bullard's "environmental racism," for the purpose of challenging entrenched thoughts and practices that construct oppressive boundaries between human animals with and without disabilities, nonhuman animals, and nature.

In Chapter Three, Janet M. Duncan explores the interdependence, capability, and presumed competence of human "disability," nonhuman animals, and the environment, as a framework for eco-ability, blending common issues and imagining a positive relationship among all three, which is mutually beneficial and enhances the conditions of all.

In Chapter Four, Robin M. Smith and Jack P. Manno present critical perspectives on Disability Studies and the social construction of environments, explicating the effects of commoditization on society and nature. Jack shows that it is not just nature that needs to be healed but society's relations to it. Robin shows that it is not the disabled that need fixing but the relationship between disability and society.

In Chapter Five, Amber George focuses a critical lens on two Disney films, *Dumbo* and *Finding Nemo*, to expose the perpetuation of ableism, speciesism, anthropocentrism, and the reinforcement by the Hollywood Industrial Complex of the binaries of ability versus disability, human versus nonhuman animals, and nature versus civilization.

In Chapter Six, Sarat Colling offers a transnational feminist and eco-ability framework to address the oppressive borders that strengthen the hegemony of global capitalism and the humanist subject, borders that are policed by force. She notes the importance of recognizing difference, while building solidarity, working across, and transcending those borders.

In Chapter Seven, A. J. Withers exposes examples of disableism engaged in by animal advocates, environmentalists, environmental justice advocates, and anarcho-primitivists, and explains disability as an oppressive political identity imposed on people who are considered unfit or less fit, unproductive, or under-productive.

In Chapter Eight, Bill Lindquist and Anna Grimm examine the impact of healing relationships between human and nonhuman animals and the natural world, drawing on case studies from PEACE Ranch, a faith-based, therapeutic environment that brings rescued horses together with human animals who are also in need of rescue. They apply this knowledge toward building symbiotic partnerships with the biotic community in urban classrooms.

In Chapter Nine, Alessandro Arrigoni draws on personal experience to delineate the discrimination against persons with disabilities in present-day Italy. He describes the issues related to the discrimination against and oppression of Italian citizens with disabilities and the treatment of nonhuman species within the environmental context.

In Chapter Ten, Deanna Adams and Kimberly Socha consider the connection between the use of aversive behavior modification techniques based on the works of B. F. Skinner and Ivan P. Pavlov, which are used in the training of animals, and the use of such techniques on people with disabilities such as autism, intellectual disabilities, and emotional or behavioral disorders. The broader implications of these control methods on the presumably insentient natural world are also explored.

In Chapter Eleven, Lynn Anderson, Vicki Wilkins, and Laurie Penney-McGee offer insights into the accessibility and inclusivity of parks and playgrounds, neighborhoods, and communities. They promote a fully just society through their unique Inclusion U training program, designed to capitalize on facilitators and minimize barriers to inclusive recreation services for people with disabilities and their families and friends.

In Chapter Twelve, Carrie Griffin Basas analyzes legislation and litigation, and what it does for people with disabilities, and nonhuman animals. She finds that when privacy is taken into account with regard to the issues faced by people with disabilities and nonhuman animals, it is used to protect the decisions of people without disabilities acting with force toward, and dominating over, the human and nonhuman animals the laws are designed to protect. She notes that the disabling language of dominant cultural narratives colors all experiences that cause discomfort for people with power over the fates of nonhuman animals and disabled people.

In Chapter Thirteen, Norm Phelps proposes the true fulfillment of a system of totally egalitarian, Infinite Ethics, first envisioned by the great sages of the Axial Age, including Confucius, LaoZi, Mahavira, and the Buddha. He traces the oldest (and still most widespread) exclusionary system of ethics to ancient times and argues that the world is still divided into "Us and Them," those who are entitled to the protections and benefits of society and those who are not.

In Chapter Fourteen, David Nibert presents a sociohistory of oppression as it manifests in the socially constructed economic value of persons with developmental disabilities, nonhuman animals, and the environment. He argues that, as U.S. and global capitalists promote a doubling of the consumption of products derived from animals in the next 40 years, increasing numbers of animals and people around the world will suffer. People in poor nations will face food shortages and will be highly vulnerable to international conflict and violence from the struggle to control finite resources in an era of climate change, drought, and increasingly severe weather.

In Chapter Fifteen, Anthony J. Nocella II deconstructs the present environmental movement and challenges its ableist context. He shows how disability is sociopolitical and economically constructed to benefit normalcy, sameness, equality, and average, rather than difference, noting that eco-ability calls for a new path to protect and live in the world. He argues that the environmental movement and environmental studies are rooted in domination, purification, and normalcy of the ecological world.

This book is a call to everyone around the world to challenge their language, perspective, politics, and location that perpetuates normalcy, speciesism, and domestication. This book argues that nothing is the same or equal, but that all are different, and it is that difference that allows all life to be in balance.

While corporations, science, and medicine see difference as flaws, blemishes, anomalies, and oddities, labeling as freakish, weird, strange, and a problem characteristics that make us all (from trees, birds, rivers, and humans to fish) who we are, we should rather respect and embrace these variations as delightfully unique. Science, medicine, school, religion, government, society, media, and all other industrial complexes were developed to construct a normal, and, if possible, perfect product, person, or plant. This book argues that all life and elements on this planet and beyond are interwoven and interdependent on one another. The contributors and editors are not interested in formulating a philosophical, jargon-based theory but instead seek to advance a radical, intersectional, multi-based, social justice movement that argues for liberation for nonhuman animals, those with dis-abilities, and the Earth. Eco-ability is a movement demanding justice for all those that are dominated and oppressed, advocating for a world that is inclusive of the differences of everyone and everything.

References

Ben-Moshe, L., Hill, D., Nocella II, A. J., & Templer, B. (2009). Dis-abling capitalism and an anarchism of 'radical equality' in resistance to ideologies of normalcy. In R. Amster, A. DeLeon, L. Fernandez, A. J. Nocella II, & D. Shannon, (Eds.), *Contemporary anarchist studies: An introductory anthology of anarchy in the academy* (pp. 113–122). New York, NY: Routledge.

Best, S., & Nocella II., A. J. (2006). *Igniting a revolution: Voices in defense of the earth*. Oakland, CA: AK Press.

Bogdan, R., & Taylor, S. J. (1987). Toward a sociology of acceptance: The other side of the study of deviance. *Social Policy*, *18*(2), 34–39.

Bullard, R. D. (Ed.). (1993). *Confronting environmental racism: Voices from the grassroots*. Boston, MA: South End Press.

The Center for Universal Design at North Carolina State University. (2010). About. Retrieved from http://www.ncsu.edu/project/design-projects/udi/center-for-universal-design/

Davis, L. J. (2002). *Bending over backwards: Disability, dismodernism & other difficult positions*. New York, NY: New York University Press.

Gaard, G. C. (1993). *Ecofeminism: Women, animals, nature*. Philadelphia, PA: Temple University Press.

Manno, J. (2000). *Privileged goods: Commoditization and its impact on environment and society* (Ecological Economics Series). Boca Raton, FL: Lewis.

Smith, R., & Manno, J. P. (2008). Disability studies and the social construction of environments. *Social Advocacy and Systems Change*, *1*(1), 1–5. Retrieved from http://www.cortland.edu/ids/sasc/vol1_issue1/index.html

Tokar, B. (1997). *Earth for sale: Reclaiming ecology in the age of corporate greenwash*. Boston, MA: South End Press.

Warren, K. J., & Erkal, N. (Eds.). (1997). *Ecofeminism: Women, culture, nature*. Bloomington, IN: Indiana University Press.

Wolfensberger, W. (1972). *The principle of normalization in human services*. Toronto, Canada: National Institute on Mental Retardation.

PART I

Pedagogy

CHAPTER ONE

Defining Eco-Ability

Social Justice and the Intersectionality of Disability, Nonhuman Animals, and Ecology

Anthony J. Nocella II

Introduction[1]

This is the first book to connect ecology, dis-ability, and animal advocacy, couched in terms of interlocking social constructions and the interwoven web of interdependent global life. Both concepts of "*the natural world*" and "*disability*" will be viewed as socially constructed entities. I suggest that for the current global ecological crisis to transform into a more sustainable global community, including nonhuman animals, the field of environmental studies needs to engage in a discussion of colonization and domination of the environment. Next, I explain and deconstruct the meaning of disability while critically examining environmentalism and environmental studies from an antioppression perspective. Finally, I demonstrate how dis-ability studies can take a position on the current ecological crisis, showing that dis-ability theory, animal advocacy, and ecology can be brought together in a philosophy of *eco-ability*. Eco-ability combines the concepts of interdependency, inclusion, and respect for difference within a community; and this includes *all* life, sentient and nonsentient.

Crisis of Ecological Domination and Normalcy

"Voice for the voiceless" is a saying that has been used repeatedly by dis-ability rights activists, environmentalists, and animal advocates. These traditionally oppressed groups—nonhuman animals, people with disabilities, and the ecological world—have much in common, and have arguably been marginalized more than any other segment of society. In today's colonized and capitalist-driven world, one of the worst things is to be considered or called an "animal," "wild," or a "freak" (Snyder & Mitchell, 2006). If one is not recognized as human by "normal society," that person is either an animal or disabled, as was the case for women and people of color less than fifty years ago, who were also once identified by law as property. Between the 17th and early 20th centuries, the predominantly white patriarchal scientists, using the racist, sexist, and ableist theory of eugenics, claimed that women and people of color had smaller brains, were "by Nature" less intelligent, psychiatrically inferior to men (labels such as "hysterical" were applied), and less than human. As Snyder and Mitchell explained,

> American eugenics laid bare the social and national goals newly claimed for medical practices. It promised an empirically sound, cross-disciplinary arena for identifying 'defectives' viewed as a threat to the purity of a modern nation-state. Turn-of-the-century diagnosticians came to rely on the value of bureaucratic surveillance tools, such as census data, medical catalogues, and intelligence testing. (p. 74)

With this mindset established, from the early 1870s onward, the rise of strategic, repressive, and pathologically medical categorization of those with mental disabilities or perceived inferior physical attributes (especially among the poor) permitted new immigration officials to deny any person with an assumed mental dis-ability entrance into the US. Next came the incarceration and institutionalization of those within the country and finally came the testing, medical experimentation, and killing of them in the name of purification (Snyder & Mitchell, 2006). The institutionalization of and Nazi experimentation on those with dis-abilities was a little-known mass genocide in the name of genetic purity and perceived normalcy promoted by the medical field (Snyder & Mitchell, 2006). Striving for a genetically and psychologically pure society was the taken-for-granted, popular view of scientists at the turn of the 20th century (Dowbiggin, 2003). The rise of intelligence testing by Binet (Binet & Simon, 1916/1973) gave scientists the "tool" to officially determine a person's competence.

In contrast, while Western colonial science constructs a "perfect norm," some theories of ecology argue that everyone and everything are interdependent and diverse, and that there exists no "norm" or "normal." The inherent philosophy within the natural world is that the environment strives to be in harmony and balance. The ecological world, or biosphere, is itself an argument for respecting differing abilities and the uniqueness of all living beings. Moreover, humans as a species are a part of the "animal kingdom" and nature, rather than separate and dominant. Ecofeminists, environmental justice scholars and activists, and environmental revolutionaries represent the antithesis of genocidal thought. They foster an appreciation and love of difference and mutual aid rather than a fetishization of sameness and individualism (Best & Nocella, 2006).

Eco-ability, a concept that I developed and explore in this book for the first time, is a philosophy that respects differences in abilities while promoting values appropriate to the stewardship of ecosystems. Eco-ability is in its infancy as a concept, and I encourage further dialogue and discussion of its implications. At this point, a basic understanding will suffice.

Dis-ability studies as a discipline also praises difference, uniqueness, and interdependency. Dis-ability studies suggests that every being has differing abilities. Each being plays an important role in the global community and is valuable within the larger ecological context. Eco-ability respects differences while challenging the concepts of "equality," "sameness," and "normalcy." These concepts are social constructions that fail to respect the uniqueness of individual abilities and differences, which, as the ecological and dis-ability communities realize, are interdependent. Further, nature, nonhuman animals, and people with disabilities have been institutionalized, tortured, and murdered, not because they have committed a crime, or for profit, but for being recognized as different, and as a commodity. "Difference" is a threat to the advancement of normalcy, which is the philosophical foundation of social control and discipline (Pfohl, 2009).

The label, *different*, is important to eco-ability because it becomes an assumed descriptor within societal institutions, as the *5Ds of Stigmatization—demonized*, *deviant*, *delinquent*, *disabled*, and *dissenter*. If you are not labeled normal by society, you are inherently viewed as abnormal, a threat that must be controlled, disciplined, and punished. The history of repressing people with disabilities has always been a complex system of stigmatization of those who are different. Even to this day, some counselors, doctors, and religious leaders state that if an individual has committed a highly controversial act that challenges socioeconomic or political norms, that person is deemed to be evil, and is demonized in the news and official reports. Critical criminology shows that there is a slippery slope of when one is stigmatized as deviant by teachers or counselors. Police and judges can more easily stigmatize an individual as delinquent when they are arrested. After the individual is convicted and institutionalized, the person is put through rigorous examinations from doctors and psychologists who are determined to finally and permanently label the individual as someone having a disability.

How Did All This Begin in Western Society?

In Western civilization, the marginalization of those who are different was first fostered and reinforced by the concept of *civilization* and its divide between nature and humans. (This divide arguably began when human beings first began cultivating the land 10,000 years ago.) Those considered wild, savage, or primitive were situated on one side, with those considered civilized, privileged, and normal on the other. This corresponded to the ideological policy of foreign relations that Kees van der Pijl (2007) called "empire-nomad relations" (p. 24). In time, civilization took the further step of establishing state borders in what we know today as Europe, amidst the project of global conquest, which today we call "colonization." In addition to establishing an elitist, antinatural culture at home (i.e., civilization), the predominant goal of empires was to conquer, assimilate, or destroy every noncolonial-influenced culture. For example, non-Christian religious sites were destroyed in the New World, and Christian churches were built on top of them. Every popular religion attempted to assimilate others through religious domination (forced conversions) in addition to economic and cultural usurpation.

With European colonialism spreading across the world, an economic system that upheld the values of capitalism was created, placing a value on everything and everyone. For example, whites were more valuable than people of color, birds, trees, water, and even land. All of nature was viewed as a natural resource, a commodity, and typically marked as property—something owned by someone—to be used any which way its owners saw fit. Over time, everything, including people (such as slaves), had an inherent worth and was viewed as a commodity.

The concept of ownership of property, critiqued by anarchists (Amster, DeLeon, Fernandez, Nocella, & Shannon, 2009), created the haves and the have-nots. Societal classes were split between the owners and the working classes. With the establishment of natural resources as a commodity and ownership of goods, the producer-consumer relationship was forged. This symbiotic relationship was the foundation of the industrialized world that became dominant in 19th-century Europe and America. The primary economic system was supported by institutions, ostensibly developed to care for others and keep the public safe and the culture orderly. Similarly, "scientific" treatments to benefit the common good were developed and hailed as improvements in a society eager to become "modern" and civilized. Institutions such as colleges, prisons, hospitals, and religious centers, worked closely with political and educational systems to justify their existence. Violent acts such as experimentation, dissection, and vivisection toward people with disabilities, nonhuman animals, plants, water, and other elements were condoned as the foundation of modern advancements toward science and knowledge.

From Personal to Political

Beating, killing, imprisonment, surveillance, raids, and framing have been taking place since the creation of a class, race, and state divide established by the elite and reinforced by governments (Bodley, 2005). Faced with dark times, survival is often the only hope for victims, both humans and nonhumans, of repressive and controlling authoritarian structures. The oppressed typically do not think of speaking out, fighting back, writing their stories, or uniting together to share their experiences (Harding, 2003). They simply want to move on, endure, and live!

It took me four years to watch a video of myself being arrested. It was too emotional to relive. I was arrensted and searched by the Chief of Police in Corpus Christi, Texas, for an act of civil disobedience in protecting dolphins from captivity (which I argue is a prison). I was subsequently framed for felony charges of possession of crack cocaine with the intent to sell. The framing was strategic. I was lead organizer of a political campaign to keep dolphins out of a nonprofit entertainment and educational facility similar to Sea World. The facility was bringing in a lot of money to the city from tourists. Law enforcement needed to figure out how to stigmatize me and other activists, as arresting us was only bringing us more sympathy from the public and the media. They needed to stigmatize me and the campaign with something that would make people disregard our efforts. Marijuana, PCP, LSD, heroin, and other drugs, although vilified, do not have the universally negative image of crack cocaine, a drug stigmatized because of its political history. Crack cocaine was strategically placed into the Black community in the 1970s by government agencies, including the CIA, to destroy those communities (Schou, 2006; Scott & Marshall, 1998; Webb, 1999). It is an interesting coincidence, if it was a coincidence or a strategic act by law enforcement, that I was framed for crack cocaine for protesting dolphins in captivity in Texas, and crack cocaine was used to destroy the Black community. Since its inception, crack cocaine has been a powerful tool to destroy and repress political and social groups by U.S. law enforcement.

After my release from jail, I did not speak much to my friends about the incident, neither did I speak to the media or make buttons or stickers about my case. Rather, I kept fighting for the dolphins. Yes, people knew about my case, but they were mainly comprised of two types of people: activists who supported me, and the media and law enforcement personnel who portrayed me as a crack-selling, vegan dissenter needing to be silenced. I remember making one flyer relating the imprisonment of dolphins to my possible imprisonment, but I only produced a hundred copies. It was then that I understood that a prisoner is a prisoner is a prisoner, no matter if the prisoner is an elephant in a zoo, a human in Attica, a bird in a cage, or a dolphin in an aquarium.

No one spoke up to write my story; if someone had done so, I would have told him or her to focus on the dolphins. Now, upon further reflection, I realize that my case tells another story. It tells how everything is connected, and that when one fights against systems of domination and oppressive institutions, she or he will be repressed. Many others in the animal rights movement have been arrested on trumped-up charges, receiving ridiculous prison sentences and fines.

I, a Quaker and straightedge practitioner (someone who does not engage in illegal drugs, alcohol, or promiscuous sex), was among the first to be framed for something I did not do. As a result, I later received numerous calls from activists wondering what to do about being targeted by police. I provided them with this advice: (a) stick with your community and protect each other, and (b) tell your story, as I am doing now. It is through our shared experiences and knowledge that we build a stronger understanding of political repression and oppression from systems of domination.

The Stigmatization of Disability, the Inclusion of People with Disabilities in Society, and Animal Rights Rhetoric[2]

At a very young age (before first grade), I was diagnosed as having severe mental disabilities. This diagnosis resulted in my being directed to special education classes from first to fourth grade. It was a nightmare for me. I could neither read nor speak well. I shook all the time, and I had difficulty focusing my energy, both in the classroom and in general. At times, I would be held down or kicked out of class. The only wonderful relationship I had in those years was with my cat, Sparkle, who was my best friend and someone that I was able to communicate with emotionally in a humane manner. While I was still a child, Sparkle was killed by three dogs. It was that death that later inspired me to become highly involved in the animal rights movement. From fifth to twelfth grade, I went to a separate school for students with mental and learning disabilities. Both the classes in "normal" school and in the separate disability school represent segregation.

It is important to connect the social construction of ableism and speciesism. Ableism, a term created by activists with disabilities, is the discrimination against people with disabilities through promoting normalcy carried out through structural barriers, personal actions, and theories (Davis, 2002). Speciesism is discrimination against nonhuman animal species by arguing that humans are more important and superior to nonhuman animals (Dunayer, 2004). Both speciesism and ableism are social constructions interwoven into society, promoting civilization, normalcy, and intellectualism grounded in modernity, which arose out of the European Enlightenment period. Modernity is "a progressive force promising to liberate humankind from ignorance and irrationality" (Rosenau, 1992, p. 5). Therefore, the intellectual movement's goal was to create theory after theory to divide themselves from everything that was savage and what they would soon deem abnormal and deviant, i.e., nature, nonhuman animals, women, and people with disabilities. Snyder and Mitchell (2006) explained how the narrative of modernity was "key" to constructing disability as deviant and undesirable:

> Modernity gives birth to the culture of technology that promises more data from less input. This unique historical terrain is characterized by Bauman as "the morally elevating story of humanity emerging from pre-social barbarity" [Bauman, 2001, p. 12, as cited in Snyder & Mitchell, 2006]. This progressive narrative is key to the development of disability as a concept of deviant variation. In a culture that endlessly assures itself that it is on the verge of conquering Nature once and for all, along with its own "primitive" instincts and the persistent domain of the have-nots, disability is referenced with respect to these idealized visions. As a vector of human variability, disabled bodies both represent a throwback to human prehistory and serve as the barometer of a future without "deviancy."
>
> In other words, for modernity, the eradication of disability represented a scourge and a promise: its presence signaled a debauched present of cultural degeneration that was tending to regress toward a prior state of primitivism, while at the same time it seemed to promise that its absence would mark the completion of modernity as a cultural project (p. 31).

To challenge this movement of domination over nature, nonhuman animals, and disability, I united the three groups together to create the field of study called eco-ability. Eco-ability is the theory that nature, nonhuman animals, and people with disabilities promote collaboration, not competition; interdependency, not independence; and respect for difference and diversity, not sameness and normalcy.

Ben-Moshe stated that the value of people with disabilities sometimes falls between humans and nonhumans, but also, depending on their physical or mental disability, they may be viewed as less than nonhuman (personal communication, January 20, 2011). Many of us in the United States are familiar with the demeaning comments directed toward humans that are exploitative of nonhuman animals—"you are such a pig," "what are you, an animal?," "stop acting like a bitch," "you are such a dog," and "you are as fat as a whale." Similarly, people with disabilities are stigmatized and marginalized when those without disabilities are faced with insults such as the following: "you are so retarded," suggesting a person is not being cool; "you are such a freak," suggesting a person has uncommon sexual behaviors; "why are you acting so lame?" suggesting that a person is boring;

and "you are acting crazy," suggesting that a person is not in control of his or her actions (Snyder & Mitchell, 2006).

In U.S. culture, and even within social movements, we are used to homophobic, racist, classist, and sexist language. While those acts of oppression are important to address, this eco-ability focuses on addressing the stigmatization of nonhuman animals as property, activists as terrorists, and people with disabilities as abnormal or less than human.

For example, a connection between ableism and speciesism has recently become manifest in the animal advocacy movement, with the concept of being a "vegan freak." The term was first coined by Bob Torres and Jenna Torres, authors of *Vegan Freak: Being Vegan in a Non-Vegan World* (2010). Torres and Torres, both dedicated animal advocates and vegans, developed the title and term ironically to spotlight the social deviance of veganism as marginalized and "abnormal" behavior. Torres and Torres wrote,

> So, regardless of how "normal" you are, in a world where consuming animal products is the norm, you're always going to be seen as the freak if you obviously and clearly refuse to take part in an act of consumption that is central to our everyday lives, our cultures, and even our very own personal identities. (2010, p. 8)

Torres and Torres are social justice scholar-activists who, like most animal advocates who challenge the norm that veganism is an "oddity," do not critically address the use of the term, *freak*, or other ableist language. In the book, a possible example connecting animal advocacy and disability is the reference to Bob's disorganization when trying to plan ahead for navigating vegan cookery. Torres and Torres wrote, "If you're like Bob, planning ahead is something for organized people without ADHD, so it may strike you as incredibly dull" (2010, p. 33). This sentence, which was not critically unraveled in the book, suggests that people like Bob Torres who have ADHD are disorganized, and that being disorganized is somehow exciting. Further, because this sentence is not examined, it is not clear if Bob has ADHD or if the authors are simply making a common ableist "joke."

Freak is a term historically associated with those with disabilities. As defined by Robert Bogdan in *Freak Show* (1988), *freak* can refer to either (a) a "non-Western world then in progress" (Bogdan, 1988, p. 6), which brought back uncommon and unfamiliar descriptions of people and cultural traditions of indigenous groups; or (b) "the second major category of exhibit consisted of 'monsters,' the medical term for people born with a demonstrable difference," (Bogdan, 1988, p. 6), i.e., "freak of nature" (Bogdan, 1988, p. 6). Bogdan provided a summary of the human attitude toward people with physical disabilities (i.e., freaks, which he is critical of, but he used the term to examine its historical and social construction). He wrote,

> Our reaction to freaks is not a function of some deep-seated fear or some "energy" that they give off; it is, rather, the result of our socialization, and of the way our social institutions managed these people's identities. Freak shows are not about isolated individuals, either on platforms or in an audience. They are about organizations and patterned relationships between them and us. "Freak" is not a quality that belongs to the person on display. It is something that we created: a perspective, a set of practices—a social construction. (Bogdan, 1988, pp. x–xi)

Therefore, from an ableist perspective, there can be only two reasons that justify and explain someone being vegan: (a) veganism is a behavior that people with disabilities adopt, or (b) people become disabled when they adopt a vegan diet. Being a "vegan freak," however, is not the only ableist term in the animal advocacy movement, for we also have *moral schizophrenia* to consider. Introduced by Gary Francione, a law professor at Rutgers University, in his book, *Introduction to Animal Rights: Your Child or the Dog?* (2000), moral schizophrenia is the action of caring for nonhuman animals such as dogs and cats but also exploiting them for food, product testing, clothes, and entertainment. In short, moral schizophrenia is hypocrisy: saying one thing, but doing the complete opposite. Francione used the term, *schizophrenia*, not in a medical manner but to stigmatize those who do not support animal liberation. While most members of the animal advocacy movement agree with the term *and* the argument, there are a few that do not agree with the term but do agree with the argument. After a number of Internet critiques that Francione's use of the term, *schizophrenia*, is ableist, he published on his blog a defense of the use of the word. He wrote,

> Some people accuse me of confusing moral schizophrenia with multiple/split personality. When I talk about moral schizophrenia, I am seeking to describe the delusional and confused way that we think about animals as a social/moral matter.... Our moral schizophrenia, which involves our deluding ourselves about animal sentience and the similarities between humans and other animals ... is a phenomenon that is quite complicated and has many different aspects. (Francione, 2009)

Francione began his argument by stating that schizophrenia is a "personality," with which people in the field of disability studies would agree; but he quickly changed his description of schizophrenia to a "condition," as seen in the following section. He then apologized to those people who were offended by his using the term in a stigmatizing manner while continuing to defend his rationale:

> Some people think that by using the term, I am stigmatizing those who have clinical schizophrenia because it implies that they are immoral people. I am sincerely sorry...if anyone has interpreted the term in that way.... Schizophrenia is a recognized condition that is characterized by confused and delusional thinking. (Francione, 2009)

Now, instead of identifying schizophrenia as a personality, he identified it as a "condition," which quickly snowballed into a condition that people "suffer" from and which is not a "desirable" condition, as stated in the following passage from that same blog post:

> To say that we are delusional and confused when it comes to moral issues is not to say that those who suffer from clinical schizophrenia are immoral. It is only to say that many of us think about important moral matters in a completely confused, delusional, and incoherent way. I am certainly not saying that those who suffer from clinical schizophrenia are immoral! (Francione, 2009)

Francione went on to provide some additional responses to the criticisms he had recieved on the original blog posting. He noted that,

> When it comes to nonhuman animals, our views are profoundly delusional and I am using that term literally as indicative of what might be called a social form of schizophrenia.... Some critics claim that it is sufficient to use "delusional." But delusion is what characterizes the clinical form of schizophrenia and anyone who objected to the use of schizophrenia as ableist would have the same, and in my view groundless, objection to "delusional."...In any event, if "moral schizophrenia" is ableist, then so is the expression "drugs are a cancer on society" or "our policies in the Middle East are shortsighted" or "we are blind to the consequences of our actions" or "when it comes to poverty, our proposed solutions suffer from a poverty of ambition." (Francione, 2009)

He made an important critique of the public stigmatization of animal advocates as "profoundly delusional." While he perceived the ableism in using the term, *delusional*, in the conclusion to his post, he strove to defend his use of the term, *schizophrenia*, to stigmatize those who eat meat and exploit nonhuman animals by arguing that using terms such as *cancer*, *shortsighted*, and *blind*, to describe a negative topic, event, or action is not ableist. On the contrary, those that use such phrases, analogies, and comments *are* ableist; whenever someone is describing someone in a negative or insulting manner by using labels that have been historically or are currently meant to describe people with physical or mental disabilities, they are ableist.

Francione strove to draw the parallel between cancer and schizophrenia, where one is a disease, while the other is a personal characteristic that makes up who that person is. In this ableist society, both of them are disabilities. Therefore, this term demeans those who have schizophrenia and reinforces that people should not be schizophrenic (as if there is a choice). Francione is certainly not the only ableist in the animal advocacy movement. There are many that use phrases such as, "we must cripple capitalism," "society is blind to the exploitation of animals," and "vivisectors are idiots." Of course, even many at the latest Conference for Critical Animal Studies at Brock University in St. Catherines, Canada, used Francione's term, "moral schizophrenia," which I addressed publicly. People who used the term at the conference took accountability and recognized their ableism.

A quick Google search can prove this, as people call each other "retard," "idiot," "crazy," "insane," "mentally ill," "freak," "mentally disturbed," "mentally unstable," "lame," "crippled," and so much more, emphasizing the "Four Ds of Dissent," which construct the individual into a deviant, delinquent, demon, or disabled. Jenkins said that there is a long history about the relationships between and among the medical, criminal justice, legal, and psychiatric fields, in that they have a record of supporting each other's work (personal communication, January 18, 2011). She further said that the largest minority group in the world is those with disabilities (S. Jenkins, personal communication, January 18, 2011). They straddle all classes, nations, ages, genders, and races. For the most part, they are nonviolent people, yet they are almost all portrayed as violent dangers to society.

I dialogued with Jenkins a few weeks after the shooting in Arizona on January 8, 2011. She mentioned that the shooter, twenty-two-year-old Jared Lee Loughner, was identified as a person with a possible mental disability, although a full investigation of his background had not been conducted (S. Jenkins, personal communication, January 18, 2011). She went on to say that this depiction was a common practice employed by media, society, and the government to convey that these types of violent actions are not acts of terrorism, and, therefore, have no validity, rationality, or reason behind them (S. Jenkins, personal communication, January 18, 2011). It is also a common practice throughout society to label constructed social, political, interpersonal, or communal enemies as "disabled" (Corrigan, 2006; Davis, 1997, 2002; Nocella, 2008; Snyder & Mitchell, 2006).

Loadenthal gave another example of the shooter, James Jay Lee, who had written a manifesto decrying what he perceived as the Discovery Channel's promotion of environmental destruction. CBS had labeled him an "environmental militant" (Effron & Goldman, 2010) (Loadenthal, personal communication, February 16, 2011). ABC's article, "Environmental Militant Killed by Police at Discovery Channel Headquarters" had witnesses who described the activities in the event using ableist language such as "!INSANE!," "crazy," and "nuts." Loadenthal stated:

> Whether Lee's critiques are valid or not, whether or not the Discovery Channel is contributing to global overpopulation or not was made kind of irrelevant. Immediately upon his attack, where he walked into the Discovery Channel building in Silver Spring, Maryland with two non-lethal starter pistols, held four hostages and was eventually killed by police, HIS POLITICAL ARGUMENT WAS MADE IRRELEVANT. How someone can be so angry about issues of overpopulation, and whether issues of overpopulation are a threat, and whether or not the Discovery Channel is to be blamed, were not examined. The analysis immediately was why is this man "crazy" and "insane," why has this man gone this far, what led this man to this "extreme" end. (personal communication, February 16, 2011)

Grubbs mentioned the horrible shooting at Virginia Tech as yet another example of an individual who was stigmatized as having a mental disability but with little attention paid to the content of his video manifesto (personal communication, January 30, 2011). It seems that, too often, these shooters in the United States are dismissed when identified as persons with mental illnesses and not as terrorists. This only reinforces the stigma that people with mental disabilities are violent and a physical threat to society, not to mention the social threat of being "abnormal."

For example, Salter noted that many homeless people are people with disabilities who are regularly arrested, jailed, and deemed "abnormal" due to their socioeconomic situations (personal communication, January 30, 2011). Swan (2002) wrote, "In the earlier scheme, disability described the degree to which one was restricted in performing an activity; handicap described the degree to which one could no longer fulfill a social or economic role" (p. 293). The term, *handicap*, reinforces the idea that people who have disabilities are poor and, furthermore, are dependent on others or are beggars. Ben-Moshe's doctoral dissertation and much of her scholarship and activism focuses on the connection between the prison industrial complex and imprisoning people with disabilities. I asked her to tell me about the incarceration of people with disabilities; she responded: "Besides being labeled for life, you could be in a psych ward for life. You know until the doctor pretty much says that you can go. So there is no end date for your imprisonment, unlike a criminal" (L. Ben-Moshe, personal communication, January 20, 2011). Jenkins suggested that people with disabilities are "labeled as being inferior, not happy, and being associated with certain kinds of pain, that is always assumed to be a negative" (personal communication, February 16, 2011). Stigmatization is a powerful tool used to imprison, silence, murder, perform tests on, and, of course, repress others (Corrigan, 2006).

Deconstructing Dis-Ability[3]

What is *disability*, and why does it have a negative connotation? *Disability* is a negative term because of the notion of being broken, not working properly, or being simply wrong. *Disabled*, *crippled*, *lame*, and *retarded* all mean similar things. They are all used commonly in U.S. society (Taylor, 1996) to conjure up negative images that are most often used to insult and label others. For example, these are common phrases: "You are being lame," "You are so retarded," "What, are you mad?" "Don't be insane!" and "What are you, crippled or something?" Thus, "feebleminded," "retarded," "special needs," and "learning difficulties" are all examples of what Corbett (1995) called "Bad Mouthing" (as cited in Armstrong, Armstrong, & Barton 2000, p. 3). Goffman (1963) wrote, "The Greeks, who were apparently strong on visual aids, originated the term *stigma* to refer to bodily signs designed to expose something unusual and bad about the moral status of the signifier [emphasis in original]" (p. 1). All of these terms indicate stigmatization.

The classic label, *dumb*, is a term historically applied to both human and nonhuman animals. For example, in St. Thomas Aquinas's (2007) thirteenth-century tome, *Summa Theologica*, one of the most influential works in Western culture, he stated that

> Dumb animals and plants are devoid of the life of reason whereby to set themselves in motion; they are moved, as it were by another, by a kind of natural impulse, a sign of which is that they are naturally enslaved and accommodated to the uses of others. (p. 2666)

Here, dumb is actually not the insult we see it as today. It indicates the nonhuman animal's inability to speak and also his or her lack of intelligence or sense of self. But *dumb* was most certainly a term used to dismiss those creatures labeled as such. Western rationalist philosophers after Aquinas would use the same terminology. More than just the import of the word itself, however, is the notion that because a being cannot speak the dominant language (i.e., human English) and process the world intellectually through the dominant framework (as white, human, able-bodied, hetrosexual males), those individuals should become slaves, be used by others as food, clothing, or subjects for scientific experimentation. This stigma against nonhuman animals is evident, but what is not as immediately apparent is the way the term similarly stigmatizes those with disabilities.

A rich example of stigma against people with dis-abilities is found in the movie, *300* (Snyder, 2006), in which the great warriors, the Spartans, battle the Persians, who are depicted as "uncivilized." A Greek who was strong and loyal, but physically disabled, approached Leonidas, and asked to join the Spartans. However, King Leonidas saw this man as a liability, rather than as a powerful and strong soldier with wit. The solider with disabilities pleaded his case to be part of the Spartans, but the king, after asking the solider to perform a few defensive and offensive moves, said that he was not at the high level of a successful warrior. This devastated the solider so much that he became a traitor for what the movie portrayed as the uncivilized, "wild" Persians.

The meaning of the story is that the Spartans, as a "perfect" society, could never have a person with disabilities among them. But for the uncivilized, "wild" Persians, the movie portrays disability as acceptable. As all marginalized groups are the same, this implies that "non-Spartan" equals nonperfect or not normal. Based on the historical battle, the story had many imperialist lessons, one of them being that "civilized men" are more powerful than all of nature. This line of thinking carried over to the era of colonial empire rule, where the concept of *disability* was seen as a normalized level of physical and mental ability, while *dis-ability* has at times been the justification to kill, test, segregate, abort, and abandon those with disabilities.

Disability, *people with disabilities* (using person-first language), or *dis-ability* (separating the prefix, *dis-*, from the root word, *ability*, which I and many others do), are terms endorsed and used by dis-ability rights activists, theorists, advocates, and allies. As noted above, there are negative connotations to the term, *disability*, but the dis-ability rights movement has reclaimed the term out of an understanding of what the definition of *disability* means and to whom it refers (Fleischer & Zames, 2001). It is also the only term used to describe the differently abled, which holds significant legal and medical value, for it "appears to signify something material and concrete, a physical or psychological condition considered to have predominantly medical significance" (Linton, 1998, p. 10). This does not suggest that the term should and must be resisted. Most dis-ability activists would not argue for doing so. However, while many in the movement embrace the term, others (including those who teach dis-ability pedagogy) are now striving to promote new terms that connote positive values of difference, such as *ability pedagogy*. The classic predicament with all names for particular identities is that not everyone will understand the term, or even be aware that it exists, thus forcing the focus group to put a great deal of energy into promoting the name and its correct and respected definition (Snyder, Brueggemann, & Garland-Thomas, 2002).

Much of the theoretical work on dis-ability studies is centered on terminology, because of the diverse array of imagery related to people with disabilities. There are currently two major points being made by the dis-ability rights movement to correct negative perceptions of the differently abled. The first of these is that they are not disabled, meaning they are not deformed, lame, or broken, nor do they have something wrong with them that needs to be fixed. They are ideal the way they are. This point has two subconcerns. The first is that societies' exclusion of difference and the reinforcement of the social construction of normalcy are a problem (Fulcher, 1999) which allows capital to exclude people with disabilities from economic life. The second concern is that until all are accepted in society, there is truly an identifiable group that needs assistance and is challenged in the current exclusionary society in which we live (Snyder & Mitchell, 2006).

The second main point is the theoretical understanding of all dis-ability activists, which is that all people are different and have unique needs. This point is critical to understanding how society identifies people's roles. We must recognize that *normal*, *average*, or *able* are all socially constructed terms that can and must change. Dis-ability rights activists are also critical of the capitalist system insofar as it tries to reduce our humanity and citizenship functions to the roles of producer and consumer, both of which support capitalism. Consumption supports the engines of production because people have to work in order to buy, and ideologically, capitalism captures their desires and economic support (Gramsci, 1989; Marcuse, 1969.)

Similarly, dis-ability activists critique the norm of a "productive" employee, student, daughter or son, and/or parent. There is no measurement for an individual except within the context of that individual. Nothing is objective and able to be measured in a detached state. Let us analyze some of the standard definitions of the names given to those identified as disabled. *Illness* is defined as, "Poor health resulting from disease of body or mind; sickness" ("Illness," 2009), while *disease* is defined as, "A pathological condition of a part, organ, or system of an organism resulting from various causes, such as infection, genetic defect, or environmental stress, and characterized by an identifiable group of signs or symptoms" ("Disease," 2009). *Disease* is also defined as, "A condition or tendency, as of society, regarded as abnormal and harmful" ("Disease," 2009). Disability has traditionally been associated with illness and disease. Yet, this socially constructed meaning cannot be understood without examining the notion of normalcy. *Normal* is defined as "Relating to or characterized by average intelligence or development" ("Normal," 2009). A standard, dictionary type definition states that *normalcy* (here derived from *normal*) means, therefore, "Free[dom] from mental illness; sane. Conforming with, adhering to, or constituting a norm, standard, pattern, level, or type; typical" ("Normal," 2009). Fulcher (1999) wrote, "Disability is primarily a political construct rather than a medical phenomenon" (p. 25.)

With this backdrop, it comes as no surprise that *disability* is understood as, "The condition of being disabled; incapacity" ("Disability," 2009). Also, it is stigmatized as, "A disadvantage or deficiency, especially a physical or mental impairment that interferes with or prevents normal achievement in a particular area" ("Disability," 2009). It is defined as, "Something that hinders or incapacitates" ("Disabiity," 2009). As the definitions build on each other, we see the repeated theme of "something wrong with" ("Disability," 2009), be it defined as incapable, harmful, or sick. In contemporary society, these are the terms that are used interchangeably with disability. But by measuring everyone according to this imaginary notion of a so-called "normal person," society is inclusive only of certain types of people, nonhuman animals, elements, and plants. Those that are excluded and identified as the abnormal include the wild, the savage, those with disabilities, the purely animalistic, and the violent. Put those five characteristics together and you construct what filmmakers and storytellers identified as monsters. Monsters are uncivilized savages; wild, not domestic; with disabilities, not able-bodied; violent, not peaceful; and animalistic, not humanistic.

The social constructions of terms such as *normalcy*, *ableism*, and *civilization* have been put in the service of domination for political power, economic gain, and social control. Those in power used them to establish a superior (dominator) versus inferior (dominated) binary, which has repeatedly played out in theories, beliefs, cultures, and identities. People are typically judged against the standard of a "normal" human; those who choose not to, or simply cannot strive towards the norm because of their identity, politics, or social and economic factors are labeled "abnormal." Within this context, ableism is a social construct, which suggests that society should manipulate those individuals whose capabilities fall outside the "norm" in an attempt to reach the same physical and mental abilities as those considered "normal," instead of being accepting and inclusive towards all.

While it has been used as a key term for unifying and bringing attention to the topic (e.g., dis-ability studies), *disability* is still a term that has been challenged and manipulated by groups attempting to "take back" the terms and own them, similar to other marginalized groups owning terms previously considered derogatory. These newer fields of inquiry include Dis-Ability, Crip Studies, Mad Studies, and others. Still, disability studies in education can be regarded as the "new" special education field, which only reinforces a socially constructed binary. All are dis-abled in some way because of exclusionary social identities which limit one's life activities. These exclusionary practices are not due to various medical conditions or factors such as being a woman, tall, short, a person of color, young, elderly, LGBTQIA, non-Christian, not formally educated, a noncitizen of a country, someone with physical and mental differences, or any other nondominate identity. Unless and until we recognize this, disability will continue to be one of the most demeaning labels and identifications human or nonhuman animals, elements, plants, water, and air can be given, even more so than being called "wild" or "an animal," because disability is a label solely constructed by those in power to stigmatize and marginalize others as abnormal.

Notes

1. I would like to thank Kim Socha for helping to edit this chapter and for her important input.
2. This section was adapted from my personal website biography, www.anthonynocella.org, and an article I wrote, "Emergence of Disability Pedagogy" (Nocella, 2008), available at: http://www.jceps.com/index.php?pageID=article&articleID=132, and http://www.jceps.com/PDFs/6-2-05.pdf
3. This section of this chapter was adapted from the article, "Emergence of Disability Pedagogy" (Nocella, 2008).

References

Amster, R., DeLeon, A., Fernandez, L., Nocella II, A. J., & Shannon, D. (Eds.). (2009). *Contemporary anarchist studies: An introductory anthology of anarchy in the academy.* New York, NY: Routledge.

Aquinas, T. (2007). *Summa theologica,* Vol. III. New York, NY: Cosimo.

Armstrong, F., Armstrong, D., & Barton, L. (2000). *Inclusive education: Policy, contexts and comparative perspectives.* London, UK: David Fulton.

Ben-Moshe, L., Hill, D., Nocella II, A. J., & Templer, B. (2009). Dis-abling capitalism and an anarchism of 'radical equality' in resistance to ideologies of normalcy. In R. Amster, A. DeLeon, L. Fernandez, A. J. Nocella II, & D. Shannon (Eds.), *Contemporary anarchist studies: An introductory anthology of anarchy in the academy* (pp. 113–122). New York, NY: Routledge.

Best, S., & Nocella II, A. J. (2006). *Igniting a revolution: Voices in defense of the earth.* Oakland, CA: AK Press.

Binet, A., & Simon, T. (1973). *The development of intelligence in children (the Binet-Simon scale).* New York, NY: Arno Press.

Bodley, J. H. (2005). *Cultural anthropology: Tribes, states, and the global system.* New York, NY: McGraw-Hill.

Bogdan, R. (1988). *Freak show: Presenting human oddities for amusement and profit.* Chicago, IL: University of Chicago Press.

Bullard, R. D. (Ed.). (1993). *Confronting environmental racism: Voices from the grassroots.* Boston, MA: South End Press.

Center for Universal Design. (2010). About. Retrieved from http://www.ncsu.edu/project/design-projects/udi/center-for-universal-design/

Corrigan, P. W. (2006). *On the stigma of mental illness: Practical strategies for research and social change*. Washington, D.C.: American Psychological Association.

Davis, L. (1997). *The disability studies reader.* New York, NY: Routledge.

Davis, L. (2002). *Bending over backwards: Disability, dismodernism & other difficult positions*. New York, NY: New York University Press.

Derrickson, S. (Director). (2008). *The day the earth stood still* [Motion picture]. Los Angeles, CA: Twentieth Century Fox Film Corporation.

Disability. (2009). *The American heritage dictionary of the English language (4th ed.)*. Boston, MA: Houghton Mifflin. Retrieved from http://www.thefreedictionary.com/disability.

Disease. (2009). *The American heritage dictionary of the English language.* Boston, MA: Houghton Mifflin. Retrieved from http://www.thefreedictionary.com/disease

Dowbiggin, I. R. (2003). *Keeping America sane: Psychiatry and eugenics in the United States and Canada, 1880–1940*. Ithaca, NY: Cornell University Press.

Dunayer, J. (2004). *Speciesism*. New York, NY: Lantern Books.

Effron, L., & Goldman, R. (2010, September 1). Environmental Militant Killed by Police at Discovery Channel Headquarters. ABC News. Retrieved from http://abcnews.go.com/US/gunman-enters-discovery-channel-headquarters-employees-evacuated/story?id=11535128#.T6cPpMWISuK

Fassbinder, S., Nocella II, A. J., and Kahn, R. (In press). *Greening the academy*. Rotterdam, The Netherlands: Sense.

Fleischer, D. Z., & Zames, F. (2001). *The disability rights movement: From charity to confrontation.* Philadelphia, PA: Temple University Press.

Francione, G. L. (2000). *Introduction to animal rights: Your child or the dog?* Philadelphia, PA: Temple University Press.

Francione, G. (2009, August 12). A note on moral schizophrenia. Animal Rights: The Abolitionist Approach. Retrieved on July 17, 2011, from http://www.abolitionistapproach.com/a-note-on-moral-schizophrenia/.

Fulcher, G. (1999). *Disabling policies? A comparative approach to education policy and disability* (new ed.). Sheffield, UK: Philip Armstrong.

Gaard, G. (1993). *Ecofeminism: Women, animals, nature.* Philadelphia, PA: Temple University Press.

Goffman, E. (1963). *Stigma: Notes on the management of spoiled identity.* New York, NY: Simon & Schuster.

Gramsci, A. (1989). *Selections from the prison notebooks of Antonio Gramsci* (10th printing.). New York, NY: International.

Harding, S. (Ed.) (2003). *The feminist standpoint theory reader: Intellectual & political controversies.* New York, NY: Routledge.

Illness. (2009). *The American heritage dictionary of the English language*. Boston, MA: Houghton Mifflin. Retrieved from http://www.thefreedictionary.com/illness

Linton, S. (1998). *Claiming disability: Knowledge and identity*. New York, NY: New York University Press.

Marcuse, H. (1969). *An essay on liberation*. Boston, MA: Beacon Press.

Nocella II, A. J. (In press). Anarcho-disability criminology. In J. Ferrell, A. J. Nocella II, & A. Brisman (Eds.), *Anarchist criminology.*

Nocella II, A. J. (2008). Emergence of disability pedagogy. *Journal for Critical Education Policy Studies*. 6(2), pp. 77–94. Retrieved from http://www.jceps.com/index.php?pageID=article&articleID=132, and http://www.jceps.com/PDFs/6-2-05.pdf

Normal. (2009). *The American heritage dictionary of the English language*. Boston, MA: Houghton Mifflin. Retrieved from http://www.thefreedictionary.com/normal

Normalcy. (2009). *The American heritage dictionary of the English language*. Boston, MA: Houghton Mifflin. Retrieved from http://www.thefreedictionary.com/Normalcy

Pfohl, S. (2009). *Images of deviance and social control: A sociological history* (2nd ed.). Long Grove, IL: Waveland Press.

Rosenau, P. M. (1992). *Post-modernism and the social sciences: Insights, inroads, and intrusions*. Princeton, NJ: Princeton University Press.

Schou, N. (2006). *Kill the messenger: How the CIA's crack-cocaine controversy destroyed journalist Gary Webb*. New York, NY: Nation Books.

Scott, P. D., & Marshall, J. (1998). *Cocaine politics: Drugs, armies, and the CIA in Central America* (updated ed.). Berkeley, CA: University of California Press.

Smith, R. M., & Manno, J. P. (2008). Disability studies and the social construction of environments. Social Advocacy and Systems Change. 1(1). Retrieved from http://www.cortland.edu/ids/sasc/vol1_issue1/index.html

Snyder, S. L., Brueggemann, B. J., Garland-Thomas, R. (2002). *Disability studies: Enabling the humanities*. New York, NY: Modern Language Association of America.

Snyder, S. L., & Mitchell, D. T. (2006). *Cultural locations of disability*. Chicago: IL: University of Chicago Press.

Snyder, Z. (Director). (2006). *300* [Motion picture]. Hollywood, CA: Warner Bros. Pictures.

Swan, J. (2002). Disabilities, bodies, voices. In S. L. Snyder, B. Jo Brueggemann, & R. Garland-Thomson (Eds.), *Disability studies: Enabling the humanities*, pp. 283-295. New York: NY: The Modern Language Association of America.

Taylor, S. (1996). Disability studies and mental retardation. *Disability Studies Quarterly*. 16(3), 4–13.

Tokar, B. (1997). *Earth for sale: Reclaiming ecology in the age of corporate greenwash*. Boston, MA: South End Press.

Torres, B., & Torres, J. (2010). *Vegan freak: Being vegan in a non-vegan world: Version 2.0* (Rev. ed.). Oakland, CA: Tofu Hound Press.

van der Pijl, K. (2007). *Nomads, empires, states: Modes of foreign relations and political economy, Vol. 1*. London, UK: Pluto Press.

Webb, G. (1999). *Dark alliance: The CIA, the contras, and the crack cocaine explosion*. New York, NY: Seven Stories Press.

CHAPTER TWO

Human Disabilities, Nonhuman Animals, and Nature

Toxic Constructs and Transformative Technologies

JUDY K. C. BENTLEY

As they are at the moment, things are rather disturbing.

—*MICHEL FOUCAULT*

Those of us in the academic profession can build careers by discussing the work of great thinkers, and presenting papers about others' great ideas to rapt audiences of other academics. Similarly, certain "paper activists" may bring forth critical theories of what is wrong with just about everything, without ever communicating clearly and directly to—or participating in solutions for—the oppressed constituencies their lofty language serves to keep out and keep down. This chapter is not for that purpose.

This chapter owes its underlying structure to the great thinker Michel Foucault but with the purpose of thinking new thoughts of our own, to birth new ideas, actions, and relationships. Although some scholars have used Foucault's work to focus on the suppression and limitation of original thought, Foucault wanted his work to inspire resistance and self-transformation. In an interview published two years after his death, Foucault summed up his intention:

> My role . . . is to show people that they are much freer than they feel, that people accept as truth, as evidence, some themes which have been built up at a certain moment during history, and that this so-called evidence can be criticized and destroyed. (as cited in Martin, 1988, p. 10)

In the 21st century, Pellow (2007a) continued in this role, conducting "self advocacy research" for environmental justice. Pellow "participate[d] in social change efforts while also stepping back and employing a reflexive analysis of that work" (p. 35). He called for scholars to achieve social change through analyzing their research and applying it to real-world activism.

Foucault gave us tools for transforming thought and action in the lived world. We can do the work of this chapter with three of them: (a) the archaeology of knowledge, (b) the genealogy of thought, and (c) technologies of the self. We will draw new parallels from Foucault's work to the discourse, knowledge, and power that connect us, or disconnect us, from people labeled as "disabled," from nonhuman animals, and from the natural world.

The Archaeology of Knowledge

The Order of Things (Foucault, 1970) began with Foucault enjoying a good laugh. Auspiciously for this book, his laughter was related to nonhuman animals. The source of his entertainment was a Chinese encyclopedia that classified animals as: (a) belonging to the emperor, (b) embalmed, (c) tame, (d) suckling pigs, (e) sirens, (f) fabulous, (g) stray dogs, (h) included in the present classification, (i) frenzied, (j) innumerable, (k) drawn with a very fine camelhair brush, (l) *et cetera*, (m) having just broken the water pitcher, and (n) that from a long way off look like flies (1970, p. xv).

It was wonderful, Foucault thought, that while we human animals could immediately understand this exotic system of classification, most of us would not have constructed it in the first place. For Foucault, the bizarre Chinese taxonomy violated, and thereby revealed, a deeply hidden "order of things."

Foucault reasoned that it was impossible for most of us to order things in such a peculiar way, because we humans are bound by a more rigid, unacknowledged, and universal order, which is situated deep in the "non-place of language" (1970, p. xvii). With credit to the Chinese taxonomist for "shatter[ing] ... all the familiar landmarks of thought" (1970, p. xv), Foucault posited his definitive "archaeology" of knowledge. Foucault's archaeology can help us recognize and analyze deep-rooted, destructive ideas about human and nonhuman animals, disability, and nature—shatter their landmarks—and transform them.

Foucault's (1970) archaeology excavated a tacit grid of existential rules by which economists, grammarians, and naturalists have collectively and unconsciously formed their theories. He showed how these impersonal structures of knowledge have changed over the millennia, from the Renaissance to the postmodern age. The underground grid of knowledge that allows thought to organize itself he called an *episteme*, and he claimed that the *episteme* limited human animals' totality of truth and knowledge, unless it was exposed and questioned. Foucault did not apply his theories to the place of nonhuman animals and the environment in structures of knowledge and power. But I will argue that they can be productively applied.

Foucault's idea of the *episteme* can be compared to a paradigm—a way of thinking that is so unconscious and entrenched in a particular time and culture that it will go unexamined, until it is challenged by discovery and analysis. Becoming conscious of an object or an idea is an act of will (Blumer, 1969; Husserl, 1913/1962; Mead, 1934/1962). We choose the ideas and objects we decide to pay attention to. And so as we dig for, unearth, examine, communicate—and, finally, question—deeply buried thoughts and ideas (so aptly named the "archaeology" of our knowledge), we change the nature of our connections to the lived world. In addition to the subconscious archaeology of knowledge, which we can willfully make conscious, we can apply Foucault's "genealogy" to transform thought and action.

The Genealogy of Ideas

A traditional historian shows us what people were doing in a particular time and place; and history can be neatly organized along a timeline, which can be seen as a form of "progress" toward some type of "civilization" or conquest. Shattering the concept of history as an orderly progression of actions and consequences, Foucault described himself as a "historian of thought" (Martin, 1988, p. 10). A historian of thought—a genealogist—deals in the complex and slippery constructs of thought that inspire people to do what they are doing and convince them to believe in what they do (Foucault, 1971/1984). A Foucauldian genealogy pays attention to the marginal, accidental, and constructed rather than what historians have labeled as significant, purposeful, and innate. Once again, Foucault opened his work on genealogy with a slice-of-life that engages the reader. But this time it is no laughing matter.

Foucault (1975/1995) began *Discipline and Punish*, his classic treatise on the genealogy of power, with a graphic description of the March 1757 drawing and quartering of Robert-François Damiens, for attempts to assassinate King Louis XV. If an execution can be described as going well or not going well for the victim, Damiens's execution did not go well. When four horses could not pull him apart, they tried again with six. When six horses failed, the executioners hacked at Damiens's joints and sinews to facilitate the quartering" (*Gazette de Amsterdam*, April 1, 1757, as cited in Foucault, 1975/1995, p. 3).

Damiens's body was individually punished for his crime, and he also suffered on behalf of the "social body," of the spectators (Foucault, 1980, p. 93). The hideous, public nature of Damiens's punishment was designed to reestablish the absolute authority of the monarch over all his subjects. Such a display punished the guilty and warned others that they were vulnerable to the same consequences (Foucault, 1975/1995).

While the crowd's attention was understandably riveted on Damiens, they also witnessed, deep in the non-place of language, a powerful demonstration of the use of nonhuman animals as instruments of destruction. We can assume, since they did not and could not draw and quarter a human being without being harnessed and forced to do so, that this act was against the horses' nature. The horses' strength was co-opted to commit torture and murder. In such a brutal environment, we can assume that the horses were driven by fear and whipping—a demonstration of the sovereign's power over nonhuman animals that the crowd could not help but internalize, whether or not they acknowledged it or cared. Nature, too, was portrayed, in front of all the king's witnesses, as subject to the sovereign's absolute will.

For the human animals involved, the spectacle of a public execution aroused feelings of empathy and pity—feelings powerful enough to make people question the "order of things." We can extrapolate these thoughts to include empathy and pity for the horses as well. At this point in history, Foucault showed us the possibility of changing deeply held beliefs and practices, weakening the existing grid that orders things on earth. But on the muddled genealogical landscape, the old "order of things"—sovereign power—remains, even as a new order emerges. But Foucault cautioned us not to misunderstand the role of this nascent empathy as leading to a more humane ethic. It leads, instead, to a new and more insidious method of control (Foucault, 1975/1995).

In the madhouse and the slaughterhouse; in "self-contained" classes and "alternative" schools for children with severe disabilities and behavior disorders; in institutions where human beings are still subject to restraint, seclusion, and aversive punishment; in the laboratory where animals are used for experimentation; and on brutal factory farms, sovereign power continues to be exercised over "kingdoms" of human and nonhuman animals. Some powerful and disruptive thoughts emerge to expose and challenge the *episteme*, when the spectacle of such abuse is brought into consciousness by activists and advocates.

From a global perspective, where the subjects of sovereign power are too numerous to be externally controlled, disciplinary power both *invents* and invades the "soul." Foucault (1975/1995) explained:

> It would be wrong to say that the soul is an illusion, or an ideological effect.... It is produced permanently around, or within the body by the functioning of a power that is exercised on those punished—and, in a more general way, on those one supervises, trains and corrects, over madmen,

> children at home and at school, the colonized, over those who are stuck at a machine and supervised for the rest of their lives. This is the historical reality of this soul, which . . . is born rather out of methods of *punishment, supervision and constraint* [emphasis added]. (p. 29)

Disciplinary power is a "policy of coercions" (Foucault, 1975/1995) that produces "docile bodies," subjects who conform to goals and practices defined by policies and politics, or "disciplines" (p. 138). In order for disciplinary power to define and subjugate individual and social bodies, it becomes necessary for each discipline to develop its own specialized discourse.

Power, Discourse, and Truth

Each discipline, possessing its own specialized language, constructs its own version of truth, resulting in "a multiplicity of new domains of understanding" (Foucault, 1980, p. 106). Each truth, as its discourse evolves, becomes a "truth of power" (p. 93) that creates and imposes a body of specialized knowledge. The discourse of discipline is derived from "a natural rule, a norm" (p. 106). When specialized knowledge achieves the status of a discipline, it brings into being a necessary binary—a distinction between what is right and what is wrong and between what was *normal* or *natural* and what is not.

Through the social construction of *normal*, with its evolving, specialized discourse, human disability has come to be portrayed as a pathological condition, so entrenched in negativity that individuals labeled as *dis-abled* are perceived as having less or other than normal lives and identities. In U.S. public schools, children are placed in special education based upon a battery of normed assessments. They qualify for special education services if their intelligence falls below a normal range, and their "abnormalities" require medical, educational, and social "interventions." Although current definitions of disabilities have evolved to more functional categories, students are still defined and prepared for restricted adult lives by specific medical diagnoses that separate them profoundly from the normal purpose and content of education (i.e., to succeed in college and make a significant economic contribution to society as taxpaying citizens).

Specialized discourse about what is *natural* has become a term of judgment as well, creating a "human/nature divide" (Crowley, 2010, p. 72). Crowley gave the example of "all-natural" sugar, which

> puts the sugar on the nature side of the human/nature divide . . . [encouraging] us to overlook the fact that it has been harvested by humans (or

> human-made machines) and its genetic code has been determined by years of selective breeding by humans ... imply[ing] that things are entirely natural or entirely artificial, with [no] intermediate degrees and interconnectedness. (p. 72)

Speciesism further splits the divide, disconnecting human from nonhuman animals. Subject to what Foucault (1975/1995) might have called an accidental consequence, and what Elstein (2003) explored as the social construction of species, there is Washoe, a chimpanzee raised in the home of experimental psychologists, Allen and Beatrix Gardner, as a deaf (and therefore "disabled") human child. Washoe was taught a highly specialized human language: American Sign Language (ASL). She developed such a distorted perception of her identity, that when Washoe first met other chimpanzees at age five, she signed to a human that they were "black bugs," denying her own essence. Washoe hated bugs and loved to squash them. She had become a "docile body" (Foucault, 1975/1995, p. 138), subject to a uniquely oppressive *episteme* or paradigm of normality—the unexamined truth of power that human and nonhuman animals are separate and unequal, with human animals superior and in charge. Roger and Deborah Fouts, who taught ASL to chimpanzees, and considered Washoe their next of kin (Goodall, 1997, p. xi), noted at the time of her first encounter with her own species that "Washoe had accepted the notion of human superiority very readily.... [She] had learned our human arrogance too well" (Fouts & Fouts, 1993, pp. 28–29).

The term, *natural*, has also been used to explain away unjust social conditions. As Foucault (1971/1984) stressed the complexity of genealogy over the inevitableness of history, Crowley (2010) noted that a normative construct of nature gives each species of nonhuman animal a particular purpose (meat, fashion, genetic manipulation, scientific experimentation, domestic service, pet therapy), toward which it is considered good and natural to work. This notion ignores both the rich, evolving variation within species and the transformative, environmental factors that shape behavior.

Grauerholz (2007) uncovered the process of commercialized imagery that blurs the connection between "animals" and "meat," so that the two are seen as distinct and unrelated. She traced the "cutification" (p. 334) of animals and the packaging of meat so that it no longer resembles anything animal. This specialized imagery promotes the consumption of animal flesh, even by people who may find "cute" animals to be loveable. Grauerholz exposed a connection between these types of objectification and the oppression of human animals in society.

Building on the work of Pellow (2007a, 2007b), who drew parallels between toxic racism and toxic chemicals, we can construct a genealogy of toxicity that connects ableism, speciesism, and the contaminated beliefs and acts that violate our world, punishing the subjects they so perversely connect: human animals mislabeled as less than able; animals mislabeled as less than human; and our punished, poisoned planet, mislabeled as the totally natural world. We can attribute a Foucauldian soul to all three entities—born of "punishment, supervision, and constraint" (Foucault, 1975/1995, p. 29).

Pellow (2007a, 2007b) identified environmental racism as the domination of the environment by human animals, a toxic behavior that reinforces social hierarchies and has a negative effect not only on the direct targets of racism but on the world as a whole. Bullard (2005a, 2005b), and Bullard and Smith (2005) gave us an example of environmental racism in Houston, Texas, where five decades of targeting Black neighborhoods for landfills, incinerators, garbage dumps, and garbage transfer stations by all-White, all-male city government and private industry have had toxic consequences. Black residents' property values have plummeted. Black neighborhoods have rapidly deteriorated and are stigmatized as dumping grounds for salvage yards, recycling operations, and auto chop shops. Comparatively high health and environmental risks have been documented in these areas as well.

Lauren Corman (2011) explored the physical and symbolic representation of "trash" and its connections to the social and cultural vilification of human and nonhuman animals. Analyzing the specialized discourse related to pests, vermin, and dirt, Corman found it contextually linked to devaluing discourses about social delinquency, race, and class. She cited as an example the idea that urban raccoons are considered trash animals, and that "freegans" (free + vegan) who forage for useful goods in the trash of retailers and residences are also considered "urban trash":

> Raccoons and freegans continue to pick their way through Western society, valuing what others deem valueless. Waste transforms into food, affluence transforms into excess, and "necessary purchases" transform into choices. [Their presence] uncomfortably reveals ideas such as civility, urban progress and economic inevitability as interrelated constructions, rather than natural realities. (2011, p. 32)

As Pellow defined human racism—"a poison that fills the air, both figuratively and literally" (2007b, p. 46)—so may we define the toxic behaviors that create ableism and speciesism. (In this chapter *ableism* is defined as privileging, and regarding as superior, individuals who are *not* labeled dis-abled, and are therefore considered to be normal or natural beings. *Speciesism* is defined as the granting of superiority and power to the human species, over all other species, and over all other living things.)

Environmental Racism, Ableism, and Speciesism: A Genealogy of Toxicity

Toxicity maims, debilitates, and kills

Pellow (2007a, 2007b) noted that toxic chemicals can maim, debilitate, and kill their victims and the environment. Likewise, ableism can maim, kill, and debilitate persons with disabilities. Linda Ware, whose son Justin was diagnosed with cerebral palsy-like symptoms a few months after his birth, described her encounter with the specialized discourse of the medical paradigm. Immediately after the diagnosis, her "once 'oh-so-healthy' baby became 'obviously blighted,' 'defective' and 'damaged'—marked by his medical fate."

Bioethicist Peter Singer (1993), insisted that "seriously disabled" human infants, and "older children or adults whose mental age is and has always been that of an infant" (p. 181) are less than human. Human personhood requires "rationality, autonomy, [and] self-consciousness" (p. 182), which Singer claimed individuals with intellectual and developmental disabilities cannot attain. He justifies the killing of any infant "born with a serious disability" because the infant's parents "may, with good reason, regret that a disabled child was ever born" (p. 183). If the disabled child could be "replaced" (p. 186) by a healthy child who would have "better prospects" (p. 185) for a happier life, Singer said "*it would be right to kill him* [emphasis added]," because the lives of all disabled people are "less worth living" (p. 188) than the lives of people who are not disabled.

Speciesism offers unconscionable examples of maiming and debilitating nonhuman animals for use and abuse as "natural" resources. Factory farming, corporate agribusiness and fast-food conglomerates profit from the torturous confinement and brutal slaughter of thousands of animals—thereafter "meat"—every hour. Tens of millions more are tortured and killed in scientific experimentation for the "good" of humankind, and hunted for the benefit of sport or fashion. Global fishing has eliminated 90% of the world's major fish species, and the vast nets that trawl the ocean floor for commercial fishing enterprises are drowning about 1,000 whales, dolphins, and porpoises every day (Kahn, 2003).

Toxicity oppressively shapes its subjects

Environmental racism literally and figuratively shapes the earth and the bodies that are subject to its power, through specialized, "professional" actions and language (Pellow, 2007a, 2007b). The chemical toxins that have physically deformed and debilitated human and nonhuman animals in communities inundated with pollution have proliferated in contexts where sentient beings are defined in terms of their market value.

The market value of a dis-abled human animal, according to ableist discourse, is that of an eternal infant and a burden on society. This powerful disability discourse emerged along with the United Way charities in the early 1950s, when polio was a particularly fearsome, dis-abling disease and a blight on the country's bright, new postwar future. In this context, disability became a complex social experience of difference, which was neither owned nor constructed by people with disabilities. Instead, disability was constructed by the nondisabled majority through a charity discourse, exemplified by the use of the "poster child" in advertising (Barton, 2001).

A poster child was selected from among children with a specific disability to serve as a "model" for that disability. The cuter the child, the better she or he was able to invoke pity and fear, erasing the legitimate interests of persons with disabilities in their own independence and autonomy. Children with disabilities held their own fearful stereotypes about the poster children they saw as the only representatives of their kind. Some of them thought they would all be cured by the time they reached adulthood. Some thought they would die before they grew up (Barton, 2001; Fleischer & Zames, 2001).

By the 1970s, the poster child shared the context of infantilism with the disabled adult, who was now portrayed as a full-grown burden on society (Barton, 2001; Fleischer & Zames, 2001; Wehmeyer, 2000). A Torch Drive poster in 1975 featured an adult with mental retardation: "The toughest handicap for a retarded child," the poster declared, "is that he becomes a retarded adult" (Walter P. Reuther Library, Wayne State University, as cited in Barton, 2001). The specialized charity discourse endures as part of the disability paradigm, galvanizing the divide between normal and disabled—Self and Other—supporting the devaluation of human animals who are labeled as dis-abled. An absurdly tragic parallel between the literal shaping of the "natural" world, and the literal shaping of the body of a child with a disability, can be drawn between the commercial "race to grow the one-ton pumpkin" (Scott, 2011) and the case of Ashley, the "pillow angel" (Gibbs, 2007).

A fierce competition among amateur gardeners to grow a one-ton pumpkin has so far resulted in an engineered squash weighing in at 1,810 pounds (210 pounds heavier than a Smart car). Hobbyist Don Young, who said he spends $8,000 a year on the great pumpkin race, said that he tucks his pumpkins in with floral bed sheets and swore that when his pumpkins are at their peak growth "they'll make a sound ... Bup. Bup." (Scott, 2011, para. 14). A complex *non sequitur* alerts us to question the order of things, when competitor Steve Connolly explained, "We're taking a natural process and we've got complete control over it" (Scott, 2011, para. 18). This "natural process" begins with forcefully cross-pollinating a male pumpkin flower from one plant by rubbing its pollen onto a female flower from another. All of the pumpkin buds and sprouting vines except the artificially pollinated one are killed. The champion pumpkin, growing up alone, is heated and cooled with fans and heat lamps to correct the weather. It is fed a home-brewed diet of worm castings, molasses, and liquid kelp. The market value of a single seed from last year's champion pumpkin was $1,600.

Respectfully comparing the literal shaping of "Ashley," the "pillow angel," to the literal shaping of the pumpkin, we can dig out the connection between human interference with what is truly *natural*, and the genealogical complexity of what *natural* has come to mean. Ashley is a child with congenital brain damage who cannot speak for herself. Her parents decided, in a careful and loving manner, to have their "pillow angel's" growth arrested so that she would be easier to carry and care for. The treatment halted Ashley's maturation before puberty, since they believed her mental capacities would remain infantile, and made it "more possible to include her in the typical family life and activities that provide her with needed comfort, closeness, security and love: meal time, car trips, snuggles, etc." (Ashley's Mom and Dad, 2007, para. 13).

Drs. Daniel Gunther and Douglas Diekema (2006) removed Ashely's uterus and breast tissue, and closed her bone growth plates with high-dosage estrogen treatments, reducing her prospective height by about 13 inches. The ethics committee of Seattle Children's Hospital gave permission for the surgery, concluding that the rewards of the Ashley Treatment outweighed the risks (Gibbs, 2007, January 7). The Ashley Treatment was subsequently performed on other children, although the original case launched a media storm of both protest and praise. In 2007, Dr. Gunther committed suicide. His family stated that Dr. Gunther had a history of depression, which they believed was the reason for his suicide, not the repercussions from the Ashley Treatment. "I think he felt good about the way he helped that family," Dr. Diekema said. "I think in many ways, it energized him" (as cited in Ostrom, 2007, para. 10).

Toxicity migrates through time

Pellow (2007) noted that toxic chemicals and toxic racism travel across generations, shaping "consciousness ... and life chances ... and the landscapes on which people depend" (p. 47). Likewise, toxic ableism and toxic speciesism persist and migrate through time until they are exposed and examined by a critical mass of stakeholders who demand an end to toxic practices.

A persistent example of toxic ableism, from which powerful advocacy has not yet drawn out the poison, is the use of restraint and seclusion for the correction or elimination of undesired behaviors in U.S. schools—a specialized discourse of "professional" education practice that originated in institutions, including schools, in 18th century France. Even in the 21st century, U.S. children with intellectual and developmental disabilities are especially vulnerable to such practices, which tend to be carried out by personnel with little or no training. There are no federal standards for monitoring and preventing restraint and seclusion, and as these toxic practices continue over time, they have caused permanent injury, trauma, and death (TASH, 2011).

In Michigan, a 15-year-old boy with autism died under restraint after four school employees held him face down on the floor for over an hour. In Wisconsin, a seven-year-old girl, restrained as punishment for blowing bubbles in her milk and disobeying time-out rules, died from suffocation, restrained by several adults. In Georgia, a 13-year-old boy hanged himself in the small, concrete seclusion room where he was locked for hours at a time. He had threatened suicide before and pleaded with teachers that he could not stand being locked up (TASH, 2011).

In addition to physical restraint and seclusion, schools may use mechanical restraint, such as straps, tape, cuffs, mats, helmets, and other devices to prevent movement and sensory perception. Chemical restraint, the use of medicine to dull a child's ability to move or think, is used in schools as well. On March 3, 2010, the U.S. House of Representatives passed legislation to protect school children from abusive restraint and seclusion. But this legislation never reached the Senate floor (TASH, 2011).

An enduring example of toxic speciesism that has migrated through time is the practice of factory farming. Factory farming refers to large-scale, industrial operations that house hundreds of food animals in obscenely cramped, captive conditions, and treat them as unfeeling commodities, exercising absolute, sovereign power over their lives. Human animals are manipulated by forced ignorance of the clandestine, toxic practices of factory farming. Its specialized discourse manipulates and perverts the natural process of life. Nonhuman animals who are "colonized . . . stuck at a [milking] machine and supervised for the rest of their lives" thus earn their Foucauldian souls and their market value through "punishment, supervision, and constraint" (Foucault, 1975/1995, p. 29).

Factory farms use automated systems to replace human-animal contact, such as feeding, moving, milking, weighing, and the detection of estrus. However, negative contact between human and nonhuman animals is still required for frightening and painful operations such as vaccination and castration. With less farmer-animal contact, animals may feel more stress when human contact occurs—and when it does occur, stress and fear are justified (Cornou, 2009). The human-animal divide in factory farming has been rationalized by admitting its brutality: "Just as we have to depersonalize human opponents in wartime to *kill them with indifference* [emphasis added], so we have to create a void between ourselves and the animals on which *we inflict pain and misery* [emphasis added]" (Rothschild, 1986, as cited in Cornou, 2009, p. 216).

More than six million pigs are kept as breeding sows on factory farms; 80% of these are kept in gestation crates—two foot by seven foot cages in which a 400-pound sow cannot turn around, lie down comfortably, or take more than one step forward or backward. Pregnant sows are moved to equally confining farrowing crates to give birth. Their piglets are taken away after two to three weeks, and then the breeding cycle begins again. After two or three years, the sow is unable to breed again, and is crowded into a truck where extreme heat and cold may kill her on the way to the slaughterhouse. If she arrives alive at the slaughterhouse, she will be inhumanely butchered. Pigs have been found to be more intelligent than dogs. Yet, on factory farms they live in constant hunger, discomfort, and frustration, developing physical and psychological scars (Farm Sanctuary, n.d.).

The majority of dairy cattle in the United States no longer get to graze in green pastures, and many spend their entire lives indoors, where cramped quarters and artificially stimulated milk production leads to tail docking for more convenient milking, inflamed, infected udders, and lameness. Dairy cattle represent the largest percentage of "downed animals" arriving at the slaughterhouse too sick or injured to walk on their own (Farm Sanctuary, n.d.).

Beef cattle, who are born and live on the range, are not adequately protected against weather. They may die of dehydration or freeze to death, with no veterinary care. A common affliction among beef cattle is "cancer eye," which, left untreated, eats away the animal's head. Downed beef cattle typically go for days without food, water, or care, and may die of neglect. Others are beaten and dragged or pushed with tractors to the slaughterhouse. Over 80% of the 35 million beef cattle slaughtered in the United States are factory farmed by four huge corporations (Farm Sanctuary, n.d.).

Thousands of factory-farmed chickens and turkeys are packed into warehouses so tightly they can barely move. The ends of their beaks are cut off shortly after they hatch, so they cannot peck each other in reaction to overcrowding. Turkeys also have the ends of their toes cut off. Broiler chickens are genetically altered to grow fast and huge, so that their hearts and lungs are not developed enough to support their bodies. Many die from congestive heart failure. They are crippled by legs too fragile to support their heavy bodies. Many succumb to heat prostration, infectious diseases, and cancer. Genetically manipulated turkeys have such large breasts that they cannot reproduce except by artificial insemination, and they are prone to heart disease and leg injuries. On their way to the slaughterhouse, many of these birds die due to extreme heat or cold (Farm Sanctuary, n.d.).

Once in the slaughterhouse, where mechanistic forms of slaughter can fail to stun them (however brutally), chickens and turkeys may be conscious when their throats are slit, or they may be boiled alive. It is particularly difficult to bleed conscious cattle who are often hung upside down, kicking and struggling. They blink and make noises. "Some survive as far as the tail cutter, the belly ripper, the hide puller. They die ... piece by piece" (Warrick, 2001, para. 4).

Toxicity and Technology: Tools for Organizing Resistance

Pellow (2007b) saw intellectual connections between toxic chemicals and toxic racism as powerful tools for "organizing resistance movements and bringing people together across social and spatial boundaries" (p. 48). Foucault (1988) saw "technologies of the self" as tools through which we nonhuman animals examine and transform ourselves "in order to attain a certain state of ... purity [or] wisdom" (p. 18). In this chapter, we have used these tools to make further connections.

To restore connections among the world and its beings, educators can employ critical pedagogy (Kincheloe, 2004), teaching that is grounded in social justice. In this era of performance-based measurement, where both teachers and students are judged and supervised by student performance on specialized tests, there is an oppressive emphasis on rigidly constructed "truths" of what students should know and be able to do. Even so, eco-able scholars can find ways to reimagine teaching, and impart the healing skills and knowledge of transformative education. For example, Sid Brown (2008) brought a Buddhist exercise to his classroom: the Council of All Beings. Each student became a nonhuman animal, or a feature of nature, and spoke from that being's perspective in a council meeting. At first, only nonhumans spoke. But later in the exercise, humans were allowed to bring their perspectives to the discussion. Participants were introduced to aspects of the environment in a memorable and personal way, so the environment became more "real and important" (p. 66) to them, and they recognized themselves as being "solidly in the web of nature" (p. 67).

When Foucault (1988) first spoke of technologies of the self, the vast reach of global media technology was just beginning its exponential growth. Today, technologies of the self, and technologies of communication can explain and expose toxic truths and actions instantly at the click of a mouse. We can resist them *en masse* just by choosing "send" on a prewritten letter to a legislator or a social justice website that brings together proponents of various causes and ideologies. But as scholars and public intellectuals, we must proceed with caution.

With this glut of information and discourse, it becomes ever more challenging to choose what we pay attention to; it is even more important to be clear and universal in our communication. Scholarly discourse too specialized to be understood by those it seeks to liberate reifies toxic inequities. Scholars who argue that their own, highly specialized field of scholarship "owns" disability, ecology, or animalia support and perpetuate an inequitable and oppressive order of things, contrary to their declared intentions.

In this chapter we have unmasked examples of toxic thoughts and practices that construct oppressive boundaries between human animals with and without disability labels, nonhuman animals, and nature. There are many more. Once these toxic ideas are exposed and challenged, we can begin to demolish the constructed, poisoned "truths" that divide and destroy us.

References

Ashley's Mom and Dad. (2007, March 25). The 'Ashley Treatment': Towards a better quality of life for 'pillow angels'. Retrieved from http://ashleytreatment.spaces.live.com/blog (no longer accessible).

Barton, E. L. (2001). Textual practices of erasure: Representations of disability and the founding of the United Way. In J. C. Wilson & C. Lewiecki-Wilson (Eds.), *Embodied rhetorics: Disability in language and culture* (pp. 169–199). Carbondale, IL: Southern Illinois University Press.

Blumer, H. (1969). *Symbolic interactionism: Perspective and method.* Englewood Cliffs, NJ: Prentice-Hall.

Brown, S. (2008). Do not cross line: Wonder and imaginative engagement. In S. Brown, *A Buddhist in the classroom* (pp. 62–71). New York, NY: State University of New York Press.

Bullard, R. D. (2005a). Environmental justice in the twenty-first century. In R. D. Bullard (Ed.), *The quest for environmental justice: Human rights and the politics of pollution* (pp. 19–42). San Francisco, CA: Sierra Club Books.

Bullard, R. D. (2005b). Neighborhoods 'zoned' for garbage. In R. D. Bullard (Ed.), *The quest for environmental justice: Human rights and the politics of pollution* (pp. 43–61). San Francisco, CA: Sierra Club Books.

Bullard, R. D., & Smith, D. (2005). Women warriors of color on the front line. In R. D. Bullard (Ed.), *The quest for environmental justice: Human rights and the politics of pollution* (pp. 62–83). San Francisco, CA: Sierra Club Books.

Corman, L. (2011). Getting their hands dirty: Raccoons, freegans, and urban 'trash.' *Journal for Critical Animal Studies, IX*(3), 28–61.

Cornou, C. (2009). Automation systems for farm animals: Potential impacts on the human-animal relationship and on animal welfare. *Anthrozoös, 22*(3), 213–220.

Crowley, T. (2010). From 'natural' to 'ecosocial flourishing': Evaluating evaluative frameworks. *Ethics & the Environment, 15*(1), 69–100.

Elstein, D. (2003). Species as a social construction: Is species morally relevant? *Journal for Critical Animal Studies, 1*(1). Retrieved from http://www.criticalanimalstudies.org/JCAS/Journal_Articles_download/Issue_1/Elstein.PDF

Farm Sanctuary. (n.d.). *Factory farming*. Retrieved from http://www.farmsanctuary.org/issues/factoryfarming/

Fleischer, D. Z., & Zames, F. (2001). *The disability rights movement: From charity to confrontation.* Philadelphia, PA: Temple University Press.

Foucault, M. (1970). *The order of things: An archaeology of the human sciences* (Trans. of *Les mots et les choses*). New York, NY: Pantheon Books.

Foucault, M. (1972). *The archaeology of knowledge; and, The discourse on language* (A. M. Sheridan-Smith, Trans.). New York, NY: Pantheon Books.

Foucault, M. (1977). *Power/knowledge: Selected interviews and other writings, 1972–1977* (C. Gordon, Ed.; C. Gordon, L. Marshall, J. Mepham, & K. Soper, Trans.). New York, NY: Pantheon Books.

Foucault, M. (1980). *Power/knowledge: Selected interviews and other writings, 1972–1977* (C. Gordon, Ed.; C. Gordon, L. Marshall, J. Mepham, & K. Soper, Trans.). New York, NY: Pantheon Books.

Foucault, M. (1984). Nietzsche, genealogy, history. In P. Rabinow, (Ed.), *The Foucault reader* (pp. 76–100). New York, NY: Pantheon Books.

Foucault, M. (1988). Technologies of the self. In L. Martin, H. Gutman, & P. Hutton (Eds.), *Technologies of the self: A seminar with Michel Foucault* (pp. 16–49). London, UK: Tavistock.

Foucault, M. (1995). *Discipline and punish: The birth of the prison* (2nd ed., A. Sheridan, Trans.). New York, NY: Vintage Books.

Fouts, R., & Mills, S. T. (1997). The island of Dr. Lemmon. In R. Fouts & S. T. Mills, *Next of kin: My conversations with chimpanzees* (pp. 117–149). New York, NY: Avon Books.

Fouts, R. S., & Fouts, D. H. (1993). Chimpanzees' use of sign language. In P. Cavalieri & P. Singer (Eds.), *The great ape project: Equality beyond humanity* (pp. 28–41). New York, NY: St. Martin's Griffin.

Gibbs, N. (2007, January 7). Pillow angel ethics. *Time*. Retrieved from http://www.time.com/time/nation/article/0,8599,1574851,00.html

Goodall, J. (1997). Introduction. In R. Fouts & S. T. Mills, *Next of kin: My conversations with chimpanzees* (pp. ix–xi). New York, NY: Avon Books.

Grauerholz, L. (2007). Cute enough to eat: The transformation of animals into meat for human consumption in commercialized images. *Humanity & Society, 31*(4), 334–354.

Gunther, D. F., & Diekema, D. S. (2006). Attenuating growth in children with profound developmental disability: A new approach to an old dilemma. *Archives of Pediatrics and Adolescent Medicine, 160*(10), 1013–1017.

Husserl, E. (1962). *Ideas pertaining to a pure phenomenology and to a phenomenological philosophy* (W. R. Boyce, Trans.). New York, NY: Collier.

Kahn, R. (2003). Towards ecopedagogy: Weaving a broad-based pedagogy of liberation for animals, nature, and the oppressed people of the earth. *Journal for Critical Animal Studies, 1*(1). Retrieved from http://www.criticalanimalstudies.org/JCAS/Journal_Articles_download/Issue_1/kahn.pdf

Kincheloe, J. L. (2004). Introduction. In J. L. Kincheloe, *Critical pedagogy primer* (pp. 2–43). New York, NY: Peter Lang.

Martin, R. (1988). Truth, power, self: An interview with Michel Foucault. In L. Martin, H. Gutman, & P. Hutton (Eds.), *Technologies of the self: A seminar with Michel Foucault* (pp. 9–15). London, UK: Tavistock.

Mead, G. H. (1962). *Mind, self, and society from the standpoint of a social behaviorist*. Chicago, IL: University of Chicago Press.

Ostrom, C. M. (2007, October 11). Doctor who backed controversial operation on child commits suicide. *Seattle Times*. Retrieved from http://seattletimes.nwsource.com/html/localnews/2003941272_gunther11m.html

Pellow, D. G. (2007a). Environment, modernity, inequality. In D. N. Pellow, *Resisting global toxics: Transnational movements for environmental justice*, (pp. 1–36). Cambridge, MA: MIT Press.

Pellow, D. N. (2007b). Race, class, environment, and resistance. In D. N. Pellow, *Resisting global toxics: Transnational movements for environmental justice*, (pp. 37–71). Cambridge, MA: MIT Press.

Scott, J. (2011, October 5). The race to grow the one-ton pumpkin. *The New York Times*. Retrieved from http://www.nytimes.com/2011/10/06/garden/the-race-to-grow-the-one-ton-pumpkin.html?_r=1&pagewanted=all#

Singer, P. (1993). *Practical ethics* (2nd ed.). New York, NY: Cambridge University Press.

TASH. (2011). *The cost of waiting: A report on restraint, seclusion and aversive procedures one year after the passage of the Keeping All Students Safe Act in the U.S. House of Representatives*. Washington, DC: Author. Retrieved from http://issuu.com/tashorg/docs/tash_the_cost_of_waiting

Warrick, J. (2001, April 10). 'They die piece by piece'; In Overtaxed Plants, Humane Treatment of Cattle Is Often a Battle Lost. Retrieved from http://washingtonpost.com/wp-dyn/articles/A60798-2001Apr9.html

Wehmeyer, M. (2000). Riding the third wave: Self-Determination and self-advocacy in the 21st century. *Focus on Autism and Other Developmental Disabilities, 15*(2), 106 – 115.

CHAPTER THREE

Interdependence, Capability, and Competence as a Framework for Eco-Ability

JANET M. DUNCAN

> This we know: All things are connected like the blood that unites us. We did not weave the web of life. We are merely a strand in it. Whatever we do to the web, we do to ourselves.
>
> —*CHIEF SEATTLE*

This chapter begins with identifying the principles of inclusion as applied to humans, nonhumans, and the environment. Next, I discuss the relevance of Martha Nussbaum's (2006) Capabilities Approach to understanding humans with disabilities, nonhuman animals, and the environment. By examining the intersection of these three spheres, we may discover an interdependence that will provide a rational way forward in this century.

When disability rights advocates consider an alliance with animal rights activists, there is often an uneasiness that overshadows the conversation. Yes, there is a shared understanding and history of maltreatment and abuse at the hand of caregivers (Taylor, 1978). There is a shared experience of being considered and known as subhuman, thereby giving people in power the "right" to disregard the needs of people with disabilities (Bogdan, Taylor, DeGrandpre, & Haynes, 1974) and animals alike (Sunstein & Nussbaum, 2004). Instead of recognizing the mutual power each could offer the other, the two camps often remain at odds and are divided on this subject. It is as if there is a hierarchy of oppression, with neither group wanting to be affiliated with the other. Often, people with disabilities and their allies hold a speciesist point of view and do not want to be compared to "animals" (Drake, 2011). Similarly, some animal rights activists do not want to detract from their arguments that support animals. This is because they view persons with disabilities as "damaged goods," with problems unique to the disability experience, and, in fact, consider them less deserving of personhood status because of their disabilities (Singer, 2004). In reality, there is a middle ground, wherein both groups can benefit from a presumption of competence, as fully capable, and deserving of a life worth living.

Adding environmentalism to the mix, as another potential intersection of oppression, baffles the former two camps. The concept of *eco-ability* is a way to blend the common issues for all three, strengthening the notions of inclusivity, capability, competence, and positive advocacy. Instead of lamenting the shared history of oppression, we can imagine a positive relationship among the three, which is mutually beneficial and enhances the conditions of all.

The intersection of these groups is an outgrowth of what Heshusius (1995) called the "contemporary discontent with the mechanistic paradigm" (p. 168). Oliver and Gershman (1989) have also referred to the mechanistic worldview as the "bits and pieces worldview" (p. 31). For example, by picking and choosing our stances on atomic energy, infant mortality, and chemicals to increase crop production, we have made significant gains for the individual at the expense of the whole. In order to achieve these "scientific advances" we have also given away our clean water supplies, safety with nuclear waste production, and security as we fight for precious resources and monetary gains in developing countries. Transnational corporations are more concerned about shareholder profits than about protecting citizens from environmental degradation.

I propose a different alliance, one based on mutuality and interdependence in a coherent argument for assuming competence and upholding the least dangerous assumption on all three accounts. In other words, to be safe in this world, we must assume the Other (including the environment) as capable and competent, even though we may not fully understand the Other, be it human, nonhuman, or an ecosystem. Just as we assume the potentiality of a human newborn—in spite of the fact that his or her skills have yet to be developed, we fully expect great things from this species (Wise, 2004)—we should carefully consider the needs of people with disabilities, with the assumption that each person is a sentient and feeling human being. Similarly, we should consider the needs of animals with the assumption that each is a sentient and feeling nonhuman being. If we extend this further, the environment, the earth, and its interdependent ecosystems also constitute a capable entity, which requires our care and support, and also responds to its needs in a competent manner.

A Brief Introduction to the Capabilities Approach

Legal and political feminist scholar, Martha Nussbaum (1999a, 2006) offered a ten-point framework for understanding quality of life for persons with disabilities and other species. This framework is based on a non-contractarian theory of justice that proposes that people and animals are entitled to live a long, fulfilling life with integrity. In real terms, how is this framework applied in today's world? What are the quality indicators that we can study and apply to the lives of persons with disabilities? Similarly, how can we determine analogues for other species? Are there indicators we can examine for supporting the health and welfare of ecosystems?

Trying to determine how many people worldwide have a disability, if such a thing could be accomplished, is one of the conundrums for today's civil society, the transnational economy, and governments concerned with providing support for their citizens. In terms of international development assistance, nongovernmental organizations (NGOs) are charged with identifying populations in need. The interests of persons with disabilities are often the last consideration for foreign aid and technical assistance (Perlin, 2007). Previously, officials would count the number of people with a medical condition that might contribute to a disability, using the medical model. This was not satisfactory for many reasons, most notably the stigma attached to cultural understandings of disability, disease, and contagion,[1] and what Perlin (2007) described as "sanist" thinking.[2] While working for the World Bank, Sen and Nussbaum set out to devise a way of thinking about people with disabilities and their functioning in society.[3] Their resulting Capabilities Approach has been much discussed and refined in subsequent iterations.

In her book, *Sex and Social Justice*, Nussbaum (1999a) used the term "Central Human Functional Capabilities," to describe the framework. She made it clear that this framework is meant to be *aspirational* in terms of capabilities of the individual, rather than relying on existing functional abilities.[4] This is an important point when we consider the current conditions of people with disabilities worldwide; when in reality many are still treated as subhuman or nonhuman.[5] The same is true for existing conditions of animals, whether living in confinement on factory farms, in sanctuaries, or in the wild with poachers at their heels. In fact, it has long been argued that since animals are not humans, we have the right to treat them as property, much in the same way that we use resources from the environment at our will and for our pleasure and profit. Animal rights activists are equally concerned about the (mal)treatment of service animals for persons with disabilities, animals which do not elect to live a life of servitude. Yet, the popular media celebrate the "noble guide dogs for the blind" and the "foster families" who raise the puppies for the select schools for canine training. There are even programs to train miniature horses as guide horses for the blind (Burleson, 2004).

The Capabilities Approach for people and animals is a hopeful way to break through this prejudice and abusive treatment. Nussbaum argued that the following ten points should be considered when supporting either humans or species:

1. *Life.* Being able to live a full normal length life, without a premature death.
2. *Bodily health and integrity.* Being able to have good health, nutrition, reproductive health and shelter.
3. *Bodily integrity.* Being able to move freely from place to place; being free of violence against you and making choices about your reproductive freedom.
4. *Senses, imagination, and thought.* Being able to use the senses, to imagine, to think, and to reason; being able to use one's mind and to express these ideas freely.
5. *Emotions.* Being able to have attachments to things and persons (species) outside ourselves; being able to love and be loved; being able to grieve, to express longing, gratitude, and anger.
6. *Practical reason.* Being able to form a conception of the good and to engage in critical reflection about one's life.
7. *Affiliation.* Being able to live for and in relation to others, to recognize and show concern for others, to engage in social interaction. Being treated as a dignified being whose worth is equal to that of others.
8. *Other Species.* Being able to live with concern for others and in relation to other species, plants, and the world of nature.
9. *Play.* Being able to laugh, play, and enjoy one's recreational activities.
10. *Control over one's environment.* Being able to participate in political activities, with free speech; and material wealth, being able to hold property. (Nussbaum, 1999a, 1999b, pp. 41–42)

The Presumption of Competence

> If you want to see *competence [emphasis added]*, it helps if you look for it. (*Douglas Biklen, as quoted in* Kasa-Hendrickson & Buswell, 2007*)*

A key point in the argument about the treatment of those who are not in a position of self-advocacy, is that there is a presumption of *in*competence, a lack of thought and conscience, and an inability to produce commodities or services (Singer, 2004). In our capitalist economy that depends on goods being produced (ever more cheaply), and expanding markets to sell commodities, being "useful" to the economy is extremely important. In some societies, being a contributing member to the household is key; thus one's status is in peril if a disabling condition prevents one from adding to the financial and social security of the family and community.

In the field of Disability Studies, there exists the counterintuitive and powerful corollary: if we do not know what a person is thinking due to an inability for "us" to understand "them," we *must* assume the person is competent, thinking, and feeling. To do otherwise is a dangerous assumption.[6] This principle of the "criterion of the least dangerous assumption" guides decision-making, personal relationships, and all aspects of care and treatment for persons with disabilities (Donnellan, 1984). Presuming competence provides the person with dignity and removes the second tier of personhood often attributed to the person with a disability (Kasa-Hendrickson & Buswell, 2007).

For persons with disabilities, issues of competence and intelligence have long plagued their lives in substantive ways. For example, individuals are often placed in untenable situations in a court of law, having to prove their reliability as witnesses and the validity of their intelligence (Crossley & McDonald, 1984; Morton, 2009). Courts of law have questioned the use of augmentative and alternative communication systems for nonspeaking individuals when giving testimony. Whereas the presumption of innocence and competence is accorded to alleged criminals, the inverse standard is the case for people with disabilities, who have to prove their competence rather than the legal system assuming their competence (Perlin, 2007). Testimony from persons with disabilities can often be discarded if the court cannot be satisfied that the witness is competent. It is an established fact that individuals with disabilities are much more likely to be victimized, often at the hand of their caregiver, because they make incompetent witnesses (Sobsey, 1991). There are numerous cases of victims being disbelieved due to their presumed incompetence (Morton, 2009).

People with disabilities are often presumed to be incompetent as parents, with the majority of society living in fear and disgust when a woman with a disability attempts to raise her child within a relationship. As people with disabilities are often deemed asexual, or promiscuous, and incompetent, their children are often removed from caring families because of the presumption of incompetence of the parents in spite of testimony to the contrary. Legal guardians are appointed by the courts to protect the needs and interests of individuals with a disability (New York State Commission on the Quality of Care for Persons with Disabilities, 2011), when in fact such persons may be able to make decisions on their own without intervention from the court-appointed guardian. Cases of guardians imposing their will and values upon adults with disabilities are well known in the media and are often romanticized in popular culture and the media (see the movie, *The Other Sister* (Rose, Iscovich, & Marshall, 1999), or, *I Am Sam* (Herskovitz, Nelson, Solomon, & Zwick, 2001)).

A dire example of this "benevolent guardianship" is the Terri Schiavo case[7] from 1998–2005 in Florida (Lynne, 2005a). In this situation, Ms. Schiavo was living in what was called by neurologists a "persistent vegetative state," supposedly rendering her incapable of indicating her wishes, including the right to nutrition and hydration. Her estranged husband claimed to know what was best for her, given their prior relationship, and was certain that she would not want to live in such a state. Ms. Schiavo's parents, on the other hand, wanted their daughter to be treated with dignity, applying the criterion of the least dangerous assumption. In other words, without *exactly* knowing her wishes, they *assumed* she would want to be kept alive. To assume otherwise amounted to a death sentence. While the courts struggled over this issue, and Ms. Schiavo became the darling of numerous advocacy groups, often for opposing reasons, the media interpreted the events in dangerous ways. The media portrayed her life as not worthy, certainly not worth living, based on culturally derived notions of quality of life. Her parents recounted stories with videotaped evidence that Terry was in fact communicative and that she was aware of her circumstances and responded to their loving touch.

Prominent physicians and elected government officials weighed in on the issue, debating health care futility policies, the definition of "vegetative state," and even whether or not she was alive. Some physicians made pronouncements, having watched her videotapes from afar, deeming her to be a "vegetable," and consigning her to a death sentence, with the suggestion that life support ought to be withdrawn. Opposing evidence attesting to her cognitive awareness was viewed as "wishful thinking" on the part of her biological family. To the majority of the public, it was inconceivable to think that she *might* be aware of her circumstances. Admitting the possibility of Ms. Schiavo's competence, while living in a state also known as "locked-in syndrome," would be tantamount to killing her, an abhorrent thought for most. In the end, her estranged husband was granted the right to determine her fate, and he chose death by starvation and dehydration for his former wife.

A more recent case, in 2007, involves a young girl from Seattle, Washington, who was born with severe developmental delays as a result of static encephalopathy. Ashley, who is much loved by her parents, according to all accounts in the media, underwent an illegal medical treatment in an effort to contain her physical body to a certain size, for the convenience of her caregivers. Her parents sought medical procedures to keep their daughter in a prepubescent state. Known as the "Ashley Treatment,"[8] doctors discussed these procedures in a prominent medical journal as a new way to assist caregivers, and to provide *comfort* to the person with a disability. The doctors attenuated her growth by removing her reproductive organs, and giving her growth-stunting hormones to keep her body in perpetual childhood. The logical reasoning was that Ashley would be *prevented* from the discomfort of menstrual periods and large breasts, and that she would remain small, enabling her parents to carry her from place to place. How did this "procedure" pass muster with the hospital's Institutional Review Board? The ethics of the case are dubious at best, and harmful, to say the least. What did Ashley want for herself? Did her parents view her as an asexual being, incapable of a loving relationship and womanhood? Without an effective means to communicate, Ashley was transformed into a small, doll-like human, denied a most basic human right to grow and age in a dignified manner.

In many schools, students with disabilities are once again assumed to be incompetent and are denied access to the general curriculum under the guise of special education being equivalent to general education in terms of quality and preparation for life (Kliewer, 1998; Kluth, 2010; Kasa-Hendrickson & Buswell, 2007). Students are placed in classrooms that gather together the most disabled students, leaving them unable to communicate with each other, model positive behaviors, and learn a rich and appropriate curriculum.

More troubling still, students with disabilities are at a higher risk of death in schools due to the specific ways they are restrained, medicated, and withheld from human interaction in "time out" rooms.[9] In a facility known as the Judge Rotenberg Center[10] staff still use aversive behavioral therapies such as electric shock cattle prods (that have been banned from use on animals); noxious fumes squirted in the nostrils; four-point restraints for hours and days on end; a special, white-noise helmet that bombards the wearer with shrill sounds; "pinching and rolling of the skin" techniques to quash behaviors; and, constant, random attacks from staff meant to keep students on guard with positive behavior. We would not tolerate this for ourselves, let alone our own children. Yet, we allow these "behavioral interventions" to continue because these students have been determined to be incorrigible, incompetent, and bothersome to the regular school system. And when students testify about their treatment in the facility, their reports are met with disbelief, again because they cannot possibly be competent witnesses.

In 2011 the Director of the Judge Rotenberg Center, Dr. Matthew Israel, was charged in the criminal courts for misleading the grand jury and destroying evidence and was sentenced to five years probation. He was forced to resign. The organization, Mental Disability Rights International (2010), submitted an urgent report to the Special Rapporteur on Torture for the UN, charging that the treatment and documented abuses at the Center met the standard for torture under the Geneva Convention.[11] Having the United Nations investigate this facility finally drew enough attention to warrant charges, and hopefully the abuse will stop.

The Sociology of Acceptance

Bogdan and Taylor (1987) proposed a different framework than one of deviance for people with disabilities. Their research has provided many examples of positive relationships between persons with and without disabilities, that call into question the taken-for-granted notion of the person with a disability as incompetent, burdensome, and in need of receiving the benefits of friendship, not reciprocating with equal measure. To think about a person with disability as a *positive, contributing member of society*, with equal value and regard, was considered radical when first proposed (Wolfensberger, 1972). How could a person who is nonspeaking, "wheelchair-bound" (presumably), incompetent (Goode, 1992), in need of 24-hour care, be capable of offering love, friendship, and intellectual pursuits? Through careful, purposeful study of loving relationships between people with and without disabilities, Bogdan and Taylor's breakthrough work provided a way of thinking about people with disabilities as contributing, caring, and reciprocating members of society (Bogdan & Taylor, 1987).

An alternative, positive worldview is in sight for those who are looking. A recent documentary, *Wretches and Jabberers* (Biklen & Wurzburg, 2011), featured two adults with autism who use augmentative or alternative communication devices to speak their minds. Their mission is to show the world how they think, feel, and enjoy their rich lives with friends around the world. In the classic road trip film style, the friends embark on a trip to Finland, India, and Japan, accompanied by their long-term friends, who provide them with support. As adults with autism, Larry Bissonnette and Tracy Thresher demonstrate throughout the documentary how they interact with the environment, which at times is chaotic, serene, and unlike anything previously known to them. They meet new friends with similar aspirations, and display their common humanity with style and elegance. It is an interpretation of life with autism that is counter to the traditional, "scientific" view of autism as a condition marked by an inability to communicate; being unable to consider the perspective of others; and being incapable of displaying or feeling emotions. In the popular media, the stereotype of Raymond from the movie, *Rain Man*, still rules. With examples of lives such as Bissonnette's and Thresher's, we catch a glimpse of what could be for individuals with autism and intellectual developmental disorders.

Another example of the significance of the presumption of competence was Anne McDonald, a woman living with spastic quadriplegia, who cowrote her life story in *Annie's Coming Out* with Rosemary Crossley (Crossley & McDonald, 1984). The book described Anne's childhood confinement in St. Nicholas Hospital in Melbourne, Australia. Her life in this institution was brutal in many ways, although considered standard treatment at the time for individuals with cerebral palsy and other disabilities. As a teenager, Anne weighed approximately 30 pounds and was transported in a stroller. Crossley worked in this institution and discovered that Anne and her nonspeaking ward-mates could communicate using a system devised by Crossley, which used the alphabet, eye-gaze, and then pointing to spell words. After a period of training with the system, Anne declared that she wanted to move out of St. Nicholas and that she feared for her life. Crossley was committed to helping Anne move out, but first they had to demonstrate that Anne was actually the one communicating, not Crossley, and that she was competent to make her wishes known to the court. The case ended up in the Supreme Court in Australia, and Anne eventually won the right to leave and was emancipated.

Anne's case teaches us much about the presumption of competence, the sociology of acceptance, and the consequences faced by those who do not have such opportunities to survive and thrive. Had Anne not met Rosemary Crossley and her partner, Chris Borthwick, Anne would not have been able to communicate, attend college, travel around the world, and become a leading advocate for nonspeech communication. She would not have lived much beyond her teenage years, as she was already starving in the institution.

The Case of Nonhuman Animals, Capabilities, and Competence

Animals are rarely thought of as sentient beings, for if we stopped to consider this possibility, it would completely change the way we do business with animals. It would mean radically changing our economic relationships with animals, our use of animals for pleasure, and the way we can (ab)use them at will. Veterinarians would have to think twice about declawing cats, docking tails for the American Kennel Club (AKC) standards of dog beauty, and euthanizing pets so they may accompany their dead person-owner to heaven. Humans would also have to reconsider their habit of eating nonhuman animals.

In the animal world, biologists have struggled for years to find scientific ways of discussing capabilities of animals without sounding romantic and *anthropomorphic* toward other species.[12] To study animal behavior and intelligence, scientists have had to swear on their lives that the positivistic science guides the study, not the emotional lives animals may or may not lead.[13] Until the recent 1980s and 1990s, many animal behavior scientists were considered to be "soft" scientists if they attributed cognitive thinking and planning to animals, even as empirical evidence was mounting in favor of animals as sophisticated thinkers. People with significant disabilities and animals have a shared mistreatment historically and continue to share negative societal attitudes toward them that define them as nonhuman or subhuman and incompetent.

In terms of nonhuman animals and their intelligence, there is a growing recognition of animals as complex thinkers, purposeful in their actions, communicative, and capable, when given a chance. The zoological science of ethology is a relatively new field that gives credence to studying the emotional and social lives of nonhuman animals. Ethology is the study of animal behavior and now examines nonhuman communication in addition to behavioral characteristics such as aggression and socialization. Field studies of animals have existed for decades; however, many scientists have been reluctant to attribute feelings and emotions to animal behavior. We love to watch videos of dolphins rescuing human swimmers; dogs in distress on YouTube videos; and interspecies love, companionship, and an unlikely friendship between a dog and an elephant. The ultimate family vacation experience, if you can afford it, is to swim with dolphins in the Caribbean, or a water theme park, ignoring the fact that these mammals have been "harvested" (and stolen) from intimate family groups offshore Japan (see *The Cove* (Pesmen, Stevens, & Psihoyos (2009)).

The situation of the bonobo chimpanzees and other primates who use sign language to communicate is equally fascinating and potentially heartbreaking. A documentary film, *Project Nim* (Chinn & Marsh, 2011), recounted the story of a chimpanzee raised by humans and then abandoned by his "family" for experimentation. These close relatives of ours develop a large repertoire of signs and can tell us about feelings, desires for favorite things, and eventually might ask for their freedom. At what point in the communicative relationship will humans take this seriously? These vivid examples of *potentiality for competence and capabilities* should give us pause. When the scientific study of nonhuman linguistics is long finished, what will our relationships be with each other? In *Songs of the Gorilla Nation*, Prince-Hughes (2004) questioned our relationships with primates and offered unique insights about her own relationship with gorillas. Similarly, Blum (1996) sought a middle ground of compassionate treatment for primates in her book, *The Monkey Wars*. The summer hit of 2011, *Rise of the Planet of the Apes* (Chernin, Clark, Jaffa, Silver, & Wyatt, 2011), featured the human dawning of the realization that apes might have intelligence, albeit created by humans in a scientific experiment gone awry.

In her book, *The Animals' War: Animals in Wartime from the First World War to the Present Day*, Gardiner (2006) described stories of animals being heroic during wartime: animals detonating bombs to assist soldiers in Iraq, camels carrying munitions in World War Two, and dolphins being employed in submarine forces. Police forces have long used dogs for solving crimes, detecting survivors in natural disasters, and assisting with public relations campaigns. At times the canines really do seem to enjoy their work and seem proud when rewarded by their human handlers. Recently, an episode of Animal Planet's cable TV show, *Pit Bulls and Parolees* (Dinco, 2010), illustrated how hardened criminals can regain their dignity through a close relationship with equally hardened and maligned pit bulls. Viewers were entertained and gratified when a personal breakthrough in these relationships was highlighted. We know that a nonhuman animal's love can cure all, and the canines at Villalobos are evidence.

Even though there is growing acceptance of nonhuman animals as sentient beings, deserving of a fulfilling life, we still have a long way to go in our thinking. In a 2011 editorial, the lofty, definitive science journal, *Scientific American*, called for a ban on the use of primates for medical research. A status of "almost human," once attributed to the higher mammals, is now being modified to include animals long thought to be lower on the evolutionary spectrum (Wise, 2004). How society will evolve toward one that embraces nonhuman animals and the environment as competent and capable remains to be seen.

The Competence of the Environment

Some advocates for the environment fall into the nature worship trap, where everything that is in nature lives in harmony, in balance, and all of nature is wise (Nussbaum, 2004). In contrast to this romantic notion, others have proposed that nature can be cruel, not in balance, and somewhat chaotic (Botkin, 1996), echoing John Stuart Mill's original comments in his essay "Nature." We should avoid arguments where nature will take its course, with or without assistance from humans, and instead find a way to recognize and appreciate the circumstances by which the environment can be supported to flourish. Following the "nature will take its course" argument, humans are relieved of the responsibility for damage caused through human activity. At the same time, "managing the environment" can be devastating, with resulting, unintended consequences, such as the release of a nonnative insect to devour a particular crop pest. At the same time, there are plenty of examples of nature responding to the discontinuation of harm caused by humans. Next, we will discuss some of these examples as a potential source of capability and competence of the environment.

Scientists have been studying the ways in which damaged ecosystems respond to recovery efforts and interventions to restore systems to their previous condition. Natural disasters such as the Mount St. Helen's eruptions in 1980 gave us a textbook case of, "nature taking its course," with multiple examples of the mountain regenerating its forest ecosystem after three decades (Carey, 2011). The initial damage caused by the volcanic eruptions was significant: over 240 miles of forest were destroyed, with all wildlife in the active zone succumbing to the lava and ash. A few short years later, seedlings appeared, underground burrowing animals reappeared, songbirds established themselves in newly treed areas, and scientists studied the progression of the new biodiverse ecosystems. After a decade, new forests developed on the north-facing slopes, interspersed with willows and deciduous trees. The entire system has regenerated without being managed, and ecologists have learned from this experience how important biodiversity in healthy ecosystems can be (McNulty, 2010).[14]

There has always been controversy over the environment, with varied approaches such as "management of resources," conservation, exploitation, preservation, and coexistence. We have seen the devastation of clear-cutting of old-growth forests; overfishing to the point of depopulation of the cod fishery off the Grand Banks of Newfoundland, Canada; near extinction of animal species due to overhunting, such as the buffalo; desertification of large tracts of land through mismanagement of water resources and wasteful logging practices; nuclear accidents with resulting deaths and ecological disaster in Japan and Chernobyl, to name only some events of many in the recent past. Finally, the 2010 oil spill in the Gulf of Mexico is a recent disaster that remains to be fully understood in terms of ecological damage and devastation.

These examples are provided not as an excuse to relieve humans of the burden of taking responsibility for their actions, with the assumption that "nature will take care of itself because it is competent." Rather, the point is that we need to acknowledge, as a global society, that we are all interdependent, including humans (with and without disabilities), nonhuman species, and the environment. This interdependence provides us with an opportunity to more fully appreciate and understand that previously discarded and misunderstood parts of our whole can contribute more meaningfully to our mutual flourishing. An example of this is recent scientific research in understanding migration patterns of monarch butterflies and their magnetic forces within their minute bodies. For decades, we have wondered how these small animals make their way from North America all the way to South America. Plants from the Amazon rainforest are providing new medicines, and large portions of that ecosystem are still undiscovered, especially in the oceans.

Our oceans are understudied and misunderstood. How many bacteria are being discovered existing in volcanic vents several miles underneath the surface of the ocean? Harnessing the energy from the world's largest tidal forces in the Bay of Fundy, Canada, is another capability we are still studying.[15] Onondaga Lake in Central New York is yet another example of a "dead lake" that has survived deep poisoning by Allied Chemical in the mid-1900s, with fish populations and eagles returning fifty years later. While scientists debated how to best clean up Onondaga Lake, considered to be the most polluted lake in all of the United States, either through dredging and removing the surface layers of heavy metals and PCBs, or by capping the toxic layers with cement, gradually the lake has begun to restore itself. While the lake is still not safe for swimming, signs of its recovery improve yearly (Williamson & Hesler, 2006.)

Letting nature take care of itself is not without controversy. Populations of wolves that have succeeded through reintroduction in the western states are considered to endanger the livestock of sheep and cattle, according to ranchers. "Management" of the wolves is a hot topic for all concerned, with some advocating culling the species. Coyotes have enjoyed a resurgence in urban areas and suburban neighborhoods, and everyone complains about the deer population gorging on shrubbery in suburban housing tracts. Overpopulation of species is the oft-cited excuse for eliminating the problem animal.

The above-mentioned "problems" with deer, coyotes, and wolves would appear to be elitist and a nice problem to have, compared to the situation in the rest of the world where famine, desertification, and deforestation affecting billions of people is more the case. Similarly, while citizens in industrialized nations are concerned about education and community living for persons with disabilities, the majority of persons with disabilities globally are not even guaranteed the most basic human rights: to live, eat, go to school, and survive childhood (Perlin, 2007). How do we reconcile such different realities and remain hopeful for our planet? By combining our collective advocacy efforts for humans, nonhuman species, and the environment, we can move forward.

The Intersection of Capabilities, Humans and Nonhumans, the Environment, and the UN Convention on the Rights of Persons with Disabilities

Let us go back to our earlier discussion of Nussbaum's (2006) Capabilities framework, and see how the intersection of humans and nonhuman animals may be illustrated with analogues for the environment. If we compare how animals and people with disabilities currently exist relative to this framework, we can itemize similarities and differences. The UN Convention on the Rights of Persons with Disabilities is a useful framework that contains articles that could parallel efforts to protect animals and perhaps the environment. At this time, there is no equivalent set of international protections for animals based on their nonhuman rights, capacity for intelligence, and competence. Equally, there is no comparable set of rights and protections for the environment on a global level. There have been, and continue to be, advocates for both animal rights and protections, in addition to environmental advocacy.

In the 1980s, disability rights activists, representing numerous groups with varying positions in the political spectrum, argued together for a new way to approach the needs of persons with disabilities. It was argued, successfully, that a new Human Rights Convention that would guarantee the right to certain freedoms was a worthy goal to pursue. At the time, there was skepticism that this would never happen in our lifetime. Indeed, at the 2008 World Congress of Inclusion International held in Ottawa, Canada, leading disability activist, Catherine Frazee, commented: "I never dreamed we would have a convention, let alone one that was signed by the UN States Parties, in such short order, and in my lifetime."[16]

The UN Convention on the Rights of Persons with Disabilities was the fastest approved convention in United Nations history. There was much agreement about the problem internationally and with potential solutions that could be implemented and monitored (MacKay, 2007). Meanwhile, significant states parties are continuing to examine the implications if the Convention is ratified and adopted (Kanter, 2007). The Convention is now in the phase of developing a framework for implementation and evaluating the progress of states parties. As of April 2012, 153 countries have adopted the Convention as signatories, and 112 states parties have ratified the Convention.[17]

> The general principles of the Convention include the following:
> a) Respect for inherent dignity, individual autonomy including the freedom to make one's own choices, and independence of persons;
> b) Non-discrimination;
> c) Full and effective participation and inclusion in society;
> d) Respect for difference and acceptance of disability as part of human diversity and humanity;
> e) Equality of opportunity;
> f) Accessibility;
> g) Equality between men and women;
> h) Respect for the evolving capacities of children with disabilities and respect for the right of children with disabilities to preserve their identities. (United Nations, 2006)

The potential for the Convention to significantly affect the lives of people globally is not to be underestimated. Countries ratifying the Convention are now obliged to establish national arrangements for coordinating Convention implementation (for example, a national Office of Disability Issues) and an independent agency with the task of promoting and reviewing progress. Countries are taking different approaches to changing their own laws to meet the Convention requirements. Some (e.g., Japan) are reviewing their legislation before ratification. Others (e.g., Hungary) are using ratification as the starting point for change. There are also differences in the way civil society organisations (like our national associations) are getting involved in this change process. For example, the Arabic countries, Mexico and Norway are each taking different routes to promoting understanding of the Convention and participation in its implementation.[18]

Of the 50 Articles presented in the Convention, there are several that have a direct link to Nussbaum's (2006) capabilities approach. The articles of the Convention describe protections for people with disabilities in the following sectors of society: education, work, healthcare, recreation, culture, and political, with protections for privacy, freedom, and accessibility. This framework can be expanded further to include a Convention on the Rights of Other Species and the Rights of the Environment. To view our systems of human, nonhuman, and environmental interactions in a holistic manner would combine advocacy efforts and lead to broader, positive outcomes and benefits for all.

Conclusion

In this chapter I have explored the ways in which humans with disabilities have a shared history of domination, subjugation, and degradation with nonhuman animals and the environment. I see the potential for common rights and protections under the United Nations with a new convention on the Rights of Nonhuman Animals and the Environment. The assumption that people are competent, capable, and deserving of equal rights and protections is an important set of principles that must be accorded to people with disabilities through the enactment of the UN Convention on the Rights of Persons with Disabilities. By extension, we can use the same positive thinking for nonhuman animals, thus providing other species with rights, an assumption of competence, and sentience. Lastly, if we assumed that interdependent ecosystems were equally alive, and competent, we could foster attitudes of respect and regard for the environment. By combining these ideas with an eye toward environmentalism with equal protections, we can find common ground with which to support the environment as a competent entity, worthy of consideration with deep regard. Anything less is a very dangerous assumption that we employ at our own peril.

Notes

1. For a thorough discussion of this issue, see Mont (2007). *Measuring Disability Prevalence.*
2. Perlin (2007) outlined the problems in the international legal system that disenfranchise persons with mental health issues based on a presumption that institutionalized persons with disabilities are held to a "sanist" standard of having to prove competency before they are afforded standard human treatment.
3. To understand the development of this approach, read *Development as Freedom*, by Amartya Sen (2000).
4. For a thorough discussion of the differences between functional and existing capabilities, see pages 41–47 of chapter 1, "Women and Cultural Universals," in Nussbaum (1999b).
5. See Laurie Ahern and Eric Rosenthal's work with Mental Disability Rights International (mdri.org), and the organization's excellent reports on the living conditions of persons with disabilities (see, in particular, Mental Disability Rights International, 2002, 2006, and 2007).

6. This principle is known as the *criterion of the least dangerous assumption*, which supports the idea that if we do not know, we cannot assume there is nothing happening cognitively. Anne Donnellan (1984) wrote a seminal article on this topic.
7. For the complete account of this story, see Lynne, 2005b.
8. See Drake, 2007.
9. See the Alliance to Prevent Restraint, Aversive Interventions and Seclusion (APRAIS) documents related to this issue, January 24, 2011, on the TASH website (TASH, 2011). TASH is an organization that stands for equity, opportunity and inclusion for persons with disabilities.
10. For a detailed account of this facility and its treatments, see Kindlon et al., 2006. Conditions are not much different today.
11. The special report is titled, *Torture not Treatment* (Mental Disability Rights International, 2010).
12. The author of this chapter, Duncan, encountered this prevailing attitude as a first-year Biology major at university, when her advisor said she would be too emotional to study animals with any scientific rigor.
13. A detailed discussion of these scientific dilemmas can be found in Moussaieff Masson and McCarthy (1995).
14. Tim McNulty is a poet, conservationist, and nature writer who lives in the foothills of the Olympic Mountains of Washington state. His books include *Olympic National Park: A Natural History* (1996), and *Washington's Mount Rainier National Park: A Centennial Celebration* (1998, with Pat O'Hara as coauthor).
15. If we can figure out how to develop turbines that do not injure sea animals.
16. Catherine Frazee, former Chief Commissioner of the Ontario Human Rights Commission, made these public comments at the World Congress, in recognition of the United Nations Convention on the Rights of Persons with Disabilities (2006), in Ottawa, Ontario, Canada, in November 2008.
17. As of April, 2012, according to the United Nations website on the Convention.
18. A complete discussion of the Convention and its development can be explored through the Inclusion International website (http://www.inclusion-international.org/).

References

Biklen, D. (1985). *Achieving the complete school: Strategies for effective mainstreaming.* New York, NY: Teachers College Press.

Biklen, D. (Producer), Wurzburg, G. (Producer, Director). (2011). *Wretches and jabberers* [Motion picture]. United States: State of the Art, Inc.

Blum, D. (1996). *The monkey wars.* Oxford, UK: Oxford University Press.

Bogdan, R., & Taylor, S. J. (1987). Toward a sociology of acceptance: The other side of the study of deviance. *Social Policy, 18*(2), 34–39.

Bogdan, R., & Taylor, S. J. (1989). *Relationships with severely disabled people: The social construction of humanness.* Syracuse, NY: Center on Human Policy.

Bogdan, R., Taylor, S. J., DeGrandpre, B., & Haynes, S. (1974). Let them eat programs: Attendants' perspectives and programming on wards in state schools. *Journal of Health and Social Behavior, 15*(2), 142–151.

Botkin, D. B. (1996). Adjusting law to nature's discordant harmonies. *Duke Law and Policy Forum, 7*(1), 25–37.

Burleson, J. (2004). *Helping Hooves.* The Guide Horse Foundation. Retrieved from www.guidehorse.com

Carey, J. (2011). Hot commodities. *National Wildlife, 49*(6), 22–29.

Chernin, P. (Producer), Clark, D. (Producer), Jaffa, R. (Producer), Silver, A. (Producer), & Wyatt, R. (Director). (2011). *Rise of the planet of the apes* [Motion picture]. United States: Twentieth Century Fox.

Chinn, S. (Producer), & Marsh, J. (Director). (2011). *Project Nim* [Motion picture]. United States: Red Box Films.

Collier, P. (2007). *The bottom billion: Why the poorest countries are failing and what can be done about it.* Oxford, UK: Oxford University Press.

Crossley, R., & McDonald, A. (1984). *Annie's coming out.* London, UK: Penguin.

Dinco, M. (Producer). (2010). *Pit bulls and parolees* [Television series] Hollywood, CA: Animal Planet.

Donnellan, A. (1984). The criterion of the least dangerous assumption. *Behavioral Disorders, 9*(2), 141–150.

Drake, S. (2007). Not Dead Yet statement on 'growth attenuation' experimentation. Retrieved from http://www.notdeadyet.org/docs/Growth_AttenuationPR0107.html

Drake, S. (2011). *Not Dead Yet blog.* Retrieved from www.notdeadyet.org

Gardiner, J. (2006). *The animals' war: Animals in wartime from the First World War to the present day.* London, UK: Portrait.

Goode, D. A. (1992). Who is Bobby? Ideology and method in the discovery of a Down Syndrome person's competence. In P. M. Ferguson, D. L. Ferguson, & S. J. Taylor (Eds.), *Interpreting disability: A qualitative reader* (pp. 197–212). New York, NY: Teachers College Press.

Herskovitz, M. (Producer), Nelson, J. (Producer), Solomon, R. (Producer), Zwick, E. (Producer), & Nelson, J. (Director). (2001). *I am Sam* [Motion picture]. United States: New Line Cinema.

Heshusius, L. (1995). Holism and special education: There is no substitute for real life purposes and processes. In T. M. Skrtic (Ed.), *Disability and democracy: Reconstructing (special) education for postmodernity* (pp. 166–189). New York, NY: Teachers College Press.

Kanter, A. S. (2007). The promise and challenge of the United Nations Convention on the Rights of Persons with Disabilities. *Syracuse Journal of International Law and Commerce, 34*(2), 287–321.

Kasa-Hendrickson, C., & Buswell, W. (2007). *Strategies for presuming competence.* Retrieved from http://soe.syr.edu/media/documents/2011/8/PresumingCompetence.pdf

Kindlon, R., Bandini, S., Suriano, C., Tyner-Doyle, P., Magyar, C., Crimmins, D., & Roll, D. (2006). Observations and findings of out-of-state program visitation: Judge Rotenberg Educational Center. Retrieved from http://boston.com/news/daily/15/school_report.pdf

Kliewer, C. (1998). *Schooling children with Down Syndrome: Toward an understanding of possibility.* New York, NY: Teachers College Press.

Kluth, P. (2010). *You're going to love this kid!: Teaching students with autism in the inclusive classroom.* 2nd. Edition. Baltimore, MD: Paul H. Brookes Publishing Co.

Lynne, D. (2005a). *Terri's story: The court-ordered death of an American woman.* Nashville, TN: WND Books.

Lynne, D. (2005b).The whole Terri Schiavo story. Retrieved from http://www.wnd.com/?pageId=29516#ixzz1MRX6LrNb

MacKay, D. (2007). The United Nations Convention on the Rights of Persons with Disabilities. *Syracuse Journal of International Law and Commerce, 34*(2), 323–331.

McNulty, T. (1996). *Olympic National Park : A natural history.* Seattle, WA: University of Washington Press.

McNulty, T. (2010) *Inner Voice.* Retrieved from afseee@afseee.org

McNulty, T., & O'Hara, P. (1998). *Washington's Mount Rainier National Park : A centennial celebration.* Seattle, WA: The Mountaineers.

Mental Disability Rights International. (2002). *Not on the agenda: Human rights of people with mental disabilities in Kosovo.* Washington, DC: Author. Retrieved from http://www.mdri.org/PDFs/reports/KosovoReport.pdf

Mental Disability Rights International. (2006). *Hidden suffering: Romania's segregation and abuse of infants and children with disabilities.* Washington, DC: Author. Retrieved from http://www.mdri.org/PDFs/reports/romania-May%209%20final_with%20photos.pdf

Mental Disability Rights International. (2007). *Ruined lives: Segregation from society in Argentina's psychiatric asylums: A report on human rights and mental health in Argentina.* Washington, DC: Author. Retrieved from http://www.mdri.org/PDFs/reports/MDRI.ARG.ENG.NEW.pdf

Mental Disability Rights International. (2010). *Torture not treatment: Electric shock and long-term restraint in the United States on children and adults with disabilities at the Judge Rotenberg Center: Urgent appeal to the United Nations Special Rapporteur on Torture.* Washington, DC: Author. Retrieved from http://www.mdri.org/PDFs/USReportandUrgentAppeal.pdf

Mont, D. (2007). *Measuring disability prevalence* [SP Discussion Paper No. 0706.]. Washington, DC: The World Bank

Morton, M. (2009). Silenced in the court: Meanings of research and difference in the US legal system. *Disability and Society, 24*(7), 883–895.

Moussaieff Masson, J., & McCarthy, S. (1995). *When elephants weep : The emotional lives of animals.* New York, NY : Delacorte Press.

New York State Commission on the Quality of Care for Persons with Disabilities. (2011). *Protection and advocacy for persons with developmental disabilities.* Albany, NY: New York State Government Printing Office.

Nussbaum, M. C. (1999a). *Sex and social justice.* Oxford, UK: Oxford University Press.

Nussbaum, M. C. (1999b). Women and cultural universals. In M. C. Nussbaum, *Sex and social justice* (pp. 29–54). Oxford, UK: Oxford University Press.

Nussbaum, M. C. (2004). Beyond 'compassion and humanity': Justice for nonhuman animals. In C. R. Sunstein & M. C. Nussbaum (Eds.), *Animal rights: Current debates and new directions* (pp. 299–320). Oxford, UK: Oxford University Press.

Nussbaum, M. C. (2006). *Frontiers of justice: Disability, nationality, species membership.* Cambridge, MA: Harvard University Press.

Oliver, D. W., & Gershman, K. W. (1989). *Education, modernity, and fractured meaning: Toward a process theory of teaching and learning.* Albany, NY: State University of New York Press.

Perlin, M. L. (2007). International human rights law and comparative mental disability law: The universal factors. *Syracuse Journal of International Law and Commerce, 34*(2), 333–358.

Pesmen, P. D. (Producer), Stevens, F. (Producer), & Psihoyos, L. (Director). (2009). *The cove* [Motion picture]. United States: Oceanic Preservation Society.

Prince-Hughes, D. (2004). *Songs of the gorilla nation: My journey through autism.* New York, NY: Harmony Books.

Rose, A., (Producer), Iscovich, M. (Producer), & Marshall, G. (Director). (1999). *The other sister* [Motion picture]. United States: Mandeville Films.

Sen, A. (2000). *Development as freedom.* New York, NY: Anchor Books.

Singer, P. (2004). Ethics beyond species and beyond instincts: A response to Richard Posner. In C. R. Sunstein & M. C. Nussbaum (Eds.), *Animal rights: Current debates and new directions* (pp. 78–92). Oxford, UK: Oxford University Press.

Sobsey, R. (1991). *Disability, sexuality, and abuse: An annotated bibliography.* Baltimore, MD: Paul H. Brookes.

Sunstein, C. R., & Nussbaum, M. C. (Eds.). (2004). *Animal rights: Current debates and new directions.* Oxford, UK: Oxford University Press.

TASH. (2011). *The cost of waiting: A report on restraint, seclusion and aversive procedures one year after the passage of the Keeping All Students Safe Act in the U.S. House of Representatives.* Washington, DC: Author. Retrieved from http://issuu.com/tashorg/docs/tash_the_cost_of_waiting

Taylor, S. J. (1978). The attendants: Attendants and their work at state institutions for the mentally retarded (Doctoral dissertation, Syracuse University, 1977). *Dissertation Abstracts International, 39,* 1145A–1146A.

Taylor, S. J. (1982). From segregation to integration: Strategies for integrating severely handicapped students in normal school and community settings. *Journal of the Association for the Severely Handicapped* (JASH), *7*(3), 42–49.

Taylor, S. J., Biklen, D., & Knoll, J. (Eds.). (1987). *Community integration for people with severe disabilities.* New York, NY: Teachers College Press.

Taylor, S. J., & Bogdan, R. (1989). On accepting relationships between people with mental retardation and nondisabled people: Towards an understanding of acceptance. *Disability, Handicap and Society, 4*(1), 21–36.

United Nations. (2006). Convention on the rights of persons with disabilities. Retrieved from http://www.un.org/disabilities/convention/conventionfull.shtml

Williamson, K., & Hesler, D. (2006, August). Return to glory—The resurgence of Onondaga Lake. *New York State Conservationist, 61*(1), 7–14.

Wise, S. M. (2004). Animal rights, one step at a time. In C. R. Sunstein & M. C. Nussbaum, (Eds.), *Animal rights, current debates and new directions* (pp. 19–50). Oxford, UK: Oxford University Press.

Wolfensberger, W. (1972). *The principle of normalization in human services.* Toronto, Canada: National Institute on Mental Retardation.

PART II

Identity Constructions

CHAPTER FOUR

Critical Perspectives on Disability Studies and Social Constructions of Environments

Commoditization and Its Effect on Society and Nature

ROBIN M. SMITH AND JACK P. MANNO

We are two scholars—Robin in Disability Studies, Jack in Environmental Studies—who have been friends and allies for decades. Together we have explored themes at the intersection of Disability Studies and Environmental Studies. Jack sees that it is just not the land (or the water or the forest or Nature) that needs to be healed, but society's relations to it, just as Robin sees that it is not the disabled that need fixing but the relationship between disability and society. In this chapter we consider how Robin's insights from disability studies can help us think and teach about environmental issues in a way that goes deeper than seeing the environment as a source of problems to be managed, and we consider how Jack's work in ecological economics on the origins and effects of commoditization can help explain the oppression of people with disabilities as a part of a larger pattern of privileging the economy of market goods and services over the interdependent economy of ecosystems and communities.

One major similarity between our analyses has been our motivation. We think about our beloved students, friends, and family members with different types of abilities and are moved to consider the lived experience of disability and what is needed for people with disabilities to flourish. We think about an ecosystem, a special place, a favorite lake or stream, or a line of turtles on a log in the pond; we think of beloved fellow beings, whose well-being is frequently trumped by something inaccurately referred to as *development*. When we think this way, our fellow creatures' homes—the swamp, the thicket at the edge of the field—can no longer be seen as problems to be drained or cleared away to make room for economic development. They become special places where life flourishes in particular fashion and abundance.

In our work we share key themes: respect for the unique, individual gifts of beings (human and nonhuman both) and an appreciation of their *intrinsic values*; a focus on *commoditization* as explanation for conditions that disable human relations among people, and between people and place; and an emphasis on *integrity* (understood as an environment that enables one's unique flourishing) and *empowerment* (understood as the social conditions that encourage flourishing). Robin has studied and lived *disability*. She has watched Disability Studies and the disability movement grow and mature, becoming increasingly complex. As a scholar, teacher, and activist she has helped to discard a simple management/charity model based on the medicalization of disability (i.e., disablement as the source of problems), and has helped to replace it by an empowerment model based on an understanding of the complex relationship between disability and society (i.e., society as much or more a source of the problems than particular impairments) (Smith, Gallagher, Owen, & Skrtic, 2009).

In the empowerment model, people with disabilities and their allies assert their rights, and society's ethical responsibility is to recognize each individual's gifts and organize societal policies and practice in ways that encourage the flourishing of these gifts. With others Robin has worked to develop core concepts and ethical principles to guide disability policy and action.

Jack, too, has focused on core concepts and principles to guide what is sometimes called *sustainability*, the challenge to imagine and create a world in which human culture and all life prospers without undermining its earth-based, ecological foundations. Jack's analysis started when he was a journalist uncovering a Cold War program code-named Project Fishbowl, that tested nuclear weapons in outer space (Manno, 1984). The "fishbowl" referred to Planet Earth. The nuclear explosion was designed to produce a stream of radioactive particles that would follow the lines of the earth's magnetic field and reenter the upper atmosphere, where it was targeted to disrupt radio and radar communication prior to a surprise first-strike attack. To Jack, the engineers of Project Fishbowl were so psychologically detached from the earth that they imagined it to be an artificially enclosed world they could observe from afar. This detachment, this metaphoric and physical transformation of the earth from a living being and a complex set of ecological relations into a tool of warfare operating within a glass fishbowl unnerved him and set him on an intellectual path to uncover the sources of that detachment. Years later, as an academic scholar, he was writing in the emerging field of Ecological Economics, tracing the dynamics of commoditization and the associated disruption of earth-based and community-based connectedness. It is from these empirical and theoretical foundations that we address the topic of disability and nonhuman animals.

The editors of this book suggested that animals (i.e., nonhuman beings) be considered a group targeted by oppression, and that this oppression bears similarities to the oppression of people with disabilities. In a previously published article we discussed alternatives to the medicalization and commoditization of ability and the environment, focusing on three key points (Smith & Manno, 2008):

1. Disability is socially constructed. Disability resides in the set of social relationships and outcomes of social practices that tend to disadvantage and marginalize people with impairments, perceived impairments, and physical differences. These relationships are institutional, cultural, and interpersonal social structures. The environment is also socially constructed. (Smith & Manno, 2008, p. 2)
2. The social construct, *environment*, is defined through a web of socioeconomic relations that privileges commodities over relationships, where a tree is regarded far more as timber and paper pulp than as oxygen producer, shelter for beings, builder of soil or the many other roles it plays in a complex set of ecosystem relations (Manno, 2000, as cited in Smith & Manno, 2008, p. 3).
3. Many of the guidelines disability studies have developed are about avoiding deficit assumptions and acknowledging the complexity of the lived experience of disabled people. (Smith & Manno, 2008, p. 4)

Animals Are Persons

Our argument begins with the assumption that animals are persons, (nonhuman beings). They matter. Individuals with disabilities are persons, fully human beings. We matter. We are all persons. We are all animals. We are all individuals with disabilities. Yes, each reader is human, and human intelligence is special, and the human spirit is glorious. But this does not mean that we are not also animals who are, in many ways, no better and no worse than any nonhuman person. And none of us has thus far come through the process of conception, birth, and growing up with all our human abilities fully developed. We all are people with disabilities. Midgley (1985) pointed out that in its English origins the term, *person*, refers to "a mask," a part in a play, "a character, relation, or capacity in which one acts" (p. 54), a part in the drama that matters to the story. The meaning turns on our ability to notice what and who matters.

Neither the categories of disabilities that we use to organize support for the inclusion, dignity, and self-determination of persons with certain disabilities nor the species categories and names we use to communicate about nonhuman animals change this fundamental reality: the universality of limitations and the earth-based physicality of all persons. Yet, most of us live in social systems that have effectively depersonalized animals and people with disabilities. For the purposes that matter most, the purposes of profit making that drive the allocation of resources in most modern capitalist economies, they do not matter as persons, only as property.

In this chapter we describe and discuss one mechanism through which this systematic depersonalization becomes *normal* rather than odd and oppressive. We argue that this results in part from what we call *commoditization*, the privileging of commodities and property over relationships and mutuality in the allocation of society's resources (Manno 2000, 2010). These resources include financial resources, energy and raw materials, and what is sometimes called human resources, for example, attention, labor, creativity, ingenuity, and time. To the extent that these resources are allocated for the purposes of producing profit or establishing and defending the conditions for profit making and continual economic growth, the depersonalization that undermines relationships becomes inevitable. In this process those who are most commoditized—those who are turned into property, such as human slaves forced into servitude and animals in industrial meat production—are the most harmed. Whenever property relations dominate over all others, everyone's humanity is diminished. In this chapter we emphasize the effects of commoditization on relations with Nature and the disabled. (In this chapter we use the term, *the disabled*, to indicate that disability is a social construct and that it is caused by external factors such as physical, social, and attitudinal barriers that exacerbate any individual impairment involved.)

Commoditization

Commoditization can be understood as a simple evolutionary process. What receives more of society's resources has a better chance of flourishing than what gets less. Commodities are, by definition, goods and services that can be bought and sold. They are readily transferable from a producer to a consumer, a seller to a buyer. The value of a commodity is not lost in its transfer. In fact, classic economic theory demonstrates that exchange of goods and services leads to greater total value, because an exchanged good or service is, by definition, of more value to the buyer than to the seller, otherwise there is simply no profit, and therefore no reason for exchange. But many important things cannot be readily transferable. They are, in a word, priceless. These include relationships of many sorts: human beings with each other, with places, animals, landscapes, and ecosystems.

Let us be clear: there are countless attempts to commoditize these relationships. Popular culture is rife with the effort. In fact, *culture* itself—the sum total of the expressions of these important relationships—has become hypercommoditized. It is important to remember that access to each individual's attention is a product that drives the nearly trillion dollar global advertising and public relations industry. When we buy products, we buy lifestyles. We establish, whether we know it or not, a depersonalized relationship with the people whose labor and creativity are embodied in the products we purchase, the land from which its raw materials have been removed, and the nonhuman beings whose lives intersect with the places and resources from which it came. Continued economic growth in highly "developed" (we prefer, "maldeveloped") societies depends on ingenious ways of commoditizing human relationships, human attention, and human feelings, and transforming them into products for sale. The result is the production of more wealth, used to import more energy, material, and human resources from throughout the material world.

This is how it works: In any competition for essential resources (finance, energy, material resources, labor, human attention, ingenuity, and creativity) between alternative approaches to meeting human needs or wants, those "satisfiers" with the characteristics of a commodity will always outcompete those that are more difficult to commoditize. For example, in health care: pills, equipment, and supplies have high commodity potential, while personal knowledge of one's own body, exercise, and hands-on care by people helping people have low commodity potential. In children's play, Barbie dolls have high commodity potential; child-led play has low commodity potential. In energy, fuels, equipment, and supplies have high commodity potential, while energy conservation and passive solar power have low commodity potential.

Thus, societies dedicated foremost to economic expansion—that is, most modern industrial societies—end up with a highly overdeveloped economy of things and commodities, and a woefully underdeveloped economy of relationships. The people in these societies tend to have overdeveloped capacities for operating in markets, and for understanding and distinguishing among a range of commodities. But they have an underdeveloped—perhaps disabled—ability to understand and distinguish among a range of relationships with other persons of all kinds. Most indigenous societies had (and have) a highly developed sense of relationships with nonhuman animals and the natural world. This is not because they are another kind of human being, but because in societies that depend on nonhuman animals and ecosystems for sustenance, the economy of relations and the knowledge of relations are of utmost importance. Thus, they pay attention. They understand that nonhuman animals are included in the phrase, "all my relations."

Despite these differences between indigenous and industrial societies, no one is actually more or less dependent on the natural world. However, some people notice their dependence more than others. In our modern, industrial societies, we live out an illusion that we are dependent on money for all that we need. But money is essentially a claim, recognized by others in the web of economic relations, for a certain amount of resources from society and nature. We are trained to think of all our relations as relations of ownership. For many, we do not "work"; we *have* a job or a career. We do not "love"; we *have* a relationship. We do not "feel"; we *have* feelings. We are not uniquely endowed with diverse gifts and skills; we *have* disabilities. We are not in relationships with nonhuman animals or ecosystems; we *own* them. This curious and damaging lack of active engagement with the world around us is the effect of commoditization, which we consider to be a form of oppression (Manno, 2010).

The concept of commoditization provides a way to understand the connection between the oppression of nonhuman persons and people with disabilities. In biophysical terms, a society can be thought of as consisting of networks of flows of materials and networks of flows of energy. Through these flows and the products that embody them we meet our basic needs for food, clothing, shelter, transportation, and warmth, as well as all our luxuries and conveniences (Vanderburg, 2005). People make daily livelihood and lifestyle decisions based on our expectations of these flows. We need to connect to them in order to support ourselves, our families, and our communities. Networks of energy and material flows involve transfers and transactions at various points of connectedness, not only through interactions with markets but also through nonmarket relations of family and community or through direct interaction with natural ecosystems.

In our interactions with markets, we are producers and consumers. In our interactions with family, politics, clubs, and other social institutions, we are participants: neighbors, family, friends, and citizens. In our direct interactions with ecosystems we are inhabitants. Each of us is a consumer, participant, and inhabitant at the same time, interacting with a range of different networks of flows. Successfully managing these multiple relations and access points to the resources that meet our needs requires a different set of skills and forms of knowledge for each role: as consumers, participants, and inhabitants. We continually make decisions about how we allocate our time, labor, and attention among various options based on our own calculus of needs, wants, and expectations. As the world around us becomes increasingly dominated by market logic, the allocation of our personal resources becomes dominated by market logic. In this manner, the realms in which commoditization operates expand, and market logic overwhelms other logics of relationships. In this way, the space for the flourishing of nature, animals, and disabled persons shrinks.

Throughout history, societies have differed in the degree to which one or another mode of connectedness to resource flows has dominated. In hunter-gatherer societies, energy and material flows were accessed through earth-based and small community-based connectedness. In other words, you flourished to the extent that you knew how to live well within ecosystems and communities. As humans became able to obtain, store, harness, and apply greater amounts of higher quality energy, cities became possible; and large community-based connections via institutions became dominant (Hall, Tharakan, Hallock, Cleveland, & Jefferson, 2003; Vanderburg, 2005). Further power to concentrate energy and material resources reduced the cost of long-range transport, and market-based or politics-based connectedness became the mode through which individuals and groups were connected to massive networks of energy and material flows. How, where, and to what degree one connects to resource flows depends on a person's place in a community, market, and ecosystem. If one is well connected to individuals and institutions of power, one has access to material and energy resources. The further away or more tenuous one's connection to power, the greater the struggle to meet daily needs. Prior to the modern era of cheap energy, networks of flows of energy and material resources were far more limited than at present. Connections to these networks were primarily through tribe, guild, family, clan, and neighborhood, or directly from fields, forests, and waters.

In most modern societies these networks of flows of energy and material resources have come to be represented by money. Each unit of currency, in effect, grants us power to lay claim to or purchase either a certain amount of embodied energy and material resources or to hold rights to claim a certain amount of future resources. The flow of money is thus the means through which present societies primarily organize the networks of energy and material flows, and it is these flows that structure society. The invention of the global system of money, and, most importantly, interest and debt, followed by its computerization, has created conditions in which claims and rights for access to energy and material resources have increased exponentially in volume and rate of flow.

The more that markets determine investment, the greater the force driving economic evolution toward the development of those traits that define a commodity, or a marketable good or service, and away from the development of those traits that characterize nonmarket satisfiers, typically those involving community-based and earth-based connectedness. Market-based and technology-based connections flourish, while others wither. Commoditization thus leads to the underdevelopment of the economy of relationships (community-based and earth-based connections) and the overdevelopment of the economy of things (market-based connectedness). What we call "highly developed societies" are societies whose development patterns have been highly distorted through the process of commoditization as a result of the colonization of the communal and ecological spheres by the logic and values of markets. A healthy, sustainable economy would, ideally, balance and optimize all three networks of energy and material flows and associated relationships—community, market, and ecosystem—in the context of each other. (For a more complete development of this argument, see Manno, 2000, 2010).

In a highly commoditized economy, oppression among human groups leaves targeted groups deprived of resources necessary to a full life. Examples are food, shelter, medical care, and the like. Oppression of people with disabilities—of people who are either less "productive" in the economy of things or whose accommodation is seen as an unprofitable expense—is seen as rational, using market logic. In this mindset, disabled people have less value and cost more. As a result, they are subject to being hidden, exploited, and sometimes killed or segregated. The movement for inclusion and full citizenship is still a concept to be fully accepted, even though written into law and practiced in schools in many countries. Even within the inclusion and rights movement, disabled people are segregated and exploited. Adults with severe disabilities, whether or not fully included in the classroom, often transition into group homes and sheltered workshops where their work is neither guaranteed nor paid full value.

Sometimes the logic of commoditization works its way into the education and services of people with disabilities throughout society. We are not referring to the new markets in assistive technology and gadgets created as people with disabilities increasingly join the workforce and traveling public but rather to the commoditization of the individuals themselves and of their behaviors. Government policies and funding, along with private and corporate provisioning of supplies and services, tend to create a large market in which people with disabilities become valued for the products they need. Much less attention is paid to how a person integrates into a community as a productive member, and much more attention is given to the market they represent.

For example, an individual on Supplemental Security Insurance (SSI) in the United States faces financial obstacles to employment by losing earned income over a fixed low amount. Individuals must think twice before earning part-time or full-time income. If they go over the eligibility amount designated by the government, they risk losing medical coverage that may include respirators or personal care assistance needed to survive. The only way to get off government assistance is to catapult into a job that enables the person to pay for his or her own help and transportation and access full medical coverage. Thus, most people with disabilities who could earn enough to pay taxes are still poor.

From the perspective of disabled people as a commodity, they provide jobs for state-funded social workers, entitlement workers, personal care workers, and manufacturers and merchants of assistive technology and mobility aids. A case that makes the point is that of Paul Longmore (2003). He described his struggles to get the California Department of Rehabilitation to fund his graduate study. Since his goal of getting a PhD to become a college teacher did not fit into their preconceived notions of what a disabled student should be learning, they only funded him part time and then told him they wanted to close his case because he was taking too long to get his degree and that his case worker was being pressured to "close cases" to improve monthly statistics. They needed to close cases to look effective. In addition, his small monthly benefit was not the reason he had to remain on Supplemental Security Insurance (SSI). His medical and personal care expenses were income dependent and tied to his SSI eligibility. This rule precludes many disabled people from working part time, as their disability is defined by the government as an inability to engage in "substantial gainful activity" earning over a certain monthly amount—around $200 in 1972 and $300 in the 1980s. This amount has increased over the years to around $1,000 depending on a complex set of regulations (see Understanding Supplemental Security Income (SSI) work Incentives: 2012 edition). Functional and medical limitations with $20,000 (exceeding $45,000 per year by 2000) in government support services were irrelevant (Longmore, 2003, p. 236). Longmore went on to describe the history of the systematic redefinition of people with disabilities, relegating them to a state of permanent and government-enforced helplessness and dependence. Still in place are government disincentives to rehabilitation, work, financial advancement, and marriage. Finally, with disabled people permanently ensconced as eternal clients, there has grown a multimillion-dollar disability industry around the physical and medical care of disabled people:

> Even those of us with disabilities at large in society pull in high profits for vendors of a great many products and services. A few years ago I designed a device for my use in the bathroom. Knowing it would prove handy for people with similar disabilities, I sought ways to make it available. It would only cost a few dollars to manufacture, but a vendor told me eagerly we could easily sell it for fifty dollars a unit. The government would pay for it, he said. Hence comes the overpricing of everything from hearing aids to wheelchairs. This greedy arrangement between government and private sector, between vendors and the government, keeps many people with disabilities in a permanent state of clientage. We have to stay clients in order to get the devices and services we require. (Longmore, 2003, p. 246)

This is an example of how commoditization intensifies negative social outcomes experienced by oppressed groups. The configuration of rules to enforce neediness precludes personal development of a sustainable, interdependent life of full citizenship. For those who manage to escape this cycle of needs enforcing regulations, the cost of services, medications, and supportive equipment consumes much of the income that for nondisabled people would be discretionary or saved for retirement.

For young people with disabilities, commoditization affects lives in the form of behavior plans. Behavior issues arise as a result of their situation. Behaviors may be related to their disability or not. They may react in socially challenging ways to the quality of their lives, to physical discomfort and illness, to the way they are treated, to the frustrations and unmet needs that accompany their disability, and the inappropriate supports they receive, or may simply need intensive support to deal with emotional distress and difficult feelings and situations. These students are the bread and butter of special educators and school psychologists. Those with emotional disabilities are a valued commodity to psychiatric institutions. Although these workers choose their occupations out of compassion and caring, society validates their seeing the behaviors as the problem, instead of looking at the causes of the behaviors. They are problem focused (the problem, a deficit, is in the person) rather than solution -focused (the solution is in the situation and environment of the student). The problem-focus or deficit-focus lends itself to commoditization of behavior. The solution-focus or competence-focus lends itself to the development of sustainable relationships and behaviors that sustain full citizenship.

For example, a young person in distress may be constantly off task in class, speak constantly out of turn, express anger in harmful ways, or completely shut down and do nothing. The typical, problem-focused professional response is to identify the solution as some sort of compliant or socially "appropriate" behavior and institute some sort of extrinsic positive or aversive consequence. These responses range from praise to rewards and bribes, isolation, and exile.

Defenders of the problem-oriented system point out that laws and speeding tickets—direct responses to behavior—mostly work. We work for paychecks and for family approval. They fail to point out that we engage in these activities voluntarily and have enough choices in our lives to keep us going through the unpleasant tasks and sometimes inconvenient laws. We would typically consider our good driving and socially acceptable behavior to have "low commodity potential," as described above, in that we do these things in the context of meaning and community. Also, the young people in question may have limited choices in life (actual or perceived) and may exert the only form of control they can manage. The result is often a behavior plan that yields external rewards—points, toys, stickers, food, etc.—and turns behavior into a commodity for sale by the student, with a concurrent risk of alienation.

Danforth (2005) referred to this social aspect of student work as alienated labor (p. 86). He wrote about students labeled Emotionally/Behaviorally Disordered (EBD) who are generally placed in segregated programs and for whom an academic curriculum is elusive. They are enrolled in a "curriculum of control," where the goals are compliant or pro-social behaviors. Whereas most students in schools are

> expected to perform "knowledge" or "academic" work," the labor of students schooled under the curriculum of control is the production of behaviors that "earn points" and are therefore commoditized into economic units of exchange. Instead of learning that human action has moral value that may be evaluated and appreciated as an expression and action of an agentic self, instead of learning that social action has and may be understood in terms of how it contributes to the lives of others, these students are systematically taught that their actions have purely economic value devoid of moral or social substance. In this sense, they are literally demoralized. (Danforth, 2005, pp. 86–87)

Rather than develop the self in a social context, the self is diminished as a moral agent in the world. This is particularly true in segregated programs for students with emotional and behavioral difficulties where the behavioral curriculum—the "curriculum of control"—typically has a point or level system, with goals that are treated as more important than academic progress. Thus the lesson of behavior becomes valued by the students as a medium of exchange, where the economic worth supplants the moral and social worth (p. 92).

In the public schools, class-wide and school-wide positive behavioral support and classroom management systems often include points redeemable for prizes at the class or school store. Because these programs also include proven ingredients such as student-centered curriculum, relationship building, meaningful praise, and learning in context, the distinctions between use value and exchange value may be less clear. Many of the students who earn their points in these programs would probably behave in the presence of clear expectations of the social contract. Students who need extra support to learn social skills experience the benefits of better peer and teacher relationships; a small percent need intensive interventions conducted with careful and sensitive analysis as to the cause and meaning of their behavior. Where prize incentives are applied indiscriminately, the desired long- and short-term results are left to chance, and teachers wonder why their incentive programs stop working.

One first-grade teacher in an inclusive classroom used an incentive system to reinforce well-executed transition routines and other good classroom behaviors. He had a thumbs-up puzzle poster on the wall. If the class was well behaved or did something well as a group, part of the hand would be put in the poster. When the students completed the thumbs-up hand, they could choose something special for Friday (such as pizza parties, a particular class game, the teacher coming to school in a funny hat). A year later, Robin asked him how his thumbs-up system was working out. He stopped it because the kids were more focused on the prize than on their learning. On a school-wide basis, we heard about an elementary school that gave out school dollars for good behavior, including "being caught doing good." Kids were leaping to pick up someone's dropped pencil. Also, the kids traded their dollars and were frequently caught gambling with them.

What is missing in these examples is a consistent policy of sustainability of personal, social, and community development. The commoditization of behavior and relationships decreased opportunity to meet human needs. In the case of people with severe physical disabilities like Longmore, the basic need for agency in how one should spend one's life, not to mention earn a living, is undermined by regulations that even defy the complex Internal Revenue Service tax code. Royalties are taxable whether or not they are the product of your labor, a distinction that caused Longmore to conduct a public book burning of the freshly published product resulting from his graduate study. Rather than encouraging a person with physical and medical limitations to use his or her mind, the system keeps many of them at home or in mind-numbing activities devoid of meaning. The stereotype of "overcoming disability" becomes even more ridiculous. No one overcomes disability; the task is to live well with disability. What needs to be overcome are the attitudes of society, social policy, and the system.

In the case of purchasing certain behaviors from children (i.e., bribing them), most kids do well with or without the bribes. These are young people who have support, meaningful relationships, and engaging activities. In fact, research synthesis of evidence-based practices on behavior change found the strongest evidence for two categories:

1. Modify the classroom learning environment to decrease problem behavior.
2. Teach and reinforce new skills to increase appropriate behavior and preserve a positive classroom climate (Epstein, Atkins, Cullinan, Kutash, & Weaver, 2008, p. 13).

These and other recommendations call upon practices that create meaningful context for the students. Epstein et al. discussed the use of rewards and found the results inconclusive—they work and they do not work. They worked in settings where relationships with and between students were primary. Defining success ("what works") informs results.

The key is understanding students and their situations and choosing meaningful "reinforcers" in meaningful contexts. The questions we wish to raise are: How narrow is the definition of success? Is it enough that the child ceases the challenging behavior but still hates school? Is it enough that students conform behaviorally but do not value the behaviors they learn or come to value the behaviors as media of exchange over the value of academic learning or relationships? What if we choose from among potentially effective strategies and techniques and frame them in the context of quality and meaningfulness of life, self-determination goals and skills and basic emotional needs of students (beyond survival)?

Many motivation theories acknowledge that belonging is a key need and motivator beyond physical survival. One we found particularly interesting is the Circle of Courage (Brendtro, Brokenleg, & Van Bockern, 2002). Needs are framed in a circle with each need supporting the other: Belonging, Mastery, Independence, and Generosity. Teachers who are trained to look at behavioral motivators such as attention, help, or task avoidance can look at the larger quality-of-life picture. In the field of positive behavioral support, improved quality of life involves the engagement of the student in meaningful activity (as defined by the student), and the increase in such quality of life indicators as belonging, mastery and responsibility, independence, relationship reciprocity, and the expression of generosity.

An example of how unsustainable behavioral approaches were overcome is a teacher who got to know a middle-school student who was off task in class, made noises, alienated peers and teachers, and was given up on by several teachers who were waiting for him to age out of school. Neither reprimands nor bribes had worked. This teacher learned that the student was a struggling reader who was interested in heavy machinery and dirt bikes. She recruited him to help the special education teacher by taking attendance, passing out papers, and some other small classroom tasks like putting the assignment on the board. He wondered why, and she told him he deserved to show off some of his good qualities that she had noticed. Plus, he could teach the class about dirt bikes on Friday. With some practice, he did his job well and delivered a compelling dirt bike lesson, which caused his peers to see him in a different light and gained him some new friends. Other teachers noticed the difference in his engagement in their classes. This is an example of how getting to show his mastery on the topic of dirt bikes and the new job reinforced the student's sense of belonging, expanded his venue to show generosity, and increased his sense of independence. Although one can make a case for the dirt bike lesson being an extrinsic reward (for doing well in his new job), the intrinsic value of the activity stands alone as something the student enjoyed doing and sharing with new friends. It raised his esteem in the eyes of others and yielded good academic behaviors as *side effects* or bonuses rather than as devalued commodities for exchange. What this teacher took into account was the lived experience of disability. She saw the student's life from his perspective of a struggling young man who felt abandoned. Taking the time to believe in him and help him fulfill valued roles went a long way. Other students have also benefitted from being placed "front and center" and relieved of their marginalized status (Smith, 2009a, 2009b).

These examples show that the key to supporting disabled adults in society, and young people in schools, is to think of them in terms of their lived experience, their strengths, their relationships, and what they find meaningful. These are all things of great value but have low potential to be commodities. A sustainable, integrated life trumps (or should trump) rules that foster or support greed (as in overpricing medical equipment and services to captive audiences) or exploitation by maintaining enforced client status.

Encouraging Directions: Looking Forward

Unfortunately, people have become used to thinking about nonhuman animals as property, as commodities in the narrow sense of the word. They are daily traded on the commodities market and eaten for dinner with mass-produced vegetables from depleted soils, without regard to suffering rainforests, climates, populations from other continents, or depleted and poisoned soil that is starving our plants and our population. The social weight and momentum of material wealth obscure the need to think about the sustainable wealth to be found in the essential value of our natural resources. Books such as this one and examples in the popular media such as *In Defense of Food* (Pollan, 2008) and *Animal, Vegetable, Miracle* (Kingsolver, 2007) shine light on directions we can take to raise awareness.

Similarly, the public is used to dehumanizing disabled people and finding it acceptable to debate whether life is worth living if you are disabled. Issues include assisted suicide, euthanasia, and withholding life support from disabled babies or poor people in need of transplants. These are not controversies when applied to able-bodied people. The commoditization of our support systems and our behavior is, however, limiting the ability of many disabled people to form sustainable social and employment relationships. Bringing the problems and perils to light is an important step in raising awareness in those who seek a sustainable and just society. Examples can be found of encouraging trends.

The United Nations sets the tone for a sustainable future for people with disabilities in its Convention on the Rights of Persons with Disabilities (United Nations, 2006). It urges governments that in order,

> to enable persons with disabilities to live independently and participate fully in all aspects of life, States Parties shall take appropriate measures to ensure to persons with disabilities access, on an equal basis with others, to the physical environment, to transportation, to information and communications, including information and communications technologies and systems, and to other facilities and services open or provided to the public, both in urban and in rural areas. (Article 9)

James Elder-Woodward (2009) summarized research that shows, "we have an in-built capacity, within our very DNA, to help others, to put others first, especially those close to us, for the benefit and future survival of our community" (p. 801). He then described two contrasting approaches to welfare reform and support of people with disabilities. One is in England, where disabled people are kept in poverty, expected to work for their stipends, but are not supported with necessities such as transportation or personal care assistance needed to get to work. They are expected to "fit" the labor market rather than having the labor market "fit" them. The author of the reforms "dismissed the view that I [Elder-Woodward] and many of my colleagues have within the disabled people's movement, that there are factors extraneous to our impairments which disable our equal participation within the labour market, and society at large" (p. 802). In contrast, the Scottish Government "has decided it will value the ideas and opinions of disabled people, and will fund their participation in a programme to mainstream the thinking and practices of independent living within transport, housing, education, social work and the environment" (p. 802). Valuing disabled people and their contributions to the development of the community is a bright light amid a sea of archaic attitudes based on "survival of the fittest" and the commoditization and exploitation of the "weak." The age of "survival of the nicest" will be more likely to support sustainability.

In the case of student behavior, rather than focus on problems and their repair, social service practitioners and educators are mounting a movement for solution-focused approaches. Strategies for person-centered planning and teaching self-determination skills are increasingly used to support people with severe disabilities to make major life choices, such as where to live and who will support them. Examples can be found of how supporting the right to communicate led to major life changes for people who cannot speak or live independently. Two such examples can be found on youtube.com: in the life of Sue Rubin, who stars in the documentary, *Autism Is a World* (Wurzburg, 2004 [available on YouTube in its entirety]), and in the lives of Tracy Thresher and Larry Bissonnette, two men with autism, as they embark on a global quest to change attitudes about disability and intelligence while promoting the importance of presuming competence (Biklen & Wurzburg, 2011).

In the United States, government laws and policies increasingly support inclusive education and positive behavioral support over segregation and aversive responses. However, the mandates include diagnostic assessments that are deficit based in the medical model. A major shift has yet to occur from dependence on problem identification to solution identification (Jackson & Panyan, 2002), and from external rewards to intrinsic, relationship-based and meaningful motivation. Promising practices include those related to "solution-building" in schools (Kelly & Bluestone-Miller, 2009; Kelly, Kim & Franklin, 2008), where teachers learn to address problems by searching for the exceptions to the problems and engage their students in noticing the resources they already have available, in order to reach the goals of a smoothly running classroom community. Alternative schools, classroom practices, and assessments based on strengths, goals, and resources already available to and within students show promising results with students with and without disabilities, who are otherwise left behind in terms of school success (Kelly & Lin, 2008), and for whom school is a meaningful endeavor in advancing life goals.

In conclusion, we end with issues to ponder and develop. The lesson is to think ecology: With what or with whom is this entity (human, nonhuman animal) in relationship, and what will be disrupted by the action we take? What are short-term gains and losses, and are they sustainable? What do we need to do to notice the value of interrelationships and enhance sustainability?

References

Biklen, D., & Wurzburg, G. (Producers), & Wurzburg, G. (Director). (2011). *Wretches and jabberers* [Motion picture]. United States: State of the Art, Inc.

Brendtro, L., Brokenleg, M., & Van Bockern, S. (2002). *Reclaiming youth at risk: Our hope for the future* (Rev. ed.). Bloomington, IN: Solution Tree.

Danforth, S. (2005). Compliance as alienated labor: A critical analysis of public school programs for students considered to have emotional/behavioral disorders. In S. L. Gabel (Ed.), *Disability studies in education: Readings in theory and method* (pp. 85–102). New York, NY: Peter Lang.

Elder-Woodward, J. (2009). Whatever happened to the human altruism gene? A service user's view of the Welfare Reform Bill, *Disability and Society*, *24*(6), 799–802.

Epstein, M., Atkins, M., Cullinan, D., Kutash, K., & Weaver, R. (2008). *Reducing behavior problems in the elementary school classroom: IES practice guide* (NCEE #2008-012). Washington, DC: National Center for Education Evaluation and Regional Assistance, Institute of Education Sciences, U.S. Department of Education. Retrieved from http://ies.ed.gov/ncee/wwc/publications/practiceguides

Hall, C., Tharakan, P., Hallock, J., Cleveland, C., & Jefferson, M. (2003). Hydrocarbons and the evolution of human culture. *Nature*, *426*(6964), 318–322.

Jackson, L., & Panyan, M. V. (2002). *Positive behavioral support in the classroom: Principles and practices*. Baltimore, MD: Paul H. Brookes.

Kelly, M. S., & Bluestone-Miller, R. (2009). Working on what works (WOWW): Coaching teachers to do more of what's working. *Children and Schools*, *31*(1), 35–38.

Kelly, M. S., Kim, J. S., & Franklin, C. (2008). *Solution-focused brief therapy in schools: A 360-degree view of research and practice*. New York, NY: Oxford University Press.

Longmore, P. K. (2003). Why I burned my book. *Why I burned my book and other essays on disability* (pp. 230–259). Philadelphia, PA: Temple University Press.

Manno, J. (1984). *Arming the heavens: The hidden military agenda for space, 1945–1995*. New York, NY: Dodd, Mead.

Manno, J. (2000). *Privileged goods: Commoditization and its impact on environment and society* (Ecological Economics Series). Boca Raton, FL: Lewis.

Manno, J. (2010). Commoditization and oppression: A systems approach to understanding the economic dynamics of modes of oppression. *Annals of the New York Academy of Sciences, 1185*(1), 164–178.

Midgley, M. (1985). Persons and non-persons. In P. Singer, *In defense of animals* (pp. 52–62). New York, NY: Blackwell.

Smith, R. M. (2009a). Fostering belonging when and where it counts: Let students shine. *TASH Connections, 35*(1), 26–29.

Smith, R. M. (2009b). Front and center: Contradicting isolation by supporting leadership and service by students with disabilities. *TEACHING Exceptional Children Plus, 5*(5). Retrieved from http://journals.cec.sped.org/cgi/viewcontent.cgi?article=1678&context=tecplus

Smith, R. M., Gallagher, D., Owen, V., & Skrtic, T. M. (2009). Disability studies in education: Guidelines and ethical practice. In J. Andrzejewski, M. Baltodano, & L. Symcox (Eds.), *Social justice, peace, and environmental education: Transformative standards* (pp. 235–251). New York, NY: Routledge.

Smith, R. M., & Manno, J. P. (2008). Disability studies and social construction of environments. *Social Advocacy and Systems Change, 1*(1). Retrieved from http://www.cortland.edu/ids/sasc/vol1_issue1/earth_smith_manno.pdf

Understanding Supplemental Security Income (SSI) work incentives: 2012 edition). Retrieved http://www.ssa.gov/ssi/text-work-ussi.htm

United Nations. (1994). Towards a society for all: Long-term strategy to implement the World Programme of Action Concerning Disabled Persons to the year 2000 and beyond. New York, NY: United Nations Division for Social Policy and Development. Retrieved from http://www.un.org/disabilities/default.asp?id=50

United Nations. (2006). Convention on the rights of persons with disabilities. Retrieved from http://www.un.org/disabilities/default.asp?id=259

Vanderburg, W. H. (2005). *Living in the labyrinth of technology.* Toronto, Canada: University of Toronto Press.

Wurzburg, G. (Producer & Director). (2004). *Autism is a world.* United States: State of the Art, Inc. Retrieved from http://www.youtube.com/watch?v=U1wsiVYCqno

CHAPTER FIVE

Disney's Little "Freak" Show of Animals in Nature

A Dis-Ability Pedagogical Perspective on the Disney Industrial Complex

AMBER E. GEORGE

Film is no stranger to reinforcing and creating images of "Otherness." The Hollywood Industrial Complex—which prides itself on constructing normalcy through means of sexist, racist, homophobic, ableist, speciesist, and humanist perspectives—reinforces the binaries of ability versus disability, human versus nonhuman animals, and nature versus civilization. While Disney has been critiqued by many, there remains a critical blind spot of its role in perpetuating ableism, speciesism, and anthropocentrism. This chapter will examine two Disney films, *Dumbo* (Disney & Sharpsteen, 1941) and *Finding Nemo* (Walters & Stanton, 2003) from a dis-ability pedagogical perspective. These two films were chosen for analysis because of the pervasive, stereotypical representations of disability, nonhuman animals, and nature that have gone largely unquestioned. Media scholar Giroux (1999), has suggested that Disney's films should be examined very closely because "the stereotypes, when learned at a young age, have a lasting impact" (p. 3). While it may be that not all Disney films could be characterized as harmful, in films such as *Dumbo* (1941) and *Finding Nemo* (2003) certain negative stereotypes persist. Disability, nonhuman animals, and nature are an important part of life on Earth; people must acknowledge the variety and value of all life experiences. Expressing negative judgments of people with disabilities, nonhuman animals, and nature constitutes a profound injustice. To express negativity to these individuals is itself an injury to them, a violation of their most fundamental right—the right to be self-determining and to qualify as beings worthy of respect.

I will begin this essay by exploring the multifaceted dimensions of corporate Disney. I am interested in understanding how influential they are as a source for children's culture and entertainment. Next, I will demonstrate some of the more well-known theories about the effects that negative media content can have on children. From there I will explain the nature of oppression, and the way in which systems of oppression are preserved within the institutional context of the media. Finally, I will analyze the role that Disney has had in perpetuating certain stereotypical cultural values, beliefs, and attitudes about social identities, starting with disability, nonhuman animals, and nature respectively in both *Finding Nemo* (2003) and *Dumbo* (1941).

The Disney Corporation

As a corporate entity, Disney is one of the largest media conglomerates in the world. The Disney Corporation has gone from amassing $22 billion in 1999 (Giroux, 1999), to earning over $37.8 billion in 2008 by selling its products and services (Iger, 2008). Its products and services include: media networks, which encompass a range of broadcast, cable, radio, publishing, and Internet services; parks and resorts located all over the world; studio entertainment, such as animated and live-action motion pictures; consumer products, including toys, books, games, food and beverages, and home décor; and interactive media that includes online, mobile, and videogame products (The Walt Disney Company, 2011). Disney is a massive multimedia corporation with considerable access to children's worlds. It is this presence that creates the strong potential to influence children's everyday lives. Disney's success relies considerably upon periodically rereleasing old films for each new generation to experience. As a result, many outdated stereotypes get recycled, as if they were accurate and acceptable reflections of contemporary society. Since teachers and parents feel safe using Disney as entertainment, these outdated and offensive stereotypes remain unchallenged for newer generations. It is imperative that parents and educators explore the ideological roots of Disney's cultural messages, which devalue people with disabilities, nonhuman animals, and nature (Artz, 2002).

The Effect of Media on Children

According to the National Association for the Education of Young Children (NAEYC, 2011), children between the ages of two and five begin to realize the meaning of difference based on ethnicity, gender, and disability. Children are less developed at the age when they begin consuming Disney's products; thus they are less able to critically evaluate the harmful messages they receive and much more likely to accept the media's portrayal. Disney's films are quite often perceived to be a trusted source for family entertainment. Parents expect that when their children watch a Disney movie, they will receive wholesome entertainment. Instead, the messages the films send do not accurately reflect the social, cultural, and political reality of contemporary society (Giroux, 1999).

There are a few key theories that explore the detrimental effects of harmful, stereotypical media on children. According to Gerbner's (1999) Cultivation Theory, exposure to mass media creates a worldview for children that is more consistent with media's distortion of reality than with reality itself (Dill & Thill, 2007). Media messages serve psychosocial functions, "to reveal how things work, to describe what things are, and to tell us what to do about them" (Gerbner, 1999, p. 9, as cited in Dill & Thill, 2007, p. 854). Likewise, Bandura's (2001) Social Cognitive Theory of mass communication suggests that when children are exposed to media figures that model these concepts, it can greatly influence their perception of the world. According to Kellner (2003), "media images help shape our view of the world and all our deepest values; what we considered good or bad, positive or negative, moral or evil" (p. 9). Seeing unreal, negative representations of the disability experience as well as similar attitudes against nonhuman animals and nature contributes to viewers' understanding, and influences their behaviors, thoughts, and feelings.

Ideologies and Systems of Oppression

For a film to be successful, it must present some cultural knowledge to which the audience can relate. The more believable the story, the more successful it is likely to be. In the film, *Mickey Mouse Monopoly* (2001), Sun & Picker explained that,

> coded in media images are ideologies—how we think about the world, belief systems, constructions of reality—and we develop our notions of reality from the cultural mechanisms around us and the most important cultural institutions is indeed the media. It gives us a whole array of images, of stereotypes, belief systems of race, class and gender.

I would also add the subject positions of disability, nonhuman animals, and nature. The prevailing attitude in many of Disney's films supports the long-standing tradition of using cultural stereotypes to reinforce oppressive ideologies targeting not only people of color and women but also people with disabilities, nonhuman animals, and nature. According to Frye (1983), oppression is systematic and involves: "a system of interrelated barriers and forces which reduce, immobilize and mold people who belong to a certain group, and affect their subordination to another group" (p. 33). As Disney is a social institution, it is responsible for institutionalizing oppression against various social identities through its use of damaging stereotypes. Furthermore, those interested in social justice have long stated that the intersectionality of experiences of oppression can help explain the pervasiveness of oppression against people on the basis of their social identity. Thus,

> as opposed to examining gender, race, class, and nation as separate systems of oppression, intersectionality explores how these systems mutually construct one another or, in the words of Black British sociologist Stuart Hall, how they "articulate" with one another ... and [how] certain ideas and practices surface repeatedly across systems of oppression. (Collins, 2011, p. 246)

This further illustrates the pervasiveness of institutionalized oppression and how important it is that we recognize that people with disabilities, nonhuman animals, and nature could be subject to the forces of institutionalized oppression in the same way as other identities that are targeted by Disney.

These forms of oppression originate from the ancient Greek philosophy of dividing reality into two distinct parts: the nonthinking, material entities (body), and the nonmaterial thinking entities (mind or soul). It was Aristotle who believed that human animals' unique ability to reason meant that they possessed intrinsic moral value. Those who could not reason were relegated to the "Other" category and were—and are still—viewed as profoundly different. The dichotomization between "us" and "them" often results in the stigmatization of this mythical "Other," who is less powerful and objectified as an object of contempt, as are people with disabilities, nonhuman animals, and nature in present society (de Beauvoir, 1952).

A Brief Synopsis of the Films

In the film, *Finding Nemo* (2003), the main character, Nemo, is a clown fish, who has an "abnormally" small fin. Nemo and his overprotective father, Marlin, live in the tropical waters of the Great Barrier Reef. As a young and adventurous fish, Nemo is eager to explore his underwater world and embarks on a dangerous journey which leads to his capture and detainment in a dentist's fish tank. Despite his fears and trepidation about the great wide ocean, Marlin takes off to rescue his son, and in doing so he becomes an unlikely hero. *Dumbo* (1941) tells the story of a baby circus elephant originally named Jumbo Junior. He has unusually large ears that cause the other circus animals to treat him maliciously and give him the rather cruel nickname of "Dumbo." Dumbo is ostracized by both the other nonhuman animals and the public, with the exception of his mouse friend, Timothy, and his mother who strive to protect him from the constant teasing and taunting.

Ableism and Disability Perspectives

For many children in the United States, their opportunity to encounter someone with a physical disability may be nonexistent or limited. When a film unrealistically portrays a person with a disability, it very well may be the first time that the child has experienced disability. Imagine a child who has never seen a little person, and having the child's first encounter be the seven dwarfs in Disney's *Snow White and the Seven Dwarfs* (Disney & Hand, 1937). These initial encounters at a very young age could have lifelong repercussions (Norden, 1994). Barnes (1992), in his report for the British Council of Organizations of Disabled People, wrote that ableism, or discrimination against people with disabilities, is on the rise. Barnes said that there is "a growing awareness among disabled people that the problems they encounter are due to institutional discrimination and that media distortion of the experience of disability contributes significantly to the discriminatory process" (p. 5). Some of the more popular stereotypes are that people with disabilities are more childlike, sensitive, dependent, miserable, and less confident than those without disabilities. These stereotypes thrive because there is a lack of information about instances where people with disabilities are active participants in society. The media contribute by rarely showing people with disabilities as independent and empowered members of society (Morris, 1991; Norden, 1994).

The characters of Dumbo and Nemo are almost identical in their portrayals of disability; both of their narratives involve a physically disabled child who has an overprotective parent. They struggle with gaining acceptance and validity as a person with a disability, with an emphasis on "overcoming" the disability through some heroic event. Norden (1994) has stated that the prominent, ableist stereotypes in film include the person with the disability as a "victim" who becomes a hero and is triumphant against all odds; and the person with a disability who is perceived as being a burden on the larger community.

The Problem of the Overprotective Parent

Marlin fears that because Nemo is made "special" by his disabled fin, he will not be accepted by Great Barrier Reef society. He spends much of his time protecting his son from physical and emotional pain. Marlin strongly believes that his malformed fin makes Nemo a weak swimmer, and he does not hesitate to remind Nemo of what he can and cannot do. Early in the film, Marlin says, "You think you can do these things, but you just can't, Nemo." Clearly, Marlin does not have much faith in Nemo because of his disability.

Dumbo learns at a very early age that his overly large ears are the reason he is stigmatized by the circus community. Dumbo is labeled as bad, called a "freak" by his peers, and relegated to being a part of the circus' "freak show." He is constantly picked on by the other elephants who laugh at his appearance and tell him how silly his ears look. The elephants jokingly call him "Dumbo" despite the fact that his name is Jumbo Junior. His mother, Mrs. Jumbo, desperately tries to make sure that Dumbo's emotional sensibilities are not damaged by constant teasing from the others. Mrs. Dumbo also has to stave off ridicule from the other elephant mothers, who react to her newborn calf with, "What a freak! He's got ears only a mother could love!" Mrs. Jumbo strives to give Dumbo all the love and tenderness that she can and, like so many other parents of children with disabilities, tries to save her child from ridicule and the pain that may come from being different.

The Problem of Overcoming Rhetoric

When a person with a disability demonstrates that he or she is in control of his or her life, or is successful in some way, it is often said that the person has *overcome* that disability. Through hard work, relentless endurance, and sheer willpower, a person with a disability is sensationalized as being "extraordinary." This rhetoric of overcoming is present in both Disney films; Dumbo is able to do the impossible by learning to fly, and Nemo survives a long, solo journey across the ocean and saves his friend, Dory, from a fisherman's net.

This type of ideology of overcoming suggests that it is up to the person with a disability to achieve a personal triumph over disability. Linton (1998) said, "it is a demand that you be plucky and resolute, and not let the obstacles get in your way" (p. 18). For instance, if there are no curb cuts at the corner of the street and you are a person using a wheelchair, then it is expected that you should learn to do wheelies and jump the curb. As a result, people with disabilities may internalize the responsibility to overcome, as opposed to demanding social change. Linton (1998) continued,

> if we, as a society, place the onus on individuals with disabilities to work harder to 'compensate' for their disabilities or to 'overcome' their condition

> or the barriers in nature, we have no need for civil rights legislation or affirmative-action. (p. 19)

Thus, in order to generate social standing, it is implied that people with disabilities need to prove that they are fully functional or *normal*. Linton surmised that because it is literally impossible to overcome disability, what they must mean is that they have overcome the social stigma of having a disability.

The pressure to overcome his disability forces Dumbo to take a role he is unprepared to fulfill, as a main attraction, involving all of the other elephants. He believes if he can be the main attraction and gain recognition it might help free his mother from imprisonment. Dumbo's mother was declared mentally ill or "mad," and was committed to solitary confinement when she tried to protect her son from merciless taunting. Unfortunately, during the monumental act, Dumbo causes the big top of the circus tent to fall, because of his clumsy ears. Because of this blunder, he is demoted to a clown and continues to face ridicule from his peers. This was his opportunity to prove to everyone that he was not a freak, or less than anyone else, and he failed. His best friend, Timothy the mouse, gives a speech after the event: "Just because he's got those big ears, they call him a freak, the laughing stock of the circus." Timothy decides that the only way Dumbo will ever overcome his disability is to learn how to fly: "Dumbo, you flew. Your ears are perfect wings. The very things that held you down are going to carry you up and up and up." Dumbo knows that acceptance requires that he prove himself in some heroic fashion, like learning how to fly. After Dumbo's friends supply him with the "magic flying" feather, he is able to demonstrate his special ability. The fame and glory that Dumbo acquires on account of overcoming his disability provide him the chance to live a normal life.

Towards the end of the film, *Finding Nemo* (2003), Nemo is given two opportunities to heroically overcome his disability. When Nemo finds himself imprisoned in the dentist's fish tank, he is presented with the opportunity to escape. Through the encouragement of the other fish in the tank, Nemo is responsible for freeing all of the fish so they can go back to the ocean. Then, as he is traveling home, he encounters Dory, who, as it turns out, was assisting Marlin in the search for Nemo. When Dory gets caught in a fisherman's net, it is Nemo who saves not only Dory but also hundreds of other fish who were en route to a not-so-fortunate fate. It is as a result of these two experiences that Nemo is finally seen by his father and the rest of Great Barrier Reef society as being a fully capable member of the underwater community. Nemo's ability to prove himself, despite his "limitations," is what allows him to live a normal life. The demonstration of Dumbo's and Nemo's ability to overcome, regardless of how realistic it may actually be in real life, provides the story with the happy ending that Disney audiences expect and enjoy.

Internalizing Oppression and Stigma

Sociologist W. E. B. Du Bois's concept of "double consciousness" helps to explain how those who are stigmatized often experience the sense of seeing oneself through the eyes of a harshly critical Other. Stigmatization creates the problem of feeling like one is constantly "on stage" (Du Bois, 1990; Hare, 1982). The stigmatized individual often experiences the sensation of being watched or on display, and often feels that others are judging them in terms of their stigma (Morris, 1991). The social stigma that both Dumbo and Nemo face as a result of their disabilities also involves objectification, (i.e., treating an individual as if he or she were an object). In objectification, the "living, breathing, complex individual" ceases to be valued, and an individual is seen as nothing more than their stigmatized status (Allport, 1958, p. 175). Thus, the mistakes that a person makes are often more likely to be noticed, noted, and ridiculed. Dumbo and Nemo both respond to the excess attention born of "being on display" by going to great lengths to overcome their condition.

Dumbo, like so many other people with physical disabilities, has internalized his disability as a source of shame. He seems to believe that his disability is his fault, and that his inability to be accepted somehow stems from his "abnormally" large ears. Dumbo's problems with disability do not come from the impairment itself but from the prejudiced attitudes, social rejection, and isolation he experiences within his community. Judgments of worth based on membership in a stigmatized category can amount to a self-fulfilling prophecy. Those who are subject to stigmatization may have difficulty establishing their merit no matter what they do. The effects of being a target of stigmatization can have major effects on one's life chances. Feelings of self-pity, self-hate, and shame are devastating because they could prevent a person from ever knowing their real self, their real options, and their real capabilities (Morris, 1991; Linton, 1998).

Nemo also exhibits feelings of shame over his disability, especially when he meets his classmates for the first time. One of his peers displays curiosity about his small fin and comments that it "looks funny." As similar comments are made, Nemo, embarrassed, begins to shy away from the group. His father, Marlin, jumps into the conversation, and explains that Nemo was born with a small fin, a "lucky fin." What is interesting about this scene is that the other small children, once they understand that Nemo has a disability, also come forth and share their own disabilities. The fact that these children are so forthcoming about their own disabilities is a unique testament to how the public perception of disability has become a bit more open-minded and accepting since the release of *Dumbo*. While it may be true that *Finding Nemo* did its best to exemplify acceptance of disability, the film still draws on some damaging disability stereotypes.

Institutionalization from the Disability and Nonhuman Animal Perspectives

In the middle of the nineteenth century, the exhibition of people with disabilities was popular in contemporary American society (Raymond, 2008). Just as Dumbo was placed in the circus' "freak show," many people with disabilities believed that they had no other means of supporting themselves unless they joined these traveling exhibitions. Although the "freaks" have disappeared from the mainstream-circus sideshow, there still remains the policy of placing people with disabilities into other institution-like settings, such as developmental centers, group homes, and nursing homes. Similarly, the process of institutionalization affects not only people with disabilities but also the exhibition of nonhuman animals in circuses, zoos, and other confined enclosures. Regan (2011), a prominent animal rights theorist, believes that all conscious beings have rights and that all beings have inherent value. Regan said that "all [animals] have an equal right to be treated with respect…to be treated in ways that do not reduce them to the status of things, as if they exist as resources for others" (p. 36). There have been widespread movements, such as those generated by grassroots organizations like ADAPT (American Disabled for Attendant Programs Today) and PETA (People for the Ethical Treatment of Animals) to end the institutionalization of people with disabilities and nonhuman animals. These organizations promote the shared themes of respect and self-determination. Deinstitutionalization for people with disabilities requires assistance with independent living outside of nursing homes, developmental centers, and group homes while nonhuman animals require assistance with living outside of circuses, aquariums, and zoos.

Mrs. Jumbo was institutionalized and labeled a "mad elephant" for coming to Dumbo's defense when a group of boys torment Dumbo by ridiculing him and tugging on his ears. Naturally, Mrs. Jumbo jumps in to protect her calf. The circus workers who respond to the scene believe that Mrs. Jumbo is far too wild and dangerous to remain in public and decide she belongs in solitary confinement. The trainers confront this distraught mother with whips, ropes, and elephant hooks to get her into a tiny wagon, and chain her feet to the floor. Mrs. Jumbo is confined in a wagon that reads "mad elephant" and "danger," fully equipped with prison-like bars. The song that is heard after the event, "Baby of Mine" (Churchill Washington, 1941) is horrifically sad, and is used to evoke pity from the audience. Even after all of these heartrending scenes of violence against circus animals, it appears that Disney made *Dumbo* to appeal to viewers who are nostalgic about the circus as a form of popular entertainment. It is quite possible that a child, after seeing *Dumbo*, could ask his or her parents if he or she could go to the circus.

In *Finding Nemo*, the clearest depiction of the institutionalization phenomenon is when Nemo is captured from his home in the Great Barrier Reef and relocated to a small aquarium in a dentist's office in Sydney Harbor. Nemo is placed on display with the rest of the "tank gang," who happened to all come from the pet store, for the amusement of all of the customers who come in for dental services. Not only does the scene support the captivity of aquatic fish, it also supports the practice of scuba-dive fishing. Shortly after the film's release, retail stores stocked "Disney's *Finding Nemo* Aquarium Kit," which sold itself thusly: "The tank features everyone's favorite clown fish, Nemo. This starter kit will peak his or her interest and stir his or her imagination about life under the sea and all its marvelous creatures" (Walmart, 2011). The film romanticizes the activity of scuba diving and aquarium ownership, which could entice children to partake in the captivity of fish and in the patronizing of places where animals are institutionalized.

Anthropomorphism, Anthropocentrism, and Speciesism: Nonhuman Animal Perspectives

Anthropomorphism is another component in Disney's successful film formula. Anthropomorphism refers to redefining a nonhuman creature using human characteristics and traits. This technique has been used in an assortment of ways to bring life to inanimate objects like toys and nonhuman animals. Viewers are drawn to anthropomorphic representations of animals because, as Serpell (2006) commented,

> Anthropomorphism and pet keeping are powerful antidotes to what John Searles once called the existential loneliness of the human condition. By enabling us to participate in nonhuman lives not just as observers but as active social partners, anthropomorphism provides us with a unique opportunity to bridge the conceptual and moral gulf that separates humans from other animals. (p. 132)

Serpell (2006) argued that instead of treating nonhuman animals as though they have intrinsic value, we humans treat animals as if they were instrumental to achieving our own self-gratification. Serpell added,

> Sadly, however, instead of accepting and appreciating companion animals for what they are, we seem more inclined to adopt them across the animal-human divide, render them in our own image, and transform them in the process into a collection of deformed or mutilated cultural artifacts. (p. 132)

Serpell (2006) seems to view anthropomorphism as conjoined to anthropocentrism, suggesting that perhaps we project our own thoughts and feelings onto nonhuman animals because we believe that we are superior and that "naturally," nonhuman animals should desire to have humanlike characteristics. While we are infusing nonhuman animals with humanlike qualities in an effort to make them more like us, we are simultaneously treating their failure to become humanlike as a form of entertainment.

The doctrine of anthropocentrism states that humans alone have moral status, placing humans above all other beings, including nature and nonhuman animals. Anthropocentrists claim that everything in nature—the animals, plants, and ecosystem—has been put on this planet for the benefit of humankind only. There is an emphasis on the instrumental value, whereby nonhuman entities are not valued as ends in themselves but rather as a means to achieving some other end. Over the past few decades, philosophers have spoken out against the traditional attitude that emphasizes the instrumental value of nonhuman beings (Philosophy, 2002). Peter Singer (2001) is a philosopher who believes that humans are guilty of speciesism, which he defined as "a prejudice or attitude of bias in favor of the interests of members of one's own species and against those members of another species" (p. 33). Singer related the prejudice and discrimination against nonhuman animals to oppression of human animals based on race and sex. He claimed that speciesism violates the principle of equality, which states that it is unjust to treat beings differently unless we can show that there is a difference between them that is relevant to the differential treatment. Disney exhibits clear examples not only of anthropocentrism but also speciesism in both *Nemo* (2003) and *Dumbo* (1941) .

That Dumbo and his mother are part of a circus speaks volumes about the anthropocentric thinking that could influence children's perceptions of nonhuman animal treatment. The very essence of a circus requires forcible, often brutal captivity, exploitation, and inevitable mistreatment and abuse. Animal rights advocates like People for the Ethical Treatment of Animals (PETA) argue that all sentient animals have an interest in not being tortured or held captive and that they have a right to live in a clean living space equipped with proper nutrition and health care. The elephants displayed in *Dumbo* are absolutely miserable. Crammed into tiny rail cars ill suited to carry them, forced to work in the pouring rain to construct the circus tent, they snarl in response to the hazardous tricks they are forced to perform in the ring.

Nature Perspectives

Environmental ethics is a field of study concerned with the moral value of nature, the preservation of species, and curbing the harmful practices of human animals. The theory of ecofeminism links environmental ethics to feminism and animals rights, arguing that the oppression of women, nonhuman animals, and nature are all founded in the same logic of dominance (Brennan & Lo, 2002). This type of oppression is also connected to social domination based on race, disability, and other forms of social difference. Plumwood (1993) has said that the "human domination of nature wears a garment cut from the same cloth as other forms of human domination, but one which, like each of the others, has a specific form and shape of its own" (p. 13). The traditional view is the idea that nature itself has no intrinsic value by itself apart from its usefulness to humans.

In terms of how nature is portrayed in these films, there are clear examples of the privileging of humans' interests and the usage of nature for instrumental purposes. In *Finding Nemo*, there are examples of humanity's indifference towards nature and scenes that demonstrate the direct effects that human interaction has had on the Great Barrier Reef habitat. These human interactions can have a direct bearing on the underwater community's ability to survive and live. There are remnants of irresponsible human behavior, such as noticeable debris from sunken ships, the draining of human waste products into the open ocean, and fishermen and scuba divers actively attempting to capture fish. Whitley (2008) noted, "most of the images depict such interactions in the film have a dark edge to them; however, the emotional force behind these images is deflected from ever becoming a full-blown critique of modern environmental practices that may be leading to disaster" (p. 136). One could argue that after seeing the film, one might be inclined to criticize the fishing industry, as well as ecotourism. But because of the way in which the underwater world is attractively depicted; it could have the exact opposite effect. Whitley also said,

> The ocean in *Finding Nemo* is represented as a source of wonder and excitement; but the film offers an imaginative stimulus for different modes of understanding the strange otherness of this watery zone of nature, rather than a sustained passionate plea to protect it (pp. 136–137).

After seeing this enchanting underwater world, people may be more likely to abduct fish from the natural habitat and patronize aquariums.

The U.S. Department of Education's Office of Educational Research and Improvement has suggested that children should be exposed to treating the natural environment with respect at an early age, to develop an appreciation and respect for nature. Seeing how Disney's films play such a critical role in shaping children's attitudes, values, and patterns of behavior, it is crucial that they present a positive relationship between humanity and nature. The goal of these films is not necessarily to improve society. But because these films provide so much of today's pedagogy for children and parents rely on them so much for education, perhaps they should furnish educational lessons for valuing nature (Dobrin & Kidd, 2004).

In conclusion, it is crucial for parents and teachers to engage in a dialogue with children about how Disney contributes to the creation and regulation of harmful, stereotypical depictions of disability, nonhuman animals, and nature. What is at stake, pedagogically speaking, is the issue of how such films teach children about domination, oppression, and social inequality. Walt Disney said it best when he explained the profound learning potential for children: "I think of a child's mind as a blank book. During the first years of his life, much will be written on the pages. The quality of that writing will affect his life profoundly" (Giroux, 1999, p. 17). Giroux claimed that "individuals must be attentive to the diverse messages in Disney films in order both to criticize them when necessary, and, more important, to reclaim them for more positive ends" (p. 3). Ideally, we should strive to teach children about a society in which individuals are both self-determining and interdependent. Parents and educators must help children develop the critical thinking tools vital to understanding oppression and their own socialization within oppressive systems. What is needed is a pedagogical response that spurs a sense of agency in children to work for social change and uproot the oppressive patterns and behaviors they observe in popular media. Using critical theories such as ableism, anthropocentrism, and speciesism provides a viable framework for parents and educators to use in questioning and challenging Disney's depictions. These theories also provide grounding for making choices about what to do and how to go about doing it. If we are to eradicate oppression, we must struggle against all its forms in all types of media. Well-informed parents and educators offer the most promising strategies for teaching transformational ideas that counter the human apathy concerning people with disabilities, nonhuman animals, and nature that is found all too readily in the films of Disney.

References

Allport, G. (1958). *The nature of prejudice*. New York, NY: Doubleday.

Artz, L. (2002). Animating hierarchy: Disney and the globalization of capitalism. *Global Media Journal, 1*(1). Retrieved from HYPERLINK "http://lass.calumet.purdue.edu/cca/gmj/oldsitebackup/submitteddocuments/archivedpapers/fall2002/artz.htm"

Bandura, A. (2001). Social cognitive theory of mass communication. *Media Psychology, 3*(3), 265–299.

Barnes, C., & British Council of Organizations of Disabled People (BCODP). (1992). *Disabling imagery and the media: An exploration of the principles for media representations of disabled people*. Derby, UK.: BCODP.

Brennan, A., & Lo, Y-S. (2002, June 3). Environmental ethics. *Stanford Encyclopedia of Philosophy*. Retrieved from http://plato.stanford.edu/archives/sum2002/entries/ethics-environmental/

Churchill, F., & Washington, N. (Songwriters). (1941). Baby of mine [Recorded by B. Noyes]. From *Dumbo* [Motion picture]. United States: Walt Disney.

Collins, P. H. (2011). It's all in the family: Intersections of gender, race, and nation. In K. E. Rosenblum & T-M. C. Travis, *The meaning of difference: American constructions of race, sex and gender, social class, sexual orientation, and disability* (p. 245–254). New York, NY: McGraw-Hill.

de Beauvoir, S. (1952). *The second sex*. New York, NY: Knopf.

Dill, K., & Thill, K. (2007). Video game characters and the socialization of gender roles: Young people's perceptions mirror sexist media depictions. *Sex Roles, 57*(11–12), 851–864.

Disney, W. (Producer), & Hand, D. (Director). (1937). *Snow White and the Seven Dwarfs* [Motion picture]. United States: Walt Disney Productions, and RKO Radio Pictures.

Disney, W. (Producer), & Sharpsteen, B. (Director). (1941). *Dumbo* [Motion picture]. United States: Walt Disney Productions, and RKO Radio Pictures.

Dobrin, S. I., & Kidd, K. B. (2004). *Wild things: Children's culture and ecocriticism*. Detroit, MI: Wayne State University Press.

Du Bois, W. E. B. (1990). *The souls of Black folk*. New York, NY: Vintage Books.

Frye, M. (1983). *The politics of reality: Essays in feminist theory*. New York, NY: Crossing Press.

Gerbner, G. (1999). The stories we tell. *Peace Review, 11*(1), 9–16.

Giroux, H. A. (1999). *The mouse that roared: Disney and the end of innocence*. Lanham, MD: Rowman & Littlefield.

Hare, N. (1982). W. E. Burghardt Du Bois: An appreciation. In W. E. B. Du Bois, *The souls of Black folk*. New York, NY: Penguin.

Iger, R. (2008). *Letter to shareholders, Part II*. Disney Investor Relations.

Kellner, D. (2003). Cultural studies, multiculturalism, and media culture. In J. M. Humez & G. Dines, *Gender, race, and class in media: A text-reader* (2nd ed., pp. 9–20). Thousand Oaks, CA: Sage.

Linton, S. (1998). *Claiming disability: Knowledge and identity*. New York, NY: New York University Press.

Morris, J. (1991). *Pride against prejudice: Transforming attitudes to disability*. Philadelphia, PA: New Society.

The National Association for the Education of Young Children (NAEYC). (2011). About NAEYC. Retrieved from HYPERLINK "http://www.naeyc.org/" http://www.naeyc.org/

Norden, M. (1994). *The cinema of isolation: A history of physical disability in the movies*. New Brunswick, NJ: Rutgers University Press.

Philosophy, S. E. (2002, June 3). *Environmental ethics*. Retrieved November 19, 2011, from Stanford Encyclopedia of Philosophy: http://plato.stanford.edu/entries/ethics-environmental/

Plumwood, V. (1993). *Feminism and the mastery of nature*. London, UK: Routledge.

Raymond, E. B. (2008). *Learners with mild disabilities: A characteristics approach*. Boston, MA: Pearson.

Regan, T. (2011). The radical egalitarian case for animal rights. In P. Pojman, *Food ethics* (pp. 31–38). London, UK: Cengage Learning.

Serpell, J. A. (2006). People in disguise: Anthropomorphism and the human-pet relationship. In L. Daston & G. Mitman, *Thinking with animals: New perspectives on anthropomorphism* (pp. 121–136). New York, NY: Columbia University Press.

Singer, P. (2001). *Writings on an ethical life*. New York, NY: HarperCollins.

Sun, C. (Producer), & Picker, M. (Producer/Director). (2001). *Mickey mouse monopoly: Disney, childhood & corporate power* [Documentary]. United States: Media Education Foundation.

Walmart. (2011). Retrieved from HYPERLINK "http://www.walmart.com" http://www.walmart.com

The Walt Disney Company. (2011). C*orporate information*. Retrieved from HYPERLINK "http://thewaltdisneycompany.com/about-disney/company-overview" http://thewaltdisneycompany.com/about-disney/company-overview

Walters, G. (Producer), Stanton, A. (Director), Unkrich, L. (Director). (2003). *Finding Nemo* [Motion picture]. United States: Disney-Pixar Studios.

Whitley, D. S. (2008). *The idea of nature in Disney animation.* Hampshire, UK: Ashgate.

CHAPTER SIX

Transnational Feminism and Eco-Ability

Transgressing the Borders of Normalcy and Nation

SARAT COLLING

> Borders: arbitrary dividing lines that are simultaneously social, cultural and psychic; territories to be patrolled against those whom they construct as outsiders, aliens, the Others; forms of demarcation where the very act of prohibition inscribes transgression; zones where fear of the Other is the fear of the self; places where claims to ownership—claims to "mine," "yours" and "theirs"—are staked out, contested, defended, and fought over.
>
> —*AVTAR BRAH, 1996, PP. 195–196*

> "Don't compete!—competition is always injurious to the species, and you have plenty of resources to avoid it!" That is the tendency of nature, not always realized in full, but always present. That is the watchword which comes to us from the bush, the forest, the river, the ocean. "Therefore combine—practise mutual aid!"...That is what Nature teaches us.
>
> —*PETR KROPOTKIN, 1972*

Today's dominant Western paradigm ignores Nature's teachings of mutual aid. The current neoliberal model of global capitalism values competition over caring, uniformity over diversity, and independence over cooperation. Relying on wage-slavery and indirect rule, the power structures of global capitalism are strengthened by the borders of normalcy and nation, in which those represented as abnormal, alien, or animal are recognized as others or strangers, disqualified from the body politic. This chapter offers a transnational feminist and eco-ability framework to address the oppressive borders that strengthen the hegemony of global capitalism and the humanist subject: borders that are policed by force. While I wish to transgress oppressive divisions, I agree with transnational feminist, Chandra Talpade Mohanty (2003), that "the lines between and through nations, classes, races, sexualities, religions, and disabilities, are real" (p. 2). Thus, it is important to recognize difference, while building solidarity, working across, and transcending those borders.

In *Mutual Aid: A Factor of Evolution*, the Russian anarchist philosopher, Peter Kropotkin (1972), explained what one sailor witnessed on a voyage to Utah: "A blind pelican which was fed, and well fed, by other pelicans" (p. 70). Kropotkin, in his own studies, found that rather than a struggle for existence among animals of shared species, there was cooperation and assistance. Those who were the most likely to survive were "not the physically strongest, nor the cunningest, but those who learn to combine so as mutually to support each other, strong and weak alike, for the welfare of the community" (Kropotkin, 1972, p. 28). He gave examples of how many different types of animals collaborate to build, travel, or hibernate, instead of compete for food:

> The ants combine in nests .... Most of our birds slowly move southwards as the winter comes, or gather in numberless societies and undertake long journeys .... Many rodents fall asleep .... The reindeer, when the lichens are dry in the interior of the continent migrate towards the sea. (Kropotkin, 1972, p. 81)

While many species succeed due to mutual aid, it is not limited to collaboration between members of a single species. Pattrice Jones (2009) told the story of an elephant known as Nana who liberated captured antelopes by undoing the latches of a stockade. Nana "not only freed those animals but let us know that elephants care about more than their own survival" (p. 241). Altruism between various animals is prevalent in nature, as many species have learned to live in mutually beneficial relationships.

Eco-ability is based on Nature's teaching of diversity. It can be read in opposition to what Vandana Shiva (1997, 2002) called the "monocultures of the mind" found in global capitalism. The monoculturing of diversity resembles the Western humanist tradition and its heir's impulse for normalization and human perfection. While anthropocentrism has led to the grim reality of widespread forest clearing, fish trawling, pollution and war, combined with the deadly practice of eugenics, this ideology has produced racial segregation, mass murder, and genocide and has led to deadly experiments on billions of human and nonhuman beings. As found when examining the core of eugenic ideology, devaluation based on ability can be likened to devaluation on the basis of species membership. While disability scholars have argued that ethics of the body must begin with the unstable category of *disability* (Snyder & Mitchell, 2006), in this chapter I suggest that the category of *animal* must also be considered as an inherent part of the equation. Those viewed as *disabled* and those viewed as animal have both been figured as strange and are devalued due to perceived biological inferiority. Within a transnational feminist and eco-ability framework, a multidirectional discourse, in which articulating atrocities side by side aids to illuminate them and build strength between movements, can assist in transgressing the oppressive discourses of normalcy and nation.

Beyond the Human

Similar to the monolithic representation of so-called "Third World" peoples and the "East" by colonizers, and the homogenous category of disability invented by eugenics, nonhuman animals have long been represented as a homogenous set under the umbrella terms, *animals*, or, *the animal*. The divide between human beings and the millions of other sentient species who become reduced to the animal has been central to the model of Western Enlightenment. As Derrida (2008) explained, "in spite of the infinite space that separates the lizard from the dog, the protozoon from the dolphin, the shark from the lamb, the parrot from the chimpanzee, the camel from the eagle, the squirrel from the tiger, the elephant from the cat, the ant from the silkworm, or the hedgehog from the echidna," this catch-all concept of the animal in the singular has been normalized (p. 34), while the "fantasy figure" of the "human" has long constructed narratives about the animal, "reminding us that the animal has always been especially, frightfully, nearby... at the very heart" of this narrative (Wolfe, 2003, p. 6). The animal has always been within the narratives constructed by the human but never truly understood. Portrayed through Cartesian dualism as biological machines, they have been subject to a never-ending cycle of confinement, slaughter, and consumption. Every year countless animals are systematically slaughtered and experimented on, similar to the way in which those thought to be *subhuman* were experimented on and murdered in the death camps and laboratories of the Nazis or by the colonial and *civilizing* conquests of White Americans. This industrial use of animals "has already had major ethical, ecological, and health implications" (Shiva, 1997, p. 32).

Atrocities have long been committed under the guise that the victims were less than human. The destruction of Indigenous people in North America, for instance, was justified due to their being perceived as part of nature: "they were not really human; they were part of the fauna" (Shiva, 1997, p. 46). Although they share similarities in critiquing a hegemonic European subject and exclusion on the basis of supposed (biological) inferiority, postcolonial and disability scholars have rarely challenged the human/animal binary. Philip Armstrong (2002) explained that this hesitancy may be due to "the suspicion that pursuing an interest in the postcolonial animal risks trivializing the suffering of human beings under colonialism" (p. 413). Labeling of a group as less than human, as an animal, in a derogatory context, has long been used to vilify, marginalize, and colonize bodies. While we can challenge the negative connotation, in Western society the term *animal* has been used in derogatory ways that reflect and strengthen speciesism.

Speciesism is the assumption of superiority of one species over another based on arbitrary characteristics. Speciesism targets human beings as well as animals. Indeed, the liberal ideal of *humanhood* has excluded those who fall under the ideal. As Gayatri Spivak has observed:

> The great doctrines of identity of the ethical universal, in terms of which liberalism thought out its ethical programmes, played history false, because the identity was disengaged in terms of who was and who was not human. That's why all of these projects, the justification of slavery, as well as the justification of Christianization, seemed to be alright; because, after all, these people had not graduated into humanhood, as it were. (as cited in Wolfe, 2003, p. 7)

Western society has constructed a speciesist division between sentient life forms: those who fall on the side of *human* and those who are constructed as *less than* human. The discourse of species privilege is entwined with discourses on normalcy and nation, with the contrived figure of the human occupying the center.

Beyond the Nation, Beyond the Norm

This ideal subject is tied to the fantasy of the normal. Lennard Davis (2002) described normality as "the alleged physical state of being normal," while "normalcy" is "the political-juridical institutional state that relies on the control and normalization of bodies, or what Foucault calls 'biopower'" (p. 107). While the universalized concept of the animal has been normalized in classical humanist discourse, so, too, has the notion of an ideal human body in opposition to queer, female, non-White, and disabled (including those seen as "degenerate" or "feebleminded")—all of which were considered categories of weakness and disability (Davis, p. 14). Preceded by the ideal of Greco-Roman culture, the ideology of normalcy arose along with the European capitalist colonization of modernity. Relating to the concept of *average*, it was constructed with the state tools of measurements and statistics in the early nineteenth century. Statistics started with the concept of counting workers and census data. It then switched over to finding ideal workers and was used for selecting ideal immigrants. Descriptive statistics changed into predictive characteristics of intelligence norms. Perpetuated by state media and discourse is the desire to reside under the mean of the bell curve: the statistical *norm*. Yet, what society is meant to perceive as normal is just an imaginary idea. There is no inherent trait that makes one disabled; rather, there is a set of social and cultural dynamics that form the meaning of disability. Bodies are measured in relation to one another through the guise of "human progress"—with one group viewing themselves as more intelligent, more developed, or civilized.

Borders, always policed by force, are perpetuated by the discourse of normality employed for order of the nation to be maintained. Language and normalcy cannot be separated from the rise of nationalism. Drawing on Benedict Anderson, Davis (2002) explained that:

> The modern nation took place largely in the eighteenth and nineteenth centuries when the varieties of polyglotism that had made up a politically controlled area were standardized into a single "national" language literature. Without this linguistic homogeneity, a notion of the modern nation-state would have had great difficulty coming into being. In addition, national literatures, both in prose and poetry, were made possible through the standardization of languages, the prescriptive creation of "normal language practices." (p. 106)

Asking the citizenship to conform to a standard language thus paved the way for nationalism by uniting people through this "linguistic homogeneity," as well as the standardized concept of bodies. Today, by expelling those viewed as strangers from the community, the "good citizen" has continued assurance of achieving the normal. Any sign of uprising or activity that may threaten the hegemony of the nation-state is a target to be extinguished by the state discourse of normality. The constructed measurements of normal versus abnormal, and chaos versus calamity, help manage conformity under a single, national ideal. Thus, self-organizing movements may be stigmatized as chaotic, abnormal, and in need of being controlled. An example of this is found in the wake of the London uprisings of 2011, when Commander Stephen Watson of the Metropolitan Police told BBC News that officers were working to enforce "calm and normality to the area as soon as possible" ("Riots in Tottenham," 2011).

This process of stigmatization is also apparent when the media, corporations, and law enforcement try to dissuade people from supporting the Occupy Wall Street movement. While the Occupy protestors in North America are heterogeneous, the movement is often depicted as chaotic and dangerous. As opposed to the normal citizen, the participants are derogatorily categorized as hippies, druggies, attention seekers, dropouts, or as persons having criminal intent. However, the movement is far too fluid to fit tightly into a container. As Allison Kilkenny (2011) wrote in *The Nation*, one of the most important aspects of the Occupy movement is its creativity and potential for resisting the self-policing that plagues the endless, permit-requiring protests. As opposed to protestors who "can protest as long as they never disrupt the normalcy of everyday living," the Occupiers refuse to be panoptisized in such a way. Indeed, at the movement's best moments, there is "no 'normal' anymore...only what Occupy chose to do, and to not do" (Kilkenny, 2011). After police cracked down on the Occupy encampment at Zuccotti Park, removing protest gear and leading to a downsizing of the occupation, a spokesperson for Brookfield Properties, on whose rules the park is based, stated that, "We are pleased that Zuccotti Park has returned to a state of normalcy" (Cherkis, 2012). In other words, normalcy refers to "a steady arrest count" (Cherkis, 2012). Whether through serving vegan food with Food Not Bombs, participating in consensus decision making, running a People's Library, spreading the anticorporate message through the arts, or giving a talk to Occupiers on decolonization and White privilege, attempts by people who resist corporate, capitalist society and recognize the need to reclaim space are unintelligible in a system where vertical power structures are normalized. When protestors are forcefully evicted from their encampments or targeted with pepper spray, this is seen as fighting chaos and abnormality. This discourse aids in maintaining a civilization in which there are vastly unequal distributions of wealth.

Intertwined Oppressions: Domestication, Industrialization, and Eugenics

The self-governing communities formed through Occupy exemplify Kropotkin's (1972) philosophy of mutual aid. Kropotkin's observations on mutual aid led him to argue that if the natural instinct of people is to join together, then governance, which assumes that society needs to be controlled, is violent and unnecessary. His distaste for government led him to speak passionately against the widespread support for sterilization of the "unfit" during the First National Eugenics Conference in London in 1992. He called instead for social welfare, such as better living conditions for the poor (Krementsov, 2010, p. 415).

While existing through millennia cross-culturally, the belief about disability as dysfunction can be traced to the eugenics era in particular. A patriarchal science, as Snyder and Mitchell (2006) wrote, "Eugenics can be recognized as a quintessential example of hegemony" (p. 73). In *Cultural Locations of Disability*, Snyder and

Mitchell (2006) discussed how eugenics functioned to maintain transnational European hegemony as a nexus for beliefs about race and biology. Eugenics, a transatlantic phenomenon, "became the site where beliefs about racial and biological inferiority dovetailed for a period of approximately one hundred fifty years in the cultural location that Paul Gilroy (1993) has named the 'Black Atlantic'" (p. 101). Drawing on Gilroy, Snyder and Mitchell (2006) identified a "Eugenic Atlantic" which placed disability into the transnational locations of exclusion. North America and Europe engaged in international collaboration through shared discussion, and what was, ultimately, a cleansing campaign (p. 104). To justify their eugenic ideologies, each nation referenced other countries' advancements in legislation and research in order to persuade support for their own.

Interconnected histories of oppressions are found in the relationship of eugenics, industrialization, and animal domestication. The field of animal agriculture, which studies breeding practices, helped lay the foundation for the field of eugenics, producing T4 Euthanasia Program personnel who staffed death camps in Nazi Germany. These included Hans Hefelmann, who coordinated the killing of disabled children and had a doctorate in agricultural economics as well as Victor Brack, a chief manager during the Holocaust who had a diploma in agriculture (Patterson, 2002, p. 107). The U.S. slaughterhouse system served as a model for the Nazi extermination program (Patterson, 2002). Europeans viewed non-European races as "psychologically nearer to the mammals than to civilized Europeans" (Patterson, 2002, p. 26), and, in another context of genocide, used racial theories to construct the Hutus in Rwanda as physically inferior and closer to animals than the Tutsis, who were seen as being closer to the European, civilized peoples. "Race science" thus paved the way for places of sanctity to become slaughterhouses.

The discourse of subhuman to oppress another persists to this day. Moammar Mashni (2010), son of a Palestinian refugee, expressed a common sentiment when he wrote, "To some, we simply do not exist, and when we do, we are terrorists, animals or sub-human." Snyder and Mitchell (2006) argued that, "While fears of racial, sexual, and gendered 'weakness' serve as the spokes of this belief system, disability, as a synonym for biological (or in-built) inferiority, functioned as the hub that provided cross-cultural utility" (p. 101). Likewise, the discourse of animality has been at the core of eugenic ideology, with those perceived as farthest from the human body equated with being weak and abnormal.

A Transnational Feminist and Eco-Ability Praxis

The preconceived notion of the normal is challenged when we consider that in nature diversity, not uniformity, equals nourishment, health, life, and abundance. Nature does not normalize. On the one hand, as a philosophy that breaks down the binaries between normal and abnormal, civilization and nature, and human and animal, eco-ability is based on the ecological principles of harmony in diversity, which include the varied social identities, cultures, and abilities of all species. All ability is respected as part of a holistic and rich ecosystem. On the other hand, intolerance for the diversity of nature is reflected in the way "civilized" human society has constructed their own rights while subordinating those who are perceived as inferior. To this day, those in power have tested and enslaved human and nonhuman animals, whether it was experimentation on Jews, Gypsies, queer people, disabled people, and other marginalized groups in Nazi Germany; the James Marion Sims reproductive experiments on Black women; or the vivisection of nonhuman animals.

A scientific worldview which relied on the domination of nature through a Eurocentric, speciesist, and sexist "objectivity" can be traced to the 17th century, with Francis Bacon, a contemporary of Descartes and the father of modern science, encouraging the exploitation of nature. As Caroline Merchant (2008) wrote, Bacon's worldview "symbolized, allegorized, and characterized Nature as female, virgin, mother and witch. The Earth too was female having deep recesses, cavities, and wombs in which grew the seeds of living things" (p. 155). Thus, the oppression of nonhuman nature has often been understood as analogous to that of the feminine. In Bacon's utopian novel, *New Atlantis* (2003), scientists develop early methods of genetic modification and control of plants and animals, illustrating modern science's desire for perfection. The corporate laboratories we find today, often hidden from public view, are based on Bacon's "parks, and enclosures of all sorts, of beasts and birds; which we use not only for view or rareness, but likewise for dissections and trials, that thereby may take light what may be wrought upon the body of man" (p. 33).

Eco-ability is a feminist philosophy, counteracting the hypermasculine ideologies of humanism, science, and civilization. Moreover, eco-ability recognizes that in all ecological communities, mutual aid and rhizomatic difference (Deleuze & Guattari, 1988) enrich the collective experience. In these communities, society and knowledge are horizontal and multiple. Like the rhizome plant whose rootstalks creep horizontally underground, and from which new life will grow from pieces that are broken off, eco-ability recognizes that rather than being dispersed from one source and moving in one direction, power is a complex network emerging from various nodes, in which every individual is different from, but on equal ground with, everyone else.

Eco-ability is in opposition to what Vandana Shiva (1997, 2002) called the "monocultures of the mind" found in global capitalism. Globalization, made possible through colonial conquests, and a form of neocolonialism, depends on a monocultured mindset in which diversity is "a threat, a perversion, a source of disorder" (Shiva, 1997, p. 101). Monoculture is the belief that every part of the Earth should be similar to every other part: the commodities, urban areas, and agricultural practices (Shiva, 2002, p. 67). Imposed on so-called "developing" countries, this model is convenient for corporations which want everything to operate quickly and efficiently without having to care for local economies and cultures or the future of the Earth. Industrial farms, chemical sprays, and increasingly mechanized work are the antithesis of nutrient-rich crops produced through farming methods that are diverse and sustainable.

Rosemarie Garland-Thomson (2006) has called for a feminism based on biodiversity as the antidote to eugenic feminism. Such feminism embraces human variation and welcomes disability, rather than going down the dangerous road of the eugenic legacy. A feminism based on biodiversity must also recognize the borders imposed on nonhuman animal life, for although "we are less likely to perceive the barriers that keep rabbits or dandelions from going where they want to go ... they may be just as destructive" (Jones, 2009, p. 237). I suggest that *transnational* feminism is an important component of bringing down these borders, because it challenges the deeply embedded belief in the Western humanist subject's experience as universally valid (Mohanty, 2003). Furthermore, transnational feminism takes this position within an anticapitalist and antiglobalist framework (Mohanty, 2003). A desire for capital provides incentives for colonialism, and Western imperialism creates more avenues for global capital while facilitating the destruction of diversity.

> Capitalism, which depends on the standardization of labor, thrives on normalcy: Normalizing normalcy is what capitalism wants and what nature rejects. Therefore, in this sense, as in others, capitalism is at war with nature. It is for this reason that nature is being genetically modified and enhanced to be controlled, normalized, and standardized for the purpose of effective production, marketing, and consumption. (Ben-Moshe, Hill, Nocella, & Templer, 2009, p. 116)

"At war with nature," capitalist society has caused mass extinctions, devastating the Earth's diversity. Under global capitalism, human society has become increasingly removed from nature. At the same time, discourses on both the right and left have argued that humans must rise above nature and exist in opposition to nature. In Western, capitalist societies the goal is to own as much as one can, colonizing women, poor people, seeds, forests, and nonhuman animals. The dominant Western belief that uniformity leads to productivity conflicts with the fact that nature thrives on diversity.

Thus, a transnational feminist and eco-ability framework opposes the "developed" world imposition of Western civilization through the so-called "green revolution" and other disastrous neocolonial measures, which operate under the common fallacy that human technology is superior to nonhuman nature and must control nature. In the next section, I draw on transnational feminist Sara Ahmed's concept of stranger fetishism to demonstrate how the discourses of Western humanism persist, particularly through analysis of the blockbuster film, *Avatar* (Cameron, 2009), produced in the techno-capitalist Hollywood Industrial Complex (Kashani & Nocella, 2010). Received favorably in terms of its leftist politics, the film is significant to understanding how those seen as alien, animal, or other, are distanced and fetishized within the colonial, White savior narrative as is the genetically engineered body.

Fetishization of the "Stranger" and the Genetically Engineered Body

In the book, *Strange Encounters: Embodied Others in Post-Coloniality*, Sara Ahmed (2000) explained that the notion of recognizing a stranger is paradoxical, because in that recognition a knowing is entailed. To recognize a stranger is a racial process in which those viewed as different from the familiar human (White, abled) body are distanced from the community. Yet, at the same time they are distanced within the paradigm of capitalist globalization, the "stranger" is also consumed, often as a source of exotic fascination and desire. The fetishization of the stranger is found in classic narratives of becoming native, but also in modern equivalents of such literature. Examining the top-grossing film of all time, *Avatar* (Cameron, 2009), I will investigate Ahmed's (2000) question: "To what extent do narratives of becoming other reconstitute rather than transgress the integrity of the Western subject who becomes?" (p. 119).

Avatar, as with another popular, "becoming other" film, *Dances with Wolves*, reworks the story of conquest so that the White male hero becomes a traitor to his people (in *Avatar*, to the human race) in order to help the Natives. *Avatar* is set in the future. Wilderness is no more on planet Earth, and human beings have set off on an imperialist mission to mine unobtanium, a mineral which will serve as a widespread energy source, from the inhabited moon, Pandora. The Pandora forest is presented as a model for the creative function of diversity. Nature is a living system of life in which all living creatures have spirits, energy flows through complex networks, and one's well-being depends on that of the forest. To some extent this view challenges Western-centric thinking and the development paradigm, including the military industrial complex. The story is told through the gaze of Jake Sully, a White marine who, significantly, has a disability. It begins with Jake narrating his experience while lying in a veteran's hospital: "With a big hole blown through the middle of my life, I started having these dreams of flying. I was free. Sooner or later though, you always have to wake up." As a wounded marine, Jake is the "Other" who has been told one too many times by doctors what he can and cannot do. So when his twin brother, a scientist trained for the Avatar program, is killed, Jake is willing to take his place.

The Na'vi "aliens" represent that which the human subject must face. Ahmed (2000) wrote: "The alien stranger is ... not beyond human, but a mechanism for allowing us to face that which we have already designated as the beyond" (p. 3). Ahmed used the analogy of human-alien encounters to discuss how the human encounter with those across borders, "aliens," allows for establishing the familiar and for the self-discovery of the human subject. The Na'vi bodies have a mixture of Ethiopian and Native American characteristics. Although they are very tall, their proportions resemble the ideal human body type perpetuated by the media. Following an Earth-based philosophy, the Na'vi adorn themselves with feathers and face paint and use tools such as bows and arrows. Similar to how people of color have historically been viewed as less than human, the Na'vi are refered to by the antagonistic humans as "blue monkeys," "roaches," and "savages who live in trees." In fact, the intrusion of a "civilized," Eurocentric human into the world of those who live at peace and harmony in nature, and who previously knew next to nothing about their invaders, is analogous to the story of the genocide of Indigenous people by Europeans in America.

With the ability to upload and download data from sacred sites in the forest, the Na'vi are part of a highly advanced biological system. As a result, they capture the imagination of Dr. Grace Augustine and other scientists. Many of the Na'vi can speak English, because the children have been subjected to what resembles a modern missionary project led by Grace, whose job is to win the hearts of the Natives, finding a diplomatic solution while she writes books and collects samples. Grace created the avatar bodies by combining human and native DNA, thus giving the humans a doorway to the Na'vi.

Jake's entrance into the forest of Pandora is filled with danger. After becoming separated from his fellow avatars, he enters the Na'vi's home alone and unprepared to face the Other. Neytiri, the leader's daughter, is the first to observe Jake and saves him from a pack of viperwolves. Moved by a sign, Neytiri takes Jake to the tribe and reluctantly agrees to teach him their ways. Thus, his wish to learn "how to see" the ways of the Na'vi is quickly granted. Traversing the borders between two worlds, he must "keep his distance *in order to see*" (Ahmed, 2000, p.120), taking on the impossible task of translating Native discourse into imperialist discourse (Chow, 1993), a process which reinforces that there is an "Other" to be found at a distance.

As the narrative progresses, Jake comes closer to the Na'vi. The viewer accompanies him as life deep in the Pandora forest begins to become a desired reality, while life in a disabled body becomes more and more a dream. He enters a relationship with Neytiri and starts to consider himself a Na'vi. Jake's dedication to being a Na'vi is proven when, despite the Colonel's promise that he can leave the planet immediately and have his legs operated on, he remains to undergo a ceremony which initiates him into the final stage of becoming a man.

As I have mentioned, the story is framed around the void in Jake's life: the void resulting from his disability. As he tells the Na'vi, "My cup is empty." It soon becomes clear that this emptiness is because of his disability. Throughout the film, the camera fixates on Jake's wheelchair and legs. His determination to do things on his own, while he lags behind the others, and is stigmatized by other marines, elicits sympathy from the viewer. He is antagonized by the soldiers, and is the subject of demeaning commentary about being a "cripple," or filling his brother's shoes, "so to speak." His challenges enhance the differentiation between his disabled body and the pleasure he experiences in the abled avatar body. So it is no surprise that after experiencing the avatar body, Pandora becomes the world of choice for Jake. In his avatar, his dreams of flying literally come true as he soars through the skies and takes leaps and bounds through the forest.

The contrast between awakening in avatar body and disabled body sets the scene for Jake's becoming. Jake's disability provides an impetus to join the Na'vi: his otherness leads him to become another Other. While he is a reluctant hero, Jake has much to gain through this encounter. His identity is reconstituted from attacker to savior. This becomes clear when Jake warns the company's indecisive manager that the blood of women and children is not something anyone wants on their hands. Feeling guilty for killing civilians in the past, Jake fills this space with what the Na'vi offer him: community, acceptance, and the opportunity to make up for his past mistakes. As Jake becomes a Na'vi, he becomes a powerful actor in their community. In fact, it is Jake, the White male subject, in his abled avatar body, not the Na'vi, who leads the clan to victory against the human warfare. When they have given up hope, he inspires the tribe not to give up their fight and leads the recruitment of other warriors from Pandora to join the Na'vi. He is also the only one who can conquer Toruk, a great pterodactyl-like creature, a feat that has not been accomplished for generations. Later, it is his prayers that are heard by Eywa, causing the Pandorian wildlife to join the fight. Thus, he is what Ahmed (2000) called a "hybrid hero" (p. 123), for it is becoming part of and hybridizing with the tribe that allows his offering to the Indigenous to occur. In her analysis of *Dances with Wolves* Ahmed (2000) described the protagonist Lt. John Dunbar's's agency as "central to this fantasy of overcoming; *not only can he make but he can unmake the border between self and other, between natives and strangers*" (p. 124). Dunbar is an anti-hero who befriends the Sioux and 'goes native' after being dispatched to a deserted (until the arrival of the Sioux) post in South Dakota. His act of becoming tied with his agency is the "energizing force behind the plot itself"

(Ahmed, 2000, p. 124). As with Dunbar, Jake's agency is crucial to the experience in which he can move back and forth between human and Na'vi.

Fantasy has an important function in the narrative of becoming. This is not a film about understanding the experience of being the other; it is a fantasy which constructs an alien to represent those differentiated from the "human," so that the White male subject may learn from "strangerness in relation to the self" (Ahmed, 2000, p.123). While the film critiques Western centrism on one level, the audience experiences the Na'vi through the lens of the White male hero; the story is narrated through Jake's reluctant video logs and voice-over as he learns the Na'vi culture. Thus, the Na'vi are relegated to the backdrop of the male subject's journey of redemption and self-discovery. Disability is used as a tool to enable the savior narrative, with Jake's becoming being more acceptable because he, too, is the Other.

As Kashani and Nocella (2010) explained in "Hollywood's Cinema of Ableism," the dramatic or exotic ways people with disabilities are represented are problematic: those actors representing the disabled rarely have a real disability while those who do often struggle to find work in the ableist institution of Hollywood, sending a message that it is okay to play someone with a disability, but it is not okay to have one (p.108). The projection of the mind of someone with a disability into the able body sends the message that it is difficult to find wholeness in the disabled body. Sam Worthington, the actor who plays Jake Sully, does not use a wheelchair in real life. Jake is portrayed as disabled not because the best actor for the position had a disability but to provide an impetus for joining the Na'vi. The ableist message is solidified as he is permanently transferred into the genetically engineered avatar body, and the disabled body is no longer of use.

Similar to Dunbar's becoming animal (Ahmed, 2000, p. 121), Jake's becoming Na'vi is related to becoming animal. The Na'vi are represented as animalistic, with long tails, cat-like eyes, and a way of expressing their distaste through hissing. As Na'vi, Jake becomes the hunter and the hunted. His becoming also relies on becoming a dominator. While a compassionate sentiment towards other animals is presented as being central to the Na'vi way of life, learning to know the ways of the Na'vi depends on the domination of animals. Many of the significant events which signify Jake's entrance into the Na'vi culture revolve around the domination of animals, whether it is to aggressively "bond" with other animals (in order to use them for transportation) or to hunt.

In one hunting scene, a "clean kill" signifies that Jake is ready to claim a Mountain Banshee, which is a pterodactyl-type creature. High on a floating mountain, each Na'vi must choose a Banshee to bond with for life, who must choose them in return. Portrayed as a collaborative and mutually beneficial experience, the connection with other creatures through the mental link is only to the benefit of the Na'vi. The creatures resist this domination and having ropes tied around their beaks. That this domination is thought to be acceptable shows how deeply the domination of other animals is accepted in Western society. What is most disturbing is the logic that one knows the Banshee has chosen their partner in return because, "He will try to kill you." That resistance somehow suggests complicity echoes narratives of abuse. As Jones wrote, in order to control an animal, the dominator will "break the spirit, by humiliating and violating the animal" (2006, p. 321). This breaking is the way that abusers treat their victims: dominating them to the point where they are subordinate to the will of the dominator. The message that it is acceptable to dominate others to get what you want echoes the ideology of colonization, while the discourse of becoming animal reinforces the human/animal binary.

"Consumer culture," wrote Ahmed (2000), "provides consumers with a fantasy that they can become the stranger, however temporarily or that they can be like the stranger, by using certain products" (p. 119). *Avatar* not only provides the fantasy of becoming stranger through the film, but there are now products being marketed to promote this fantasy. Mattel toys are offering Avatar action figures in McDonald's (well known for their own global conquest) "Happy Meals" around the world, thus ironically marketing the film on the neocolonial stage of global capitalism. The European colonial legacy is carried on in narratives in which the subject disappears and reemerges as the stranger. Transferring the method of agency, the discourses of Western humanism persist.

Eco-Ability as a Multidirectional Discourse

While colonial, capitalist, patriarchal hierarchy has long exploited women, nonhuman animals, and people with disabilities, the recognition of shared histories of genocide, displacement, and exclusion brings forth new possibilities for solidarity and mobilization. Michael Rothberg's (2009) concept of multidirectional memory, "subject to ongoing negotiation, cross referencing, and borrowing; as productive and not private," can help us understand how recognizing conjoined histories of exploitation can be productive (p. 3). In a multidirectional memory, the events that are strongly embedded in social consciousness, such as slavery or genocide, can be platforms for understanding the suffering occurring today. Remembering them productively can unravel the unique, yet unifying memories and identities. This unraveling must occur through recognition of the "social vulnerability" of bodies (Butler, 2004, p. 20), while moving away from the recognition of vulnerability as a precondition for human—that which is in a process of becoming—and engaging in dialog of the meaning of the human as the site of social critique. Rather, we should be concerned with a shared recognition of vulnerability, based upon what it means to *be* a sentient animal of diverse abilities.

New narratives based on productive memory, instead of the normalized colonial story, empower rather than repeat the old stories of domination, fetishization, and exclusion. Through them we may begin to embrace a spectrum of abilities that transgress borders and lead to new ways of being a compassionate presence in the world. This new way of living includes embracing a lifestyle of nonviolence toward other creatures in recognition that the current mode of consumption is cruel, unsustainable, and unhealthy. Linda Fisher, a Native American Ojibway vegan inspired by Chief Seattle, seeks to dispel the common notion that because her ancestors engaged in ("limited") meat consumption this must be desirable today. Fisher (2011) expressed concerned about the treatment of nonhuman animals, which is prevalent today. She noted that Hollywood's depiction of the Native American diet and lifestyle is incorrect, and that most tribes in North America lived off an abundance of plant-based foods. Fisher suggested that if her ancestors were to comment on the "right to hunt... they, who listened to the land and killed only as was necessary, would not be wasteful... [they would] tell us that it is time to stop the suffering and the killing." For those deprived of healthy, plant-based diets due to slavery and colonization, a sustainable practice of veganism can be a powerful practice of *decolonization* (Harper, 2010). This decolonizing lifestyle is a result of productive memory that calls for simultaneously freeing oneself *and* nonhuman animals from colonization.

The restructuring of harmony between human beings, and between human and nonhuman nature, is central to the decolonizing project: transgressing normalcy and nation, not through assimilation or failing to acknowledge that borders exist, but through the rejection of those oppressive nationalisms, borders, and binaries which aid in hegemonic state control. A transnational feminism emphasizing rhizomatic difference and the value of diversity is an antidote for the violence of the Western humanist tradition. While it is important to challenge the uniformity created by global capitalism, this should not lead to believing that one's culture or identity is separate from everything else. All sentient beings who inhabit the Earth are linked in sharing this planet. An eco-ability philosophy that respects the Earth is empowering for all who depend on its well-being.

Note

1. As Barker and Murray (2010) have noted it is important to situate one's analysis in the correct context. *Normalcy* has different meanings in different cultures. For instance, in certain Indigenous American cultures, the degree of normalcy rests on whether one is in balance with the natural world and with one's relationships. Thus, in certain postcolonial contexts *normal* might actually refer to the experience of having a disability (p. 229).

References

Ahmed, S. (2000). *Strange encounters: Embodied others in post-coloniality*. New York, NY: Routledge.

Armstrong, P. (2002). The postcolonial animal. *Society & Animals, 10*(4), 413–419.

Bacon, F. (2003). The new Atlantis. In F. Bacon & T. Campanella, *The new Atlantis and the City of the Sun: Two classic utopias* (pp. 1–40). Mineola, NY: Dover.

Barker, C. & Murray, S. (2010). Disabling postcolonialism: Global disability cultures and democratic criticism. *Journal of Literary & Cultural Disability Studies, 4*(3), 219–236.

Ben-Moshe, L., Hill, D., Nocella II, A. J., & Templer, B. (2009). Dis-abling capitalism and an anarchism of 'radical equality' in resistance to ideologies of normalcy. In R. Amster, A. DeLeon, L. A. Fernandez, A. J. Nocella II, & D. Shannon (Eds.), *Contemporary anarchist studies: An introductory anthology of anarchy in the academy* (pp. 113–122). New York, NY: Routledge.

Brah, A. (1996). *Cartographies of diaspora: Contesting identities*. New York, NY: Routledge.

Butler, J. (2004). *Precarious life: The powers of mourning and violence*. London, UK: Verso.

Cameron, J. (Producer/Director). (2009). *Avatar* [Motion picture]. United States: Twentieth Century Fox.

Cherkis, J. (2012, January 11). Occupy Wall Street activists could see more arrests at newly reopened Zuccotti Park. *Huffington Post*. Retrieved from http://www.huffingtonpost.com/2012/01/11/occupy-wall-street-zuccotti-park-arrests-civil-rights_n_1200247.html

Chow, R. (1993). Where have all the natives gone? In R. Chow, *Writing diaspora: Tactics of intervention in contemporary cultural studies* (27–54). Bloomington, IN: Indiana University Press.

Davis, L. J. (2002). *Bending over backwards: Disability, dismodernism and other difficult positions*. New York, NY: New York University Press.

Deleuze, G., & Guattari, F. (1988). *A thousand plateaus: Capitalism and schizophrenia*. (B. Massumi, Trans.). London, UK: Continuum

Derrida, J. (2008). *The animal that therefore I am*. New York, NY: Fordham University Press.

Fisher, L. (2011, August 14). On the 'right to hunt' by a Native American vegan. *The Scavenger*. Retrieved from http://www.thescavenger.net/animals/on-the-right-to-hunt-by-a-native-american-vegan-768.html

Garland-Thomson, R. (2006). Welcoming the unbidden: The case for conserving human biodiversity. In A. Schrager Lang & C. Tichi (Eds.), *What democracy looks like: A new critical realism for a post-Seattle world* (pp. 77–87). New Brunswick, NJ: Rutgers University Press.

Gilroy, P. (1993). *The black Atlantic: Modernity and double consciousness*. Cambridge, MA: Harvard University.

Harper, A. B. (2010). Social justice beliefs and addiction to uncompassionate consumption: Food for thought. In A. B. Harper (Ed.), *Sistah vegan: Black female vegans speak on food, identity, health, and society* (pp. 20–41). New York, NY: Lantern Books.

Jones, P. (2006). Stomping with the elephants: Feminist principles for radical solidarity. In S. Best & A. J. Nocella II (Eds.), *Igniting a revolution: Voices in defense of the Earth*, (pp. 319–334). Oakland, CA: AK Press.

Jones, P. (2009). Free as a bird: Natural anarchism in action. In R. Amster, A. DeLeon, L. A. Fernandez, A. J. Nocella II, & D. Shannon (Eds.), *Contemporary anarchist studies: An introductory anthology of anarchy in the academy* (pp. 236–246). New York, NY: Routledge.

Kashani, T., & Nocella II, A. J. (2010). Hollywood's cinema of ableism: A disability studies perspective on the Hollywood Industrial Complex. In B. Frymer, T. Kashani, A. J. Nocella II,

& R. Van Heertum (Eds.), *Hollywood's exploited: Public pedagogy, corporate movies, and cultural crisis* (pp. 105–114). New York, NY: Palgrave Macmillan.

Kilkenny, A. (2011, November 21). Occupy Wall Street and the importance of creative protest. *The Nation*. Retrieved from http://www.thenation.com/blog/164729/occupy-wall-street-and-importance-creative-protest.

Krementsov, N. (2010). Eugenics in Russia and the Soviet Union. In A. Bashford, & P. Levine (Eds.), *The Oxford handbook of the history of eugenics* (pp. 413–429). New York, NY: Oxford University Press.

Kropotkin, P. A. (1972). *Mutual aid: A factor of evolution*. London, UK: Allen Lane.

Mashni, M. (2010, March 5). Palestinians painted as animals while Israel goes scot-free. *National Times*. Retrieved from http://www.theage.com.au/opinion/society-and-culture/palestinians-painted-as-animals-while-israel-goes-scotfree-20100304-plog.html

Merchant, C. (2008). Secrets of nature: The Bacon debates revisited. *Journal of the History of Ideas, 69*(1), 147–162.

Mohanty, C. T. (2003). *Feminism without borders: Decolonizing theory, practicing solidarity*. Durham, NC: Duke University Press.

Patterson, C. (2002). *Eternal Treblinka: Our treatment of animals and the Holocaust*. New York, NY: Lantern Books.

Riots in Tottenham after Mark Duggan shooting protest. (2011, August 7). *BBC News*. Retrieved from http://www.bbc.co.uk/news/mobile/uk-england-london-14434318

Rothberg, M. (2009). *Multidirectional memory: Remembering the Holocaust in the age of decolonization*. Stanford, CA: Stanford University Press.

Shiva, V. (1997). *Biopiracy: The plunder of nature and knowledge*. Toronto, Ontario, Canada: Between the Lines.

Shiva, V. (2002). Monocultures of the mind. In A. Kimbrell (Ed.), *Fatal harvest: the tragedy of industrial agriculture* (pp. 67–70). Washington, DC: Island Press.

Snyder, S. L., & Mitchell, D. T. (2006). *Cultural locations of disability*. Chicago, IL: University of Chicago Press.

Wolfe, C. (2003). *Animal rites: American culture, the discourse of species, and posthumanist theory*. Chicago, IL: University of Chicago Press.

PART III

A Challenge to Oppressive Relationships

CHAPTER SEVEN

Disableism Within Animal Advocacy and Environmentalism

A. J. WITHERS

This chapter explores some examples of disableism in which animal advocates, environmentalists, environmental justice advocates, and anarcho-primitivists have engaged. *Disableism* (also referred to as *ableism*) is discrimination against people who are labeled as disabled, and/or the belief that disabled people are inferior to nondisabled people. Influential individuals, organizations, and existing social structures have perpetuated, within these movements, these notions: that disability is bad, that disability should be eliminated, that disabled people are a drain on resources, and, at times, that disabled people are subhuman or marginally human. Further, the needs and demands of disabled people are often ignored, even when environmental or animal advocates are addressing issues that specifically relate to us. Disableism, both overt and subtle, endemic to these movements, is not only oppressive; it also undermines any claims that these movements make about being committed to social justice. While considerable damage has already been done because of disableist attitudes and practices, I still believe that there are possibilities for how these movements can move forward in anti-disableist ways.

Before I continue, however, I need to define who I am talking about when I talk about disabled people. *Disability* is a political identity imposed on people, rather than an individual defect or shortcoming (Withers, 2012). Disability is a social construct imposed upon some of us because we are considered unfit or less fit, unproductive or underproductive. Therefore, disableism is a form of oppression, because of our social devaluation unrelated to who we actually are, or to our actual capabilities and incapacities as individuals.

Animal Advocacy

There is a multitude of perspectives within animal advocacy. Among them are supporters of animal welfare, "advocating humane or kind use of animals"; animal rights, "the idea of abolishing all use or exploitation of animals" (Sztybel, 2010, p. 50); and animal liberation, which "rejects *speciesism*" (p. 49). There are often divergent ideas and aims within these ideologies. For the purposes of this chapter, I will refer to these groups of people as animal advocates. There are also diverse perspectives regarding which animals these notions of welfare, justice, rights, and/or liberation should be extended to, and on what grounds—if, for instance, they should be extended on the basis of intelligence, length of life and relational ties (Aaltola, 2005), or intrinsic value (Anderson, 2004). However, particularly within animal rights and animal liberation, disability and disabled people are frequently invoked in the pursuit of welfare and/or justice for animals.

Disability is used as a cautionary tale by some animal advocates for those who consume animals: If you eat animals, you could become disabled. People for the Ethical Treatment of Animals (PETA) warned that eating fish "can cause mental retardation and physical disability in children" (PETA, n.d.b, para. 7). PETA also ran a billboard campaign called "Got Autism?" that depicted a bowl of milk with Cheerios arranged in a sad face that (falsely) linked dairy consumption to autism (PETA, n.d.a). The imagery implies that an autism diagnosis leads to a future of sadness and unfulfilled potential. This campaign reinforces the disableist notion that a diagnosis of autism is a diagnosis of an unhappy life that needs to be avoided. This, however, runs counter to how many autistic people view their own lives (Trivedi, 2005).

Similar, negative depictions of disabled people are also reflected in anti-vivisection campaigns, which oppose the use of animal testing. Groups like the National Anti-Vivisection Society (NAVS, n.d.) and In Defense of Animals (IDA, n.d.) also depict disability as solely negative, and something that resources should be used to avoid. Both organizations argue that "birth defects" should be prevented, and call on human genetic research to achieve this. NAVS also raises alarm bells about the cost of disabled babies in terms of "health care, special education and lost work" (NAVS, n.d., para. 2). Here, in order to protect animals from being experimented on, disabled people are undermined, belittled, and depicted as drains on resources.

In addition to this *prima facie* disableism, these organizations support genetic testing on humans as an alternative to testing on animals, something to which many disabled activists and academics are vociferously opposed. These medical interventions are often *in utero* tests to identify disabled fetuses so they can be aborted. According to Lisa Blumberg (2002), "The social purpose of these tests is to reduce the incidence of live births of people with disabilities" (p. 234). These tests are designed to reduce the number of disabled people, not to make our lives better or provide care. As many disabled people have argued, what we need are things like accessible transportation, affordable housing, food security, attendant care, and an end to discrimination—not eradication.

Disabled people have been some of the most articulate and vocal critics of the medical industrial complex. They have fought for and won change within the medical system, such as the deinstitutionalization of many disabled people from medical institutions into the community (Fleischer & Zames, 2001). Rather than working with disabled people as allies against industries that cause harm to both disabled people and (nonhuman) animals, anti-vivisection activists have chosen to reinforce disabled people's oppression in an attempt to win gains for animals. In adopting this position, anti-vivisection activists work to end one aspect of the abuse of animals at the expense of disabled people, which is, at best, a problematic trade-off.

Perhaps the most dramatic example of disableism within animal advocacy, however, is the argument from marginal cases (AMC), a term coined for the idea that some disabled people, specifically those with profound intellectual disabilities, are "marginal cases" or even "marginal humans" (Garner, 2005, p. 29). While there are variations on AMC, the gist of it is that some "profoundly disabled people" are not capable of rational thought or reason, and, therefore, cannot be considered human in the same way that others are (Anstötz, 1993). For example, Christoph Anstötz wrote:

> There is nothing that humans with the most serious intellectual disabilities can do or feel that chimpanzees or gorillas cannot; moreover, there is much that a chimpanzee or a gorilla can do that a profoundly mentally disabled human cannot do. (1993, p. 165)

Additionally, ethicist Peter Singer, who has been called an "icon of the animal rights movement" (Aaltola, 2005, p. 42), argued that one using life support or diagnosed with persistent vegetative state (PVS) is "obviously not equal to a healthy person" (as cited in Hari, 2004, p. 1). Singer (2011) also advocated the murder of disabled infants, saying:

> When the death of a disabled infant will lead to the birth of another infant with better prospects of a happy life, the total amount of happiness will be greater if the disabled infant is killed. The loss of happy life for the first infant is outweighed by the gain of a happier life for the second. (p. 163)

Singer (2011) also asserted that "killing a disabled infant is not morally equivalent to killing a person. Very often it is not wrong at all" (p. 167).

For many disabled people this statement is terrifying and hateful. While Singer may argue that he is not advocating that disabled people be treated worse but that animals be treated better (Hari, 2004), the dehumanization and marginalization of disabled people can help to justify and legitimize worse treatment of disabled people. Disabled people have been actively fighting for social justice for decades (Fleischer & Zames, 2001), and the AMC undermines many of the claims that disabled people, or at least certain disabled people, make for better treatment in society.

The criteria for marginal humanity would appear to be, according to Christoph Anstötz (1993), possessing the ability to "respond to any stimuli in a perceptible way," having the ability "to take part in communication," as well as the ability to "react to other people or his or her surroundings" (p. 162). However, the lack of ability to perceive responses, communication, or reactions only says something about the assessor, not necessarily about the person being assessed. Such tests often also require that one not be deaf in order to respond to sound, and that one have the motor abilities to physically respond to stimuli, things that someone may not have while understanding what is going on around them, being conscious, and, even, thinking rationally (Crossley, 1997). For example, Rom Houben was diagnosed with persistent vegetative state (PVS), and for twenty-three years it has been argued he was conscious, with no one able to perceive his communication, rationality, or awareness of his surroundings. Indeed, some experts estimate that many people diagnosed with PVS are actually conscious at times. As many as 40% of people with this diagnosis could fall into this category (Charter, 2010). The argument from marginal cases would say that Houben and others who are diagnosed with PVS, what Crossley calls, "the postcoma catchall" (Crossley, 1997, p. 53), are marginally human and question their claim on humanity, at least while labeled as being in a PVS. It is, however, very probable that Houben, and everyone else who has been in the same situation, would have taken offense to this position.

The assumption that Singer (2011) made, that a nondisabled person has "better prospects of a happy life," is also very troubling, and imposes on us disableist notions about our lives and our capacity to be happy. By this logic, would it then be acceptable to advocate the killing of, or to actually kill, infants from other marginalized communities, based on the presumption that their chances of happiness would be lower due to systemic oppression? Would it be acceptable to kill a homosexual or a female infant if it would be replaced by a heterosexual male who has more access to privilege, and, therefore, might be more likely to be happy? No external body—no person, no organization—has the right to determine anyone else's quality of life.

The AMC criteria is arbitrary and originates from a disableist position. Because disabled people are devalued, our ways of being in the world are also devalued. To be clear, valuation of disabled people is a social one, not necessarily a biological one. A century ago, indigenous people in Australia may have been the focus of the AMC. Eugenicist and feminist Margaret Sanger, echoing a commonly held sentiment, called Indigenous Australians "the lowest known species of the human family, just a step higher than the chimpanzee in brain development" (Sanger, 2003, p. 45). By this standard, Indigenous Australians were "marginal cases," or even "marginal humans"; however, the racism and social injustices in such a view are clearly apparent today.

Even from an animal advocate's perspective, many animals are excluded from access to rights or reduction of suffering under the argument for marginal cases, which underlines an important, fundamental contradiction to this disableist line of argument. Daniel Salomon (2010) argued: "Singer grants nonhuman animals moral consideration based on their demonstrating a certain standard of self-awareness—a criterion that many nonhuman animals cannot meet" (p. 52). If animal advocates want to ensure that all animals are not subject to oppression, suffering, and/or the withholding of rights or freedoms by humans, maintaining a human disability analysis is important. I would think that an animal welfare, rights, or liberation platform should be extended to all animals, not simply those that are not considered disabled. If animal advocates support animals that are affected by pollutants, injured by hunters, saturated by oil, etc., then a disability analysis is key. Otherwise those animals' bodies that are injured or changed, or whose health is compromised by human or environmental factors, would as easily be, by the same logic, designated as defective, marginal, unworthy of life or dignity.

Environmentalism

Like those engaged in animal advocacy, environmentalists are an ideologically diverse group. Also like animal advocacy, mainstream environmentalism routinely engages in disableist practices and rhetoric. There is a wide array of issues that fall under the environmentalist umbrella, but for the purposes of this chapter, I will discuss a few of the main environmental issues, and how they are articulated by prominent organizations and individuals within the environmental movement.

One key area of concern within the mainstream environmental movement is transportation. Cars are major emitters of carbon and other pollutants; as such, campaigns like Bike to Work Week, Car-Free Day, and CarFree City, USA have been developed. Some of them are time-specific events, while others are campaigns to make certain blocks, neighborhoods, or even cities car-free, either permanently or for certain days of the week. These campaigns encourage people to get rid of their cars and take up biking, walking, or, sometimes, public transportation.

Of course, an obvious problem with campaigns like these is that many physically disabled people are not acknowledged—either by their bodies or by their transportation needs. This is especially apparent in campaigns that solely call for people to bike. Many disabled people require cars to meet their transportation needs (at least in communities, and particularly cities, as they are currently organized). Many disabled people cannot bike or walk considerable distances or at all. This is coupled with the fact that public transit, where it is available, is frequently inaccessible physically and/or financially. In areas where there is a transit service specifically for disabled people, it is often inadequate, difficult to book, full of arbitrary rules, or even dangerous—for example, there have been a number of documented sexual assaults on Toronto's WheelTrans (Canadian Press, 2007, 2008). Disabled people may not have their needs met by or be comfortable with these segregated forms of transit. So we turn to cars or more pollutant-producing, wheelchair-accessible vans, to get around. All of these and other transportation barriers faced by disabled people are typically ignored by anti-car campaigns.

Occasionally, however, disability is discussed in campaigns like these. For example, an article by Alexander Berthelsen on *Carbusters.org* said:

> Kids, people with disabilities and elderly, people living in suburbs far away from their work and people living in cities where the weather just isn't suitable for being outside most of the year—for all of them biking or walking is hardly ever an option and this is something that needs to be addressed. (Berthelsen, n.d.)

Carbusters.org, however, does not actually address the needs of disabled people, beyond simply acknowledging that for them, car use is necessary. Of the organizations that I have mentioned, this is the only acknowledgment I came across of the fact that many disabled people have needs that cannot be met within the current car-free framework. In fact, it is one of the few organizations whose campaign acknowledges disabled people at all.

These campaigns demonize disabled car users along with others, as people who stubbornly refuse to abandon their autos. Further, their failure to put forward materials that are inclusive of disabled people suggests that those of us who rely on cars, in the car-free advocate's ideal world, should simply stay home. As disabled people have fought for many years to get access to their communities (Fleischer & Zames, 2001), campaigns that appear to be promoting further segregation are threatening and frightening.

In a similar manner, campaigns that focus on consumer activism as an environmental movement frequently ignore the needs and realities of people living with disabilities and other marginalized communities. Examples of this phenomenon are various, but for the purposes of this chapter, this brief mention will suffice.

Another focal point for environmentalists is pollution and toxin emissions. This is also a common site of disableist rhetoric. In spite of the fact that many disabled people experience our minds and bodies, and our lives, positively, anti-emissions campaigns tend to frame disability as wholly negative. For example, the *Earth First! Journal* website features articles condemning the cause of birth defects by depleted uranium (Puck, n.d.) and coal ash (Jameson, n.d.). Others rebuke the "toxic surroundings that... deform" (Best & Nocella, 2006, p. 13). In British Columbia, a group of eighteen environmental and health organizations called for a ban on cosmetic pesticide use because, among other things, they cause "birth defects, and neurological illness" (David Suzuki Foundation, 2010, para. 5). When people discuss "birth defects" or babies born with "deformities," what they are really talking about is the birth of disabled *people*. The desire to prevent "birth defects" is the (eugenic) desire to prevent disabled people from being born. It is deeply problematic to publicly advocate a reduction of disabled people in coded environmental rhetoric. There is a marked difference between advocating the reduction of harm and advocating for the culling of a certain population. It is very possible to condemn toxic chemicals, chemicals that cause harm to people (that cause, among other things, cancers) without devaluing an entire segment of society.

The only exception to disability being addressed as wholly negative that I have found within environmental campaign discourse is when activists use direct action and sabotage to break industrial equipment. Environmental organizations proudly proclaimed that "activists physically disabled the machine" (Molland, 2006, p. 50), that a "deep sea destroyer [was] disabled" (Walsh, 2004, headline), and that "access [was] denied" to a "disabled coal truck" (Coal Dust, n.d., para. 12). Here, disability is evoked in order to describe an enemy or villain. Some may argue that it is an acceptable usage of the word, *disabled*, to describe making something unable to work. However, if these words "have acceptable usages about things other than people, in terms of what dictionaries say," Chris Chapman (2010) argued, "it is impossible to use these words without evoking people." Chapman continued: "whatever dictionaries say, it would be impossible for me to say gay and have it only signify 'happy.'" The use of the word, *disabled*, in this context, reinforces notions that disability is negative, undesirable, and even worthless.

Environmental Justice

Environmental justice (EJ) addresses both social justice issues and environmental issues. The movement emerged in the late 1980s with the argument that civil rights should be included in environmental issues, particularly regarding the disproportionate impacts of hazardous wastes on racialized communities (Bullard, 1990). Unlike mainstream environmentalism, whose leadership is largely monopolized by White men (Rhodes, 2005), the environmental justice movement is led largely by women, racialized people, and working class or poor people (Gandy, 2003; Pulido, 1997; Warren, 1997). This movement, according to Dorceta Taylor (1993), responds to the "injustice in the distribution of environmental hazards and envisions a world where these burdens would be eliminated, reduced, or, where unavoidable, distributed equally in the future." The shift from a sole focus on the natural world within traditional environmentalism to a recognition that "human societies and the natural environment are intricately linked and that the health of one depends on the health of the other" was what Taylor called "a revolution within the history of U.S. Environmentalism" (p. 57).

While the environmental justice movement is far more inclusive, it rarely, if ever, addresses disabled people and our issues. Proponents of EJ commonly list women, racialized people, and poor people as unequally bearing the brunt of environmental degradation and toxins (Stein, 2004; Warren, 2000). Notably, disabled people seem to be consistently absent from this list. Disabled people, who are disproportionately women, racialized, and/or poor, are also disproportionately impacted by environmental injustices, as a result. Additionally, disabled people can experience the consequences of environmental injustices in unique ways. For some disabled people, different types of environmental pollutants, toxins, or degradation could have greater negative consequences. For example, smog is an annoyance or even a long-term health hazard for many people, but for some disabled people it can require that they stay indoors, resulting in isolation, loss of work, and any other number of negative consequences.

As in the mainstream environmental movement, disability is spoken of in almost exclusively negative terms by the environmental justice movement. Some in the EJ movement, Peter S. Wenz (*Environmental Justice*, 1988) for example, adopt the argument from marginal cases. Further, an increase in learning disabilities linked to lead and mercury are primary reasons given to get rid of or reduce use of the metals (Bullard, 2005; Faber, 2007). Robert Bullard, called the "father of environmental justice" (Dicum, 2006, p. 1) also warned of the "significant health costs, education costs related to lead-caused learning disabilities, and other social costs" (p. 27). Arguments such as these are used to devalue disabled people. We are depicted as drains on resources, and it is argued that our existence should be prevented. This same argument was used by eugenicists to justify the abuse of disabled people, which included forced sterilization—even murder (Withers, 2012). As social justice movements are becoming more aware of disability issues (Goodlad & Riddell, 2005), it becomes increasingly evident that the environmental justice movement should stop actively excluding disabled people and reinforcing disabled people's oppression. If this movement does not reconcile its claim to fight for justice while effecting injustice on disabled people, it is both at risk of losing support from the broader social justice movement and losing credibility.

Primivitism

The primitivist, anarcho-primitivist, or anticivilizationist paradigm promotes the idea that civilization is unsustainable, and that humans should live in small, hunter-gatherer communities. Primitivists are often disableist, both in how they discuss disability and in their envisioned ideal futures. A central theme within anarcho-primitivism is the notion that humans have surpassed the earth's carrying capacity. In order to correct this, according to primitivism, either a dramatic change in lifestyle, or reduction of the population, or both, are needed (Jensen, 2006a, 2006b).

While primitivists rarely speak about *disabled people*, they frequently talk about disabilities. Many primitivists discuss disability as a (negative) consequence of technology and civilization. Well-known primitivist, John Zerzan (2002), with an impressively disableist double hook, maintained that mental health issues are the result of life being "crippling, alienated, bizarre" (p. 87). Paul Shepard (1998) argued that "adult infantility—madness" is caused by the failure to observe rites, largely attached to the hunt and other hunter-gather observances (p. 317). Zerzan (2002) contended that "Nearly all diseases are diseases either of civilization, alienation, or gross habitat destruction"(p. 79). The creation of disease, or disability, is one of the central arguments that primitivists use against technology and civilization. Therefore, eliminating civilization, according to Zerzan, "will eradicate the suffering" (p. 118). It is unclear here if he means the eradication of those people he considers to be suffering, or the act of suffering, or both.

In order to correct the instances of disability and the superseding of the planet's carrying capacity, primitivists argue that civilization must be undone. A key aspect of eradicating civilization and technology is the elimination of the division of labor (Zerzan, 2002). This includes, according to Zerzan, eliminating the "form of dependence that comes from relying on others who have specialized skills you don't" (p. 73).

What, then, happens to disabled people when technology and division of labor are gone? Many disabled people rely on mutual aid and forms of assistance from others. Attendant care and other forms of support are integral to many disabled people's survival, and the dissolution of labor roles that include these would mean that many disabled people would die. Similarly, the elimination of certain medicines, assistive devices and mobility devices would mean that many disabled people lose their mobility, lose important ways of interacting with the world, and, might even lose their lives.

When Zerzan was asked what the end of civilization would mean for disabled people, he responded:

> Are we supposed to keep this whole industrialized suicide going for the sake of the people that you don't want to pull the plug on? If you discover that what is it that creates the problem and the problem just keeps on being created, whatever it is, like more people with all kinds of conditions, all kinds of problematic things ... these are creations of mass society so ... where is the healthy direction? I don't know what to do about disabled people. I don't want to pull the plug on people. I'm getting old, I don't want to pull the plug on people but we have a reality too. (Zerzan, 2008)

The primitivist ideal is one where disabled people have been killed. While Zerzan is hesitant to say it, his "reality" requires that people "pull the plug" on disabled people. We need to be eliminated in order to create their Utopia. Zerzan (2002) also wrote:

> Many say that millions would die if the present techno-global fealty to work and the commodity were scrapped. But this overlooks many potentialities. For example, consider the vast numbers of people who would be freed from manipulative, parasitic, destructive pursuits for those of creativity, health, and liberty. (2002, p. 116)

While millions dying is, perhaps, unfortunate, it is necessary, according to the primitivist ideology. I am not arguing that the millions who Zerzan asserts will die are all disabled; many different people will die in primitivist predictions. "Pulling the plug" in this context doesn't only mean a literal, physical life-support plug. "The plug" includes all forms of technology. People who rely on medication, most assistive devices, and/or electricity to survive would be cut off—would be killed. this is necessary in order for a very select few to achieve Zerzan's "creativity, health, and liberty," disabled people must no longer exist.

It can also be gleaned from other primitivist writings that we are not a part of their idealized hunter-gather societies. Manning (2004) wrote: "There are beings ... that see, smell, hear, remember, sense more than we do .... The human beings who maintain these hyper-refined senses are hunter-gatherers" (p. 6). Glendinning (2007) wrote of hunter-gatherer women who have "lean bodies," and possess "physical conditions that are reproduced among today's female athletes" (p. 52). The primitivist Utopia does not include people with poor or no sense of sight, smell, hearing, or memory, or people who do not have the bodies of athletes. (We can assume that Glendinning's athletes do not include paralympians, wheelchair athletes, etc.). It can also be assumed, based on the previous comments about how civilization and technology are the cause of so-called psychiatric disabilities, that the primitivist Utopia does not include people who are currently considered to be neuroatypical, have mental health issues, or have been psychiatrically labeled.

Conclusion

All of the movements and ideologies discussed here have caused harm to disabled people by, at best, perpetuating disableism, and, at worst, calling for our eradication. I do not believe that anarcho-primitivists have any common goals with disabled people or organizations—in fact, it is clear that disabled people are incompatible with the primitivist ideal. I would argue that anarcho-primitivism is fundamentally disableist; and this oppressive ideology cannot be reconciled with notions of social justice.

However, this is not true of the animal rights/liberation, environmentalism, or environmental justice movements. Anti-disableist principles and practices can be complementary to the practices of these movements, strengthening both these forms of organizing and disability organizing. There is also a great deal of potential for disabled people and our organizations to work together with environmentalists and animal advocates on common campaigns or to support each other in the furtherance of justice and solidarity.

Yet, while there are certainly disabled animal rights/liberation proponents and environmentalists, disabled people have been actively excluded from these movements. Not Dead Yet, a disability rights organization, said: "if there is a 'schism' between animal rights and disability rights, it's mostly been caused on one side" (Drake, 2010, para. 17). The damage done by these movements to disabled people and our causes has been deeply felt, and I do not believe that any allied relationship can be developed until these movements acknowledge their disableism and work to correct this. This is especially true with respect to those animal advocates and, to a far lesser extent, environmentalists and proponents of environmental justice, who adopt the argument from marginal cases. Drake (2010) wrote that it is implausible to imagine "us joining hands with a group that holds Peter Singer in such high esteem and at best expressing 'regret' for his writings on disability" (para. 26).

Should these movements choose to stop reinforcing disabled people's oppression in order to try to win gains for animals or the environment, there is potential to make real victories together. This, however, will never be possible until these movements make an effort for reconciliation with disabled people.

Note

1. I use the term, *disabled people*, in this chapter rather than *people with disabilities* because I view disability as a social construct rather than an individual trait. The label of disability is imposed on people; therefore, we are disabled people. For an in-depth discussion of this topic, see Oliver, 1990 and Withers, 2012.

References

Aaltola, E. (2005). Animal ethics and interest conflicts. *Ethics and the Environment, 10*(1), 19–48.

Anderson, E. (2004). Animal rights and the values of nonhuman life. In C. R. Sunstein & M. C. Nussbaum (Eds.), *Animal rights: Current debates and new directions* (pp. 277–298). New York, NY: Oxford University Press.

Anstötz, C. (1993). Profoundly intellectually disabled humans and the great apes: A comparison. In P. Cavalieri & P. Singer (Eds.), *The great ape project: Equality beyond humanity* (pp. 159–172). New York, NY: St. Martin's Press.

Berthelsen, A. (n.d.) Travel doesn't have to cost the Earth. *Carbusters: Journal of the Carfree Movement, Internet Edition*. Retrieved from http://carbusters.org/2010/02/04/travel-doesn%E2%80%99t-have-to-cost-the-earth/

Best, S., & Nocella II, A. J. (2006). A fire in the belly of the beast: The emergence of revolutionary environmentalism. In S. Best & A. J. Nocella II (Eds.), *Igniting a revolution: Voices in defense of the earth* (pp. 8–29). Oakland, CA: AK Press.

Blumberg, L. (2002). Eugenics and reproductive choice. In B. Shaw (Ed.), *The ragged edge: The disability experience from the pages of the first fifteen years of the disability rag* (pp. 228–239). Louisville, KY: Advocado Press.

Bullard, R. (1990). *Dumping in Dixie: Race, class and environmental quality*. Boulder, CO: Westview Press.

Bullard, R. (2005). *The quest for environmental justice: Human rights and the politics of pollution*. San Francisco, CA: Sierra Club.

Canadian Press. (2007, Nov. 28). Cabbie pleads guilty to sex assault on Wheel-Trans passenger. *The Canadian Press.* Retrieved from http://ezproxy.library.yorku.ca/login?url=http://proquest.umi.com.ezproxy.library.yorku.ca/pqdweb?did=1390220221&sid=3&Fmt=3&clientId=5220&RQT=309&VName=PQD

Canadian Press. (2008, July 4). Driver for disabled transit service charged with assaulting passenger. *The Canadian Press.* Retrieved from http://ezproxy.library.yorku.ca/login?url=http://proquest.umi.com.ezproxy.library.yorku.ca/pqdweb?did=1505615821&sid=3&Fmt=3&clientId=5220&RQT=309&VName=PQD

Chapman, C. (October 8, 2010). Crippling narratives and disabling shame: Disability as a metaphor, affective dividing practices, and an ethics that might make a difference. Paper presented at the conference *The space between: Disability in and out of the counselling room.* University of Toronto, Ontario, Canada.

Charter, D. (2010, November 24). Belgian man in 'deep coma' was awake, aware for 23 years. *The Ottawa Citizen.* Retrieved from http://proquest.umi.com.ezproxy.library.yorku.ca/pqdweb?index=0&did=1908808331&SrchMode=1&sid=1&Fmt=3&VInst=PROD&VType=PQD&RQT=309&VName=PQD&TS=1302825001&clientId=5220

Coal Dust. (n.d.). Access denied: Anatomy of a power plant blockade. *Earth First! Journal.* Retrieved from http://www.earthfirstjournal.org/article.php?id=274

Crossley, R. (1997). *Speechless: Facilitating communication for people without voices.* New York, NY: Dutton.

David Suzuki Foundation. (2010, January 14). *Unprecedented coalition of 18 health and environment groups band together to support BC ban on lawn and garden chemicals.* Retrieved from http://www.davidsuzuki.org/media/news/2010/01/unprecedented-coalition-of-18-health-and-environment-groups-band-together-to-sup/index.php

Dicum, G. (2006, March 14). Meet Robert Bullard, the father of environmental justice. *Grist.* Retrieved from http://www.grist.org/article/dicum/

Dombrowski, D. A. (1997). *Babies and beasts: The argument from marginal cases.* Champaign, IL: University of Illinois Press.

Drake, S. (2010, October 11). Connecting disability rights and animal rights—a really bad idea. *Not Dead Yet Blog.* Retrieved from http://notdeadyetnewscommentary.blogspot.com/2010/10/connecting-disability-rights-and-animal.html

Faber, D. (2007). A more 'productive' environmental justice politics: Movement alliances in Massachusetts for clean production and regional equity. In R. Sandler & P. C. Pezzullo (Eds.), *Environmental justice and environmentalism: The social justice challenge to the environmental movement* (pp. 135–164). Cambridge, MA: MIT Press.

Fleischer, D., & Zames, F. (2001). *The disability rights movement: From charity to confrontation.* Philadelphia, PA: Temple University Press.

Gandy, M. (2003). *Concrete and clay: Reworking nature in New York City.* Cambridge, MA: MIT Press.

Garner, R. (2005). *The political theory of animal rights.* Manchester, UK: Manchester University Press.

Glendinning, C. (2007). My name is Chellis and I'm in recovery from Western civilization. Boston, MA: Shambhala.

Goodlad, R., & Riddell, S. (2005). Introduction: Disabled people and social justice. *Social Policy and Society,* 4(1), 43–44.

Hari, J. (2004, July 1). Peter Singer—On killing disabled babies, saving animals, and the dangers of superstition. Retrieved from http://www.johannhari.com/2004/07/01/peter-singer-on-killing-disabled-babies-saving-animals-and-the-dangers-of-superstition

In Defense of Animals (IDA). (n.d.) The truth about vivisection. Retrieved from http://www.vivisectioninfo.org/humane_research.html

Jameson, J. (n.d.). Kingston power plant toxic waste spill in Tennessee. *Earth First! Journal.* Retrieved from http://www.earthfirstjournal.org/article.php?id=442

Jensen, D. (2006a). *Endgame: The problem of civilization* (Vol. 1). New York, NY: Seven Stories Press.

Jensen, D. (2006b). *Endgame: Resistance* (Vol. 2). New York, NY: Seven Stories Press.

Jensen, D., & McBay, A. (2009). *What we leave behind.* New York, NY: Seven Stories Press.

Manning, R. (2004). *Against the grain: How agriculture has hijacked civilization.* New York, NY: North Point Press.

Molland, N. (2006). A spark that ignited a flame: The evolution of the earth liberation front. In S. Best & A. J. Nocella II (Eds.), *Igniting a revolution: Voices in defense of the earth* (pp. 47–58) Oakland, CA: AK Press.

National Anti-Vivisection Society (NAVS). (n.d.). *Birth defects*. Retrieved from http://www.navs.org/site/DocServer/Birth_Defects.pdf?docID=361

Oliver, M. (1990). *The politics of disablement*. Basingstoke, UK: Palgrave Macmillan.

People for the Ethical Treatment of Animals (PETA). (n.d.a). *Got autism? Learn about the link between dairy products and the disease*. Retrieved from http://www.peta.org/features/got-autism-learn-about-the-link-between-dairy-products-and-the-disease.aspx

People for the Ethical Treatment of Animals (PETA). (n.d.b). *Toxins in fish*. Retrieved from http://www.peta.org/living/vegetarian-living/Toxins-in-Fish.aspx

Puck. (n.d.). The war this time. *Earth First! Journal*. Retrieved from http://www.earthfirstjournal.org/article.php?id=167

Pulido, L. (1997). Community, place, and identity. In J. P. Jones, H. J. Nast, & S. M. Roberts (Eds.), *Thresholds in feminist geography: Difference, methodology, representation* (pp. 11–28). Lanham, MD: Rowman & Littlefield.

Rhodes, E. L. (2005). *Environmental justice in America: A new paradigm*. Bloomington IN: Indiania University Press.

Salomon, D. (2010). From marginal cases to linked oppressions: Reframing the conflict between the autistic pride and animal rights movements. *Journal for Critical Animal Studies*, *8*(1–2), 44–72. Retrieved from http://www.criticalanimalstudies.org/wp-content/uploads/2009/09/4-JCAS-Vol-VIII-Issue-I-and-II-2010-Essay-FROM-MARGINAL-CASES-pp-47-72.pdf

Sanger, M. (2003). What every girl should know: Sexual impulses—Part II. In E. Katz (Ed.), *The selected papers of Margaret Sanger: Volume I: The woman rebel, 1900–1928* (pp. 41–45). Chicago, IL: University of Illinois Press.

Shepard, P. (1998). A post-historic primitivism. In J. M. Gowdy (Ed.), *Limited wants, unlimited means: A reader on hunter-gatherer economics and the environment* (pp. 281–326). Washington, DC: Island Press.

Singer, P. (2011). *Practical ethics* (3rd ed.). New York, NY: Cambridge University Press.

Stein, R. (2004). Introduction. In R. Stein (Ed.), *New perspectives on environmental justice: Gender, sexuality, and activism* (pp. 1–20). New Brunswick, NJ: Rutgers University Press.

Sztybel, D. (2006). The rights of animal persons. *Animal Liberation Philosophy and Policy Journal*, *4*(1). Retrieved from http://www.animalliberationfront.com/Philosophy/sztybel-rights.pdf

Sztybel, D. (2010). Animal welfare and animal rights, a comparison. In M. Bekoff (Ed.), *Encyclopedia of animal rights and animal welfare* (2nd ed, Vol. 1, A–H, pp. 49–51). Santa Barbara, CA: Greenwood Press.

Taylor, D. E. (1993). Environmentalism and the politics of inclusion. In R. D. Bullard (Ed.), *Confronting environmental racism: Voices from the grassroots* (pp. 53–62). Cambridge, MA: South End Press.

Trivedi, B. (2005). Autistic and proud of it. *New Scientist*, 2504, 36–40.

Walsh, D. (2004, November 13). Deep sea destroyer disabled. *Greenpeace International*. Retrieved from http://www.greenpeace.org/international/en/news/features/deep-sea-destroyer-disabled/

Warren, K. (1997). Taking empirical data seriously: An ecofeminist philosophical perspective. In K. Warren (Ed.), *Ecofeminism: women, culture, nature* (3–20). Bloomington, IN: Indiana University Press.

Warren, K. (2000). *Ecofeminist philosophy: A Western perspective on what it is and why it matters*. Lanham, MD: Rowman & Littlefield.

Wenz, P. S. (1988). *Environmental justice*. Albany, NY: State University of New York Press.

Withers, A. J. (2012). *Disability politics and theory*. Black Point, Nova Scotia, Canada: Fernwood.

Zerzan, J. (2002). *Running on emptiness: The pathology of civilization*. Los Angeles, CA: Feral House.

Zerzan, J. (2008, June 18). *Anarcho-primitivism, archeology and anthropology. Montreal Anarchist Bookfair* [Video 8/10]. Retrieved from http://www.youtube.com/watch?v=FomlQHwqlpk

CHAPTER EIGHT

Therapeutic Relationships Within the Biotic Community

BILL LINDQUIST AND ANNA GRIMM

The relationship that exists between the natural environment, nonhuman animals, and their human partners draws on thousands of years of coevolution as species. As these players come together within a synergistic alliance, the ensuing relationship can be one of transformation and healing. Human separation from the natural world leaves a sense of imbalance. Transforming this relationship offers healing, calm, and growth. This chapter examines the impact of that relationship. We draw on case studies from PEACE Ranch,[1] a faith-based, therapeutic environment bringing rescued horses together with human clients. Examples of the powerful relationships between nonhuman animals, people, and the natural world that are respectful of the unique gifts each brings are presented. An examination of parallels between the dynamics within the therapeutic arena and today's urban classrooms is offered. And finally, we offer a further exploration of lessons we might learn in order to integrate a symbiotic partnership within the biotic community in urban classrooms.

Horses

Humans have a long history of relationships with horses. Some 5,000 years ago, humans made their first effort to capture, train, and breed wild horses, leading to the domestication of today's horse. This relationship had a phenomenal impact on human and nonhuman life, especially economically, including the use of horses to transport humans and goods, and as weapons in war. Through this relationship based on domestication and domination of horses by humans, horses have made their way into the very fabric and foundation of human culture. Today, children grow up with the near mythological stories of Black Beauty, the Red Pony, Trigger, and Gandalf the White's triumphant steed, Shadowfax. The coinciding evolution of horse and human has resulted in a unique ability of horses to acutely respond to their human partners. For example, I watched as a young woman in a wheelchair entered the arena at PEACE Ranch. A mare approached, rested her head in the woman's lap, and proceeded to gently lick her arm. This woman could not physically reach out to the horse, but the horse perceived this woman's needs and responded in a loving and gentle manner.

Temple Grandin (Grandin & Johnson, 2006), one of the first people publicly to make the philosophical connection between the oppression of people with disabilities and the oppression of nonhuman animals, described people and nonhuman animals as meant to be together. Her own connection with animals played a significant role in her growth and development as an autistic person. Horses were particularly important to her. She tells of a psychiatrist friend who has developed an altered set of expectations for teenagers who rode horses.

> He says if you take two kids who have the same problem to the same degree of severity, and one of them rides a horse regularly and the other one doesn't, the rider will end up doing better than the non-rider (Grandin & Johnson, 2005, p. 5).

The kids with horses have had to assume the responsibility for the care of such a large animal. They developed a real relationship with the animal, a relationship fed with love. The very act of riding requires a partnership of caring. "Real riding is a lot like ballroom dancing or maybe figure skating in pairs" (p. 5). Horses learn their riders and begin to respond to the rider's needs even before the rider is aware.

Equine-Assisted Therapy

Horses are uniquely situated for use in therapy situations. Through structured and specialized activities involving a therapeutic herd, clients are able to surmount fears, improve communication skills, learn emotion regulation, gain assertiveness and confidence, and increase self-esteem. Horses' status as prey animals position them well for this work. Their very survival depends on their ability to accurately read their environment. They must be able to quickly assess the congruence of another being, and clearly judge their intention. To survive, horses have become acutely sensitive to body language.

The majority of human communication is nonverbal, yet people often lack awareness of this type of communication. In an equine-assisted session, horses help bring awareness to nonverbal messages. To get the horse to respond in an ideal manner, the client must first gain awareness of his or her own behavior and posturing as well as potential ramifications. From that awareness begins the process of making changes in one's life. Because it is experiential in nature, preverbal experiences in people's lives can be accessed and worked through—resolving issues that may never arise in traditional talk therapy. Additionally, the element of pressure is removed, as interaction in sessions takes place with the horses. For this reason, equine-assisted therapy can be a powerful approach for the treatment of resistant individuals.

Among the first nationally recognized organizations offering therapeutic services involving horses and people was the North American Handicapped Riding Association (NAHRA), now the Professional Association of Therapeutic Horsemanship (PATH). Individuals experienced in this discipline recognized the physical and mental therapeutic benefits of horseback riding for individuals with special needs. As this field became more recognized and respected, other therapies involving the use of horses began to emerge. Among the first of these was the Equine Assisted Growth and Learning Association (EAGALA). Established in 1999, EAGALA has grown to be an international nonprofit organization with 3,500 professional members. Professionals offering EAGALA-model, equine-assisted therapy all follow a code of ethics and adhere to very clear standards. Other organizations have formed as well, creating a variety of ways to utilize horses in therapy.

The employment of a treatment team, the exclusion of riding, and a solution-focused approach all help EAGALA stand apart from other equine therapies. A licensed mental health professional and an equine specialist work together in the design and implementation of activities for clients to engage in with the horses. In adhering to a solution-focused approach, equine-assisted psychotherapy and learning (EAP/L) professionals recognize that client(s) "have their own best solutions if just given the opportunity to discover them" (EAGALA, 2009, p. 25). The EAP/L treatment team is skilled at asking open questions, clean of their own perspectives, biases, and agendas. In asking these questions, symbols and metaphors begin to emerge. "Many cognitive scientists now conclude that people not only talk in metaphor, but also think and reason in metaphor; they make sense of their world through metaphor, and they act in ways that are consistent with their metaphors" (Lawley & Tompkins, 2005, p. 18). For this reason, there is a strong emphasis on the development of metaphors as a context with which to begin the work of changing a client's metaphorical landscape. As the therapeutic team works to bring awareness to the symbols and metaphors organizing a person's life, work can be done to change the landscape, thereby changing the client's life.

A Tale of Healing at the PEACE Ranch

The following is an account of the relationship between a rescue horse that has found a home at PEACE Ranch and a teenage client referred to the services at PEACE Ranch.

The large chestnut mare ran wild. Her mane and tail were a tangled mess, so lost in burrs there was no hair to be seen. Ten horses, 15 dogs, and numerous cats were abandoned along with her, left on their own to survive. By the time local law enforcement and rescue professionals arrived, two horses had died of starvation, and parts of their bodies had been consumed by the dogs. Seven of the horses were caught and trailered—but not this mare. To her, survival depended on escaping the humans' touch. Four hours and 12 tranquilizer shots later, they were finally able to coax her into a trailer. Veterinary care was waiting at her first rescue home, yet she fiercely resisted any attempt by the vet to examine her. Seven of her fellow horses were able to be placed in foster homes, but no one would take this "dangerously wild" animal.

At age fifteen, the teenage boy ran wild. Multiple legal encounters related to drugs, alcohol, and expulsion from school had earned him a tether by which local authorities maintained continual surveillance of his whereabouts. In their own struggles with addiction, his parents had lost custody of him and his siblings two years before. His continued drug and alcohol use and frequent absconding put his current pre-adoptive foster placement at risk. If something did not change, the next step would be residential placement.

As a last resort for the struggling adolescent, he was referred to an eight-week intensive program at PEACE Ranch. He was to be part of an experiential, multidisciplinary treatment approach. Upon completion of the first eight weeks, the *Behavior Assessment System for Children*, Second Edition (BASC-2) was administered for a second time. The BASC-2 is a comprehensive set of rating scales and forms including Teacher Rating Scales, Parent Rating Scales, Self-Report of Personality, Student Observation System, and Structured Developmental History, that help with understanding the behaviors and emotions of children and adolescents (see Reynolds & Kamphaus, 2004). The instrument showed significant to moderate improvement in every area but one—the scale assessing his involvement in school. He had repeated negative experiences in the educational setting, including expulsion from his last school. At the completion of his first eight weeks, his probation officer asked for one more eight-week course, this time targeting education. All parties agreed, and the course immediately commenced.

In the first session of the second eight weeks, he and Jackie, the Executive Director and mental health treatment professional at PEACE Ranch, walked to the pasture with a halter and lead rope to get his horse. The objective for this session was to provide an experience that corresponded with his moving to yet another new school. During his first eight weeks, he had successfully haltered a horse of his choosing multiple times, routinely choosing a tall, rescued thoroughbred he named Prince. However, this time, things did not go as planned. Greeting Prince this time, he found the horse would have nothing to do with him. Each time he began to approach, Prince quietly moved out of reach. Trusting the horse's instincts, Jackie watched and waited.

At the same time Prince was moving away, a young haflinger-cross mare approached. The more intensely he sought Prince, the more insistently this new mare stayed by his side. He finally stopped, asked Jackie to watch, and demonstrated how the mare kept in stride wherever he went. "What is happening?" Jackie asked. "The mare wants to be with me," he said. "She likes me!"

During the first eight weeks, he had expressed his belief that, while he was able to halter Prince, Prince really did not like him. He thought Prince was stubborn and just wanted to be on his own. Despite this, Prince had been the horse he had continued to choose to work with. He eventually was able to make the connection that this was how he perceived himself: a stubborn loner. Now, here he was in a new situation, spontaneously orchestrated by the intuition of his equine friends, projecting positive feelings about himself and this new horse. He asked, "Can I just take this horse instead? She wants to be my friend!"

This insightful moment laid out by the equine cotherapists gave way to discovery and breakthrough in the area of letting go of old friends and forging new relationships. It became a foundational piece for that session and changed the course of the boy's treatment program. At the close of the second eight weeks, the BASC-2 was administered for the third time, and all 20 areas, including the education segment, showed significant improvement. During the sixth week of the program, this troubled young man was elected president of his class. He went on to finish that school year. One year later, he remains in his home. He has successfully completed his probation and no longer needs intensive, therapeutic support services.

An interesting parallel occurred with the chestnut mare. As a last resort, she, too, was sent to PEACE Ranch for a 90-day evaluation. If she could not be rehabilitated in that time, she would be put down. When she first arrived at the ranch, she continued her wild run for three straight days, unwilling to be touched by any human. She was given fresh water and food daily. Slowly, she began to tolerate Jackie standing near while she ate, first outside the pen, then inside. It was not until children came to visit that she really began her transformation. They called to her while standing outside the fence. With head lowered, she slowly approached and sniffed their small, gentle hands filled with grass dangling hesitantly inside the fence. She carefully took their peace offerings and allowed them the privilege of lightly touching her head before she moved away. That moment was a turning point, the opening of one very injured spirit to healing and the slow process of rebuilding trust. It was not long after this gentle connection with the children that she began to allow Jackie to slowly remove the matted burrs, first from her forelock, then from her mane, and eventually from her tail.

With a healthy diet and a chance for positive relationships with other horses and humans, her beautiful chestnut coat began to shine. She now approaches you in the pasture with eyes full of life and curiosity. She allows people to come near, groom her, and teach her new things. Her 90-day evaluation at PEACE Ranch turned into a permanent placement. Her journey has been filled with retraining and new experiences. One year later, this "dangerous" horse is living a safe, productive, and healthy life. On top of that, she has now found a place in the educational and therapeutic programs at the ranch. She is an active member of the therapeutic herd and has earned celebrity status, as her story of transformation offers hope to all who hear it.

Beyond Horses

The isolation and pain shared by these two individuals are not anomalies. Healing is a transformative process. We have been examining the transformative power of reconnecting people with the natural world, with a particular focus on the role horses play within the model of equine-assisted therapy. To look beyond the work being conducted with horses, we begin by looking to E. O. Wilson, a Harvard University scientist, who drew from his work in evolutionary biology to describe a concept of "biophilia" as an innate need to "affiliate with other forms of life" (as cited in Louv, 2005, p. 43). When we bring together the wonderful complexity of the natural world in the forms of children, plants, and nonhuman animals and utilize the woods, streams, and prairies as extensions of the classroom, we help support the healthy development of the children in our classrooms.

Wilson argued that humans' biological needs were honed through an evolutionary need to remain in connection with the natural world. The rise of eco-psychology, or nature therapy, describes the transformative power of what we can do for the earth, and, in turn, what the earth can do for us. Our mental, physical, and spiritual well-being is connected to our experiences with the natural world. It grounds us, connecting us with the base of our being. Separated from this connection, as so many of our children are today, we suffer the negative impact on our development.

In the late 1700s, Dr. Benjamin Rush declared digging in the soil to have "a curative effect on the mentally ill" (as cited in Louv, 2005, p. 45). Today, we recognize that connection with animals can fill a special niche in our mental health. Nursing homes and doctors' offices tap into this understanding and provide aquarium fish to lower blood pressure and reduce stress.

The significance of the natural world to the well-being of children was recognized as early as the late 19th to early 20th centuries. During that period, Nature Study emerged as a popular movement in the country's elementary schools. Anna Botsford Comstock (1854–1930), a leader in the Nature Study movement, is recognized as one of the first teachers to actively take her pupils outside, using the natural world as part of her classroom. She went on to become a noted speaker, teacher trainer, and developer of classroom materials.

> Nature study gives the child a sense of companionship with life out-of-doors and an abiding love of nature.... Out-of-door life takes the child afield and keeps him in the open air.... This is an age of nerve tension and the relaxation which comes from the comforting companionship found in woods and fields is, without doubt, the best remedy for this condition. (Comstock, 1911, p. 2)

Access to nature can help children deal more effectively with stressful events they encounter. Those children considered most vulnerable, facing a higher degree of stressful events in their lives, appear to benefit the most (Wells & Evans, 2003). Louv (2005) described a modern phenomenon of increasing separation from experiences in nature, leading to what he described as nature-deficit disorder. The absence of unstructured free play in nature has played a significant role in the onslaught of obesity, attention disorders, and depression. "Two out of ten of America's children are clinically obese—four times the percentage of childhood obesity reported in the late 1960s." The rate at which "American children are being prescribed antidepressants almost doubled in five years" (p. 47). Louv described studies that support exposure of children to nature as a form of therapy for attention-deficit disorders and other maladies.

A Personal Connection to Nature

I (Bill Lindquist) grew up with ample freedom to build tree forts in the nearby woods, wage naval battles in the nearby gravel pit pond, and navigate kites flying high overhead. I spent countless hours in the nonjudgmental and creative blank slate that nature provides, free from the pressures I faced at school and at home. The world was mine.

"Given a chance, a child will bring the confusion of the world to the woods, wash it in the creek, turn it over to see what lives on the unseen side of that confusion" (Louv, 2005, p. 7). I learned many life lessons through the interactions with nature that provided skills I would later call upon, as the need for calm, focus, and serenity arose in my life. I went on to teach in the urban core of Saint Paul, Minnesota. Every winter, we took the sixth-grade students for a three-day immersion in the natural world at the Audubon Center of the North Woods, a residential environmental center. For many, this was their first time out of the city. Kids appearing street-tough in school shed that toughness as nature evened out the playing field and placed these kids in an unfamiliar world. It was that immersion that set the stage for long conversations at night, pleas to leave a night-light on, and teddy bears tucked in.

It is vital that educators today recognize this innate need to affiliate with other forms of life. It may be impossible to maintain a stable of horses outside each classroom, but it is entirely possible to fill classrooms with other forms of life, from mealworms to hamsters. It is entirely possible to take our students outside to breathe in the air, study the skies, listen for birds, and explore the natural world found within the cracks in the sidewalks.

Interspecies Understanding: The Tao of *Equus*

There are numerous schools of thought regarding the gentling and training of horses. On one end is the use of spurs and whips in an attempt to tame through domination. An alternative approach is Natural Horsemanship, a way of working with horses relying on the trainer's ability to understand the *tao of equus*, or *the way of the horse*. The trainer must first learn the language of the horse and then learn to communicate with horses in *their* language.

Horses rely on their ability to communicate nonverbally. Subtle movements such as the shifting of feet, lowering of the head, or licking of lips, send clear messages to others within and outside the herd. One horse is able to *move* another horse with a simple shift of his eyes. A newcomer is able to discern the precise timing for joining a herd by observing the nonverbal messages each horse is sending.

Rather than *demand* that a horse come to you and do as they are told, Natural Horsemanship focuses on the relationship developed between horse and human and encourages the human to find a common space to meet the horse. Pat Parelli is a successful horse trainer that helped shape the methods of Natural Horsemanship. The Parelli method "allows horse lovers at all levels and disciplines to achieve success without force, partnership without dominance, teamwork without fear, willingness without intimidation, and harmony without coercion" (Parelli, 2012, para 4).

Within this model, horses are perceived as capable of growth independent of their presenting behavior. It is in this natural partnership between human and horse that mutual understanding and respect emerge. Monty Roberts (1997), often referred to by followers as a real-life horse whisperer, believed his success came solely from his ability to communicate gently with horses in horse language. Roberts has drawn numerous parallels between the relationships we have with horses and the relationships we hold with other humans in our lives, helping to deepen our understanding of human psychology. "What works with horses, he says, also works with humans. The name of the game is communication" (Scanlan, 1997, p. xiv).

During a Natural Horsemanship class at PEACE Ranch, horses were "re-arranged" in their pastures for an observation of herd dynamics. Jackie rotated the horses in the pasture, splitting two herds up and joining four horses together. The new group was made up of two families, each horse joining the new crowd with a friend. One horse in each pair had previously established themselves as leaders in their respective herds. Participants were observing how those two leaders would relate to one another as they attempted to establish a new hierarchy.

Roxy. Roxy, the chestnut mare described earlier, waited expectantly with a new horse in her pasture, both content to quietly eat their dinner. Yet, she was intensely aware that her best friend remained in the adjacent pasture with the rest of the herd. A gelding that typically falls lower in the hierarchy approached. He was keenly aware that this hefty mare was doing everything she could to let him know that he just stepped foot onto *her* territory. Roxy fussed, while the little gelding did little to challenge but did everything to avoid her bites and kicks. Roxy moved the gelding's feet. A horse person can quickly recognize the ranks within the herd. Roxy was in charge. She walked toward the gelding. He ran. She ran toward him; he bolted.

The next horse that entered was Vinnie, the recognized leader of the entire herd. In an attempt to again establish her place, Roxy charged, squealed, and made herself loom as large as she possibly could. Something was different this time; Vinnie stood his ground. He arched his neck, extended his nose, and stood firm. No biting, no kicking, no chasing. The message was clear. With adrenaline pumping, Roxy charged, but at the last second, ran off. He was calling her bluff. The gelding that had allowed himself to be moved by Roxy stood near. With Vinnie there, he no longer seemed as nervous. Appearing confused, Roxy ran to the adjacent pasture and whinnied for her buddy, who continued to munch the new grass around her. The fence between them blocked any chance of them getting together. So she charged the newcomers in her pasture again. Roxy ran a few circles trying to get them to move. Vinnie continued to quietly stand his ground. Despite her charges and her snorts, he was solid. Roxy continued to protest, never quite accepting his leadership. The other mare had quickly acquiesced, and was contentedly eating on the other side of the hay bale. The next morning found Roxy in the adjacent pasture, reunited with her buddy. The fence was untouched. The only explanation was that she had jumped it. The power of friendship and the need for comforting and familiar connections run deep.

Anna. Anna grew up with horses. In her adult life she seized every opportunity to be around them. It had been years since she had been on one of many trail rides around her rural childhood home in the country or lay near her horse as she grazed in the yard. Early in her relationship with PEACE Ranch, she could hardly contain her excitement at the promise of a trail ride. One of those days presented a particularly vivid encounter. It was a morning when her second grader and preschooler were at home. She had made a loaf of bread before they woke, to bring along as a gift. Her children were more clingy than normal, making Anna's exit from the house emotional. In her haste, she forgot the bread. Rather than go back and risk another dramatic scene, she chose to let it go. When she arrived at the ranch, she was provided a young mare assured to be cooperative and pleasant. During grooming, the mare grew fidgety. She kept moving away from Anna, making the job difficult. It took Anna a full five minutes to get on the horse once she was finally saddled. Anna's energy had been continually mounting for the past half hour. Anna was led around the arena for a time to calm herself down before finally venturing out, only leaving once she pronounced that *she* felt fine. Anna's anxiety and unregulated energy that morning had been clearly read by the horse, as the horse mirrored what Anna unconsciously displayed. Finally aware, Anna worked at letting it go. As she did so, the horse responded, perceptibly calming. As a rider learns to regulate her energy, so does the horse, intuitively mirroring the emotions the rider brings to the relationship.

Connecting to the Classroom

A similar construct exists in the classroom. A teacher cannot successfully lead a classroom from the vantage of the cowboy riding hard to impose his will on the herd. Doing so may create a classroom that appears orderly, but students obey out of fear, not respect and are unable to engage in the spirit of learning. They are trained, but not taught; they are compliant, but not attentive and engaged. "Short-tempered intimidating teachers that habitually put students on the spot plunge emotionally unstable students into the fight, flight or freeze mode, a process that literally shuts down higher processes" (Kohanov, 2001, p. 154). It is here that we can unravel the difference between educating and schooling. Schooling promotes discipline, and teaching is based on lecturing at students, while educating fosters creativity and exploration and teaching is a shared dialogue (Freire, 1993). Freire, the founder of critical pedagogy, argued against the banking method, which emerged out of the standardization approach to education. Freire argued for a collaborative, transformative learning experience for social justice, where the teacher facilitates the dialogue with his or her students.

Teachers communicate strong and clear messages through nonverbal language. Differing expectations of students based on ethnic background have been shown to result in reduced opportunities for quality instruction. Teachers have been shown to hold higher expectations for European American students than for students of color. A dialogue of more positive questions, feedback, and encouragement follows (Tenenbaum & Ruck, 2007).

Ladson-Billings (2009) described the impact on urban learners of teacher belief systems and the manner in which teachers carry themselves. She described a number of teachers that follow culturally relevant practices as possessing a high self-esteem and high regard for others. Culturally competent teachers see themselves as professionals with a strong identification with the teaching practice. Their actions come out of a deeply held belief system that all students can succeed through a safe place, which fosters a liberatory, transformative experience (hooks, 1994). A safe place promotes social justice and challenges systems of domination, such as racism, sexism, ableism, and classism (hooks, 1994). In the midst of a typical urban school, Ladson-Billings described the power of one teacher that carried herself with a calm and confident presence. Entering her classroom you were "overcome with a feeling of calm and peace" (p. 51). To be effective, it is important that teachers learn to recognize and manage their fears and anxieties and dispel any notion that runs counter to success for all. Teachers project their emotions and beliefs, and students will behave in a manner that mirrors what they read.

The novice teacher may fail to recognize the significance of her stance in the classroom. Unsure of her boundaries, and not confident in her stance, she may find herself reacting to her students out of fear or anxiety. Like Anna's ride, she remains unaware of how she is projecting her own anxiety onto her students. Students will mirror the emotions the teacher brings into the classroom and may mirror the teacher's unease by acting out their own unease. Teachers benefit from learning to be conscious of their emotions and allowing the positive stance of their congruent selves to be the nuance that students read.

Teachers must learn to step into the culture of the classroom and learn the language of their students. From entering their students' world, they can begin to form the necessary relationships within an appropriate learning environment that allows all students to succeed. Not doing so can lead to cultural conflicts with "incongruence, and inconsistencies that educators and students encounter in the classroom can limit students' learning opportunities" (Milner, 2010, p. 23). To operate only from your own experience without taking the time to know the students' world may set a learning environment in place with few points of reference for the students. Delpit (1995) described attitudinal differences in the classroom between teachers and students of differing backgrounds. Failure to understand these differences can result in the inability of students to properly read their teacher's intent. "If teachers are to teach effectively, recognition of the importance of student perception of teacher intent is critical" (Delpit, 1995, p. 168).

Carl Pickhardt (1978) described the impact of "fear" in the classroom with a focus on the nonverbal games students can play to instill fear within the teacher. "Keenly observant, they notice the slightest tremors of insecurity or fright, and move with incredible speed and accuracy to exploit their momentary advantage. They do not 'see' fear so much as they 'sense it'" (p. 108). Pickhardt interviewed students who were experts at utilizing their posturing stance to move power to their advantage. He concluded with suggestions from the same students on what a teacher can do in response:

- *Don't back away*—physical distancing is one of the most easily identifiable indicators that a teacher is afraid
- *Don't back down*—relenting on a demand can indicate sensitivity to pressure from fear
- *Don't fight back*—fighting fear by fighting the student indicates your susceptibility to the fear game being played (Pickhardt, 1978, p. 112).

Interesting parallels exist between Pickhardt's findings and Vinnie's behavior in the herd dynamic. Not unlike horses' ability to read the level of congruence within their human partners, students are skilled at reading behaviors emanating from our emotions. Awareness and control of these emotions, followed by a calm and confident stance in our classrooms, will go a long way to the creation of a learning environment where all members of the learning community within the classroom can thrive.

Conclusion

Paralleling a model of natural horsemanship, a successful teacher enters the classroom in partnership, surveys his or her students, checks in with *their* language, and seeks to get to know each of them for the individuals they are in a holistic process, rather than trying to break, tame, or control them. She learns to be keenly aware of the subtle nuances each student presents. From that position, she squares herself with both feet planted firmly on the ground. She knows herself well; her boundaries are clear. She clearly asserts herself as leader, while honoring the individual spirit of each of her students. Discipline is created while dignity is maintained. As students test her, as Roxy tested Vinnie, she learns to project confidence and calm because she knows who she is. Her students read her. They respect her. They mirror her. Because the necessary ingredients are present, students are able to be quiet and allow their teacher to lead them as a facilitator. They do not see her as intimidating or as someone to be feared, but as someone to respect, someone who will work alongside them and lead them in the learning that is to take place.

Every day, teachers face classrooms of Roxys—students in need of a stable, nonjudgmental environment in which to learn and thrive. They need teachers who can stand squarely in the classroom, undeterred by the challenges thrown their way. They need teachers who know themselves and allow their students to mirror the calm and caring they project. They need teachers who seek to learn the language of the student, who will enter their world, and listen, and whisper. Students and the community need teachers who recognize the healing power of plants and garden in the classroom, a dog lying down near a student's desk, windows overlooking a park, a walk in the field, the miraculous world found between the cracks in the city sidewalk. They need teachers who know the transformative power of the natural world. The world needs students who fully discover themselves through a liberatory process that is empowering within the classroom and the world.

Note

1. PEACE Ranch (Professional Equine Assisted Counseling and Education). See http://www.peaceranchtc.com

References

Comstock, A. B. (1911). *Handbook of nature study*. Ithaca, NY: Comstock.

Delpit, L. (1995). *Other people's children: Cultural conflict in the classroom*. New York, NY: New Press.

EAGALA. (2009). *Fundamentals of EAGALA model practice training manual: Supplemental material to the EAGALA Equine Assisted Psychotherapy and Learning training and certification program* (6th ed.). Layton, Utah: EAGALA.

Freire, P. (1993). *Pedagogy of the oppressed*. New York, NY: Continuum.

Grandin, T., & Johnson, C. (2006). *Animals in translation: Using the mysteries of autism to decode animal behavior*. Orlando, FL: Harcourt.

hooks, b. (1994). *Teaching to transgress: Education as the practice of freedom*. New York, NY: Routledge.

Kohanov, L. (2001). *The Tao of equus: A woman's journey of healing and transformation through the way of the horse*. Novato, California: New World Library.

Ladson-Billings, G. (2009). *The dream-keepers: Successful teachers of African American children* (2nd ed.). San Francisco, CA: Jossey-Bass.

Lawley, J., & Tompkins, P. (2005). *Metaphors in mind: Transformation through symbolic modelling.* London, UK: Developing Company Press.

Louv, R. (2005). *Last child in the woods: Saving our children from nature-deficit disorder.* Chapel Hill, NC: Algonquin Books.

Milner IV, H. R. (2010). *Start where you are, but don't stay there: Understanding diversity, opportunity gaps, and teaching in today's classrooms.* Cambridge, MA: Harvard Education Press.

Parelli, P. (2012). *Natural horsemanship: The Parelli program.* Retrieved from http://www.parelli-naturalhorsetraining.com/natural-horsemanship/

Pickhardt, C. E. (1978). Fear in the schools: How students make teachers afraid. *Educational Leadership, 36*(2), 107–112.

Reynolds, C. R., & Kamphaus, R. W. (2004). *BASC 2, Behavior assessment system for children* (2nd ed.). Circle Pines, MN: American Guidance Service.

Roberts, M. (1997). *The man who listens to horses: The story of a real-life horse whisperer.* New York, NY: Ballantine Books.

Scanlan, L. (1997). Introduction. In M. Roberts, *The man who listens to horses: The story of a real-life horse whisperer.* New York, NY: Ballantine Books.

Tenenbaum, H. R., & Ruck, M. D. (2007). Are teachers' expectations different for racial minority than for European American students? A meta-analysis. *Journal of Educational Psychology, 99*(2), 253–273.

Wells, N. M., & Evans, G. W. (2003). Nearby nature: A buffer of life stress among rural children. *Environment and Behavior,* 35(3), 311–330.

CHAPTER NINE

Institutional and Common Oppression of People with Disabilities, Nonhuman Species, and the Environment in Italy

ALESSANDRO ARRIGONI

Introduction

This chapter is based on a personal research project concerning discrimination against persons with disabilities, with particular regard for civilians in modern Italy. Civilians with disabilities are, according to Italian law, people with disabilities that are not the result of war, work, or service. They are discriminated against in many different ways, which will be clarified in this chapter. In the European Union, Italy is one of the latest countries to have social and economical concerns, despite claims by the former and present governments and the political milieu in general. The lack of social cohesion has historical and economical reasons (currently, the black market economy represents 40% of the GDP), which must be highlighted in order to understand the topic. This chapter describes the issues related to discrimination against and oppression of Italian citizens with disabilities and the treatment of nonhuman species within the environmental context.

Since the end of WWII, Italians had to face a hard period of structural, industrial reconstruction, with many internal conflicts (poverty, domestic terrorism—both "black" or fascist, and "red" or communist—workers oppression, organized crime, industrial pollution), in addition to the pressures of the Cold War. Italy is still the sole European country with active, Soviet-inspired communist parties. With few exceptions, during the last four decades, Italy was ruled by Catholic-inspired parties and socialists, in addition to postcommunist forces after 1989. The chronic instability of government never solved these problems, which increased their negative effects after the advent of economic globalization, during the 1990s.[1]

Nowadays, in the era of national politicians such as Berlusconi (which many have called the "postfascist" era), we face a general lack of a welfare state (by European standards), and a dramatic increase of youth unemployment (34% average, 60–70% in the South). The environmental devastation in many areas of the South is the highest rate of chemical pollution on the European continent. The industrial North suffocates by the fumes of millions of cars and thousands of factories built near or in cities. High illegal immigration rates, not only due to the North African rebellions, combined with high crime rates (organized and not) are other major problems. Finally, general impoverishment of the educational system, which was considered one of the best in Europe until the end of the 1980s, results in poorer academic outcomes for students. Public transportation is close to a general collapse, while the increase of cement consumption is second only to China's (Settis, 2010).

Many public universities are close to bankruptcy, and the investments in research are among the lowest in Europe. Architectural barriers are still widespread (both in public and private buildings) and make the lives of people with reduced mobility a living hell in many towns and cities. In this respect, Italy resembles a developing country.

A lack of urban planning has been the rule in 80% of Italy since the 1950s, with only a few small towns counting on sustainable urban planning. In the southern regions, 40% of private houses are improperly and illegally constructed, and there is a total absence of services for people with disabilities. This is also the case for elders and children who need a nursery, with rare exceptions held by volunteer or religious associations or groups.

To take a train, for a blind person or a person in a wheelchair, requires a long procedure, beginning with alerting the rail company. In many cities, like Rome (the capital), most public buses and many subway stops are not accessible. Only 10% of the Italian railway system is accessible (Schianchi, 2009, p. 62). Inter-city buses are 90% inaccessible, and 60% of Roman buses have fake[2] or nonworking platforms for persons with disabilities. Northern Italy is surely better, but is nothing compared to other European or U.S. towns I have visited in the last 15 years. For example, in 2010 I travelled by train and bus from Cortland (NY) to Miami (FL), and I never found a single architectural barrier, and where there was a "critical" point, I always saw people helping persons with disabilities or elders in need, myself included. In Washington, DC, an Amtrak crew reversed the escalators when they saw me with a crutch. In NYC and Miami I have seen bus drivers stop the bus and help persons with disabilities to get onto the platform, as did the Amtrak crew. In Italy, such a thing is rare—of course not everywhere—and it is a continuous fight just to ask "normal" people to not park their cars in reserved, accessible spaces.

The meaning of the word, *oppression*, is something that Italian citizens with disabilities know very well. In many cases, oppression becomes a form of open racism and discrimination, carried out by public institutions and people, because people are not educated in citizenship, as we will see below. Societal stigma is still the norm, with devastating results for persons with disabilities.

Historical Frame

If we look at Italian history we can easily see that, as a republic, Italy is a very young country—compared to other European nations: only 150 years since unification, which has been likely an annexation by the kingdom of Sardinia (Piedmont Savoia) over the other medieval realms (Papal states included), and this is still visible in the different lifestyles of the present twenty administrative regions and three geographical areas (Northern-Central-Southern). In 1861, 75% of the Italian population was illiterate, compared with only 30% in the UK and 20% in the US (in 1870). After two lost World Wars, both begun in alliance with the Germans, the Kingdom of Italy was abolished by popular referendum in 1946. It was only in the 1960s that industrial reconstruction led to an economical, industrial boom (at the end of WWII Italy was really backward, with an agriculture-based economy). Average salaries of Italians have been similar to China's or India's for centuries. Only after 1945 was there a major effort to generate modern, industrial development, mostly in northern cities (the South again lagged behind, for many reasons which would be hard to identify here).

One of the causes of this backwardness is certainly the historical fragmentation dating back to the medieval municipalities, governed by powerful families, who were also often fighting each other on the basis of the old rivalry between the Guelphs and the Ghibellines, which corresponds to the ancient division between supporters of the Roman Empire and the papacy. This dichotomy is deeply rooted in Italian culture, society, and politics even today, where it is evident that forty years of stunted social reforms benefited only those people, families, or groups connected to the power centers of the Roman Catholic Church (Vatican State) or the masons (which acts very differently from other E.U. countries, because it is always hidden from the visible political and social layers).

Political parties are "infiltrated" by emissaries of the lodges and the church—whether conservative/right, or progressive/left, is irrelevant (Dolcetta, 1999). These people do not respond mainly to the Italian constitution but to the "higher" rules of the masonic codes or the canonical law. This generated (and still generates) a sort of widespread, "hidden" patronage, which is formally illegal but is very common at any level of economical, social, and political life. Patronage and familial relationships have degenerated into a shared culture of lawlessness, which, after centuries, often becomes violent with the mafia in many regions of the country (and it has been exported abroad in many other countries). It is in this culture of lawlessness that Bettino Craxi (former president of the Socialist Party who became prime minister in 1922) declared in Parliament, before his arrest and the implosion of the "first" Republic in 1992: "If we, the Socialists, have stolen public funds for so many years, so did the other parties' officials." The vast majority of citizens are only partially aware of these issues, for they are distracted by mainstream media (50% of which are the property of Berlusconi's family), soccer games, religious holidays, and problems of daily survival (it.wikipedia.org, n.d.).

Generally speaking, Italians are very proud of their medieval and Renaissance traditions and history. This is understandable and wonderful as well, but they refuse to acknowledge the damages caused by historical social fragmentation and familial relationships. Likewise, they refuse to compare their social achievements to those of other E.U. citizens concerning public health systems, average wages, retirement benefits, tax levies (an Italian employee works for the Government until the end of June, compared to a U.S. employee for whom the "no tax day" is near the end of April), public transportation, press freedom, civil freedom (gay people will never marry in Italy and still do not have social security when they live together), technological development, environmental protection, and, generally speaking, quality of life.[3]

Concerning all of the parameters mentioned above, Italy lags behind other European countries, and it is often surpassed even by developing nations, particularly in categories such as press freedom (see Freedom House, 2010) and educational and technological development.[4] The Freedom House report said: "The Italian government is in 113th place in the world for what concerns openness to innovation and at the 89th for the use of technology." According to the 2010 Freedom House report:

> Corruption remains an issue in politics despite the changes in government over the past decade. Italy was ranked 63 out of 180 countries surveyed in Transparency International's 2009 Corruption Perceptions Index, the second lowest rating for Western Europe. [...] Freedoms of speech and of the press are constitutionally guaranteed. However, the prime minister controls up to 90 percent of the country's broadcast media through state-owned outlets and his own private media holdings. (Freedom House, 2010)

These are just a few examples of what it is like currently to live in this country. The difference is almost tangible, something that one can "feel in the air" when one travels abroad and then returns to Italy.

Back in the 1950s, when the American sociologist, Edward C. Banfield (1958/1967), came to southern Italy for a field inquiry, he compared a small town in the Basilicata region to St. George (Utah), highlighting that in St. George there was a whole set of group activities in pursuit of goals that go beyond the immediate, material interests of a single family: new members for the Red Cross; raising funds managed by an association to build a new dormitory at the local middle school; and a collection of shelters for antiaircraft defense in case of alien attack. And in Basilicata? None of that. The orphanage and convent were falling down; farmers were not willing to cede even one working day to fix anything that was public, and no one was willing to sacrifice a modicum of their time and resources without a personal return. In short, in southern Italy, all behaviors of individuals are "family oriented." "Why?" asked Banfield. For cultural and psychological reasons, was the answer. In "Montegrano" there was an absence of that particular form of sociability, called civicness, or having a "civic sense," which is the backbone of democracy. The civic sense is nothing but the spirit of association (which Tocqueville considered the basis of democracy in America) according to which the citizens offer their time, their specific attitudes, and sometimes their own money, contributing to an organization that pursues goals that do not fall in the direct and immediate interests of the individual but that benefit the community (see Banfield, 1958/1967). Banfield maintained that Italians act in this way because their moral basis is the opposite of civic sense, i.e., it is based on the amoral familial relationships, namely, the rule to "maximize the immediate, material benefits of the nuclear family, and to assume that everyone else should behave in the same way." This is also the opinion of the anthropologist, Carlo Tullio Altan (1995, 1997, 1999, 2000). In my opinion, this attitude continues even today and is embedded in so many aspects of Italian society, heavily influencing the possibility of obtaining respect for the civil rights of the most fragile population, including persons with disabilities.

When the ordinary Italian citizen needs to approach the public institutions—central or peripheral—he or she collides with a series of bureaucratic difficulties that are unparalleled in continental Europe. This is true for every kind of social need, health care, or fiscal and retirement services. Persons with disabilities are the most exposed to the risk of individual failure, poverty, and social exclusion because of the reduced possibility of expressing their problems and requirements in workplaces and other social environments (Schianchi, 2009). As we will see, the family is the only institution that literally saves the lives of hundreds of thousands of persons with disabilities, although, unfortunately, increasing their exclusion. Italians are so eager to evade taxes, and they are always complaining about the poor performance of public services, ignoring the vicious circle of not having strong social controls and not receiving decent social services.

Definitions and Laws Pertaining to Persons with Disabilities in Italy

Italian law defines "invalid civilian" as a citizen with congenital or acquired disabilities—physical or mental—which cause an (at least) one third (33%) permanent reduction in working capacity. Persons with disabilities at work, service, or in a war are protected by different laws. It means that the definition of persons with disabilities implies a general concept, i.e., that the concept of disability supports all the impairments that a person experiences, except for those impairments that were caused by war, work, or service. In fact, victims of war, service, or work injuries have special insurance and rights that, put simply, citizens with disabilities[5] do not have, a constitutional discrimination that has been obvious to all politicians for fifty years, and yet remains unresolved. In addition to that, I recently discovered that if you become disabled after the age of 65, you do not have any right to access financial benefits, except the support due in critical cases to all citizens who are not self-sufficient.

The duty of solidarity enshrined in the Constitution obliges the state to ensure every citizen unable to work and without the means to live, the right to maintenance and social assistance (Article 38 of the Italian Constitution). Italy ranks 23rd (out of 30 countries) in salary classification (EURISPES data, 2011) and has the lowest social allowances for retirement and disability in Europe (for which the European Council condemned Italy again in 2010). The institution of Strasbourg said, among other things:

> [Italy did] not guarantee to the elderly and persons with disabilities an income that enables them to not be at risk of poverty, the Italian authorities were not able to guarantee adequate social and health care to all those who needed it or that it had introduced measures to ensure that waiting lists for visits and medical examinations did not exceed an acceptable period of time (blitzquotidiano, 2010).

In Italy in 2011, persons with disabilities can receive a disability check of €260 per month only if they earn less than €4,470.70 per year (gross income) and have a disability certified from 75% to 99% of "reduced capacity to work." They can receive a disability check of €260 per month only if they earn less than €15,305.79 per year (gross income), and have a disability certified at 100%. After the 65th birthday, the check is converted—not added!—into a social security check (as for other citizens without regular retirement allowance) of €409. 05, or €580 if you do not have other income! If you consider that the net average income in Italy is around €14,500 per year—and that the cost of living is fairly high—the level of public financial support of people with disabilities can only be called shameful.

Of course, a disability check is not the only way to help people with disabilities to be integrated in society. The best solution is to give them a job (and the means of getting to work, which is very difficult—and often impossible—in many areas of the country), but the general situation of precarious employment in our country also affects persons with disabilities (civilians), worsening their situation, pushing many into suicide or violent crime within the family (as newspaper reports attest). Another shameful discrimination for persons with disabilities is that if they work, they lose the right to public financial support (as their disability payments decrease while they are working). On the other hansd, if a person is disabled because of a job accident and goes back to work, he or she does not lose the public financial support of a person with a disability!

Matteo Schianchi in his book, *The Third Nation of the World* (2009), talking about the social disintegration of persons with disabilities in Italy, described what the National Institute of Statistics reported: 27% of people with serious disabilities could not work, only 19.3% of persons with disabilities who could work had a job, whereas 55.8% of people without disabilities did work (p. 65). There also is a law for compulsory recruitment of persons with disabilities, which is very often ignored or bypassed because companies prefer to pay the fines rather than hire people with disabilities. Very often, jobs offered to persons with disabilities never meet their high qualifications, for they are often forced to accept work as doormen or telephone solicitors. In other words, the disability becomes a disqualifier that is useful to satisfy the legal recruitment obligations for few big companies, without care for the person they hire and his and her abilities. Of course, there are exceptions, but the mainstream situation is as I described. Italy—as often happens, such as in the case of the law for conscientious objection to vivisection (L. 413/93)—has originally inspired laws, like the one regarding the inclusion of children with disabilities in primary schools, but—equally often—these laws are left without appropriate financial and operational resources by the current government, even though it formally ratified the UN Convention on the Rights of Persons with Disabilities in 2009.

The 1948 Declaration of Human Rights claims that everybody has the right to social security in case of unemployment, disease or disability. Article 3 of the Italian Constitution provides that,

> It is the duty of the Republic to remove all economic and social obstacles that, by limiting the freedom and equality of citizens, prevent full individual development and the participation of all workers in the political, economic, and social organization of the country.

Article 38 provides that,

> All citizens unable to work and lacking the resources necessary for their existence are entitled to welfare support. Workers are entitled to adequate insurance for their needs in the case of accidents, illness, disability, old age and involuntary unemployment. Persons with disabilities are entitled to education and vocational training. Responsibilities laid down in this article are entrusted to public bodies and institutions established or supplemented by the State.

Both these charters have been and are betrayed by the men and parties who ruled this country in the First (1946–1992) and Second (1992–present) Republic.[6] This betrayal is takes place, in my opinion, in many spheres, and not only for what regards the national and regional laws and regulations concerning the life of Italian citizens with disabilities. Of course, discrimination in Italy—as in other countries—does not only affect persons with disabilities but also all women. We are a E.U. country with one of the lowest percentages of working women. Politicians pay as little attention to women's concerns as they do to issues related to babies, immigrants, or gay people, not to mention the sad situation of nonhuman animals in factory farms, vivisection farms, and slaughter houses.

The specific laws which govern disability issues (like Law 104/1992) are full of good principles, but, as Matteo Schianchi (2009, pp. 115–116) wrote, the full realization of the civil, political, and property rights of persons with disabilities is unfulfilled because of the lack of systematic, practical implementation of those same laws: "These structural deficits become [part of the] real life of real people, in not finding answers to specific needs, unable to establish appropriate measures to deal with the trauma, physical, psychological and social difficulties related to disability." This regards almost three million people in Italy. This figure almost doubles if we count mild forms of disabilities. Since, on average, Italy invests less in social spending than other EU countries—with a severe lack of expenditure controls, which permits the existence of the fake invalids[7] phenomenon, amongst other deplorable, widespread illegalities—persons with disabilities are more vulnerable than able-bodied people to the risks of poverty and social exclusion.

Not wanting to talk only about negative things, let me finish this section by talking about a nice zoo-anthropological project that could be of relevance to both disability studies and animal studies.[8] The "Almost Project" (Progetto Quasi) was created to honor Quasi ("Almost"), a dog with an extremely rare genetic condition which makes her look "almost" like a wild boar, who was adopted after some years of wandering and abuse. This project aims to rescue disabled and abused dogs, curing them when possible, hosting them in a foster homes and looking for new families to adopt them. In addition, the loving foster family, hosting up to three dogs at a time, is made up of a needy woman with a child with disabilities. Thirty volunteers donate €10 a month to give this family €300 a month for caring for the dogs while they look for new families. In this way, the project helps both dogs and needy families.[9] After all, Italian persons with disabilities are funded less per month than these dogs.

Forms of Discrimination in Italy: From Sexism to Ableism, Speciesism, and Disregard for the Environment

Italy is a very weird country because it is very contradictory. Italians, known as "hot Latins" who are open to the world, actually deal very differently with their local or familiar, ordinary background, as demonstrated in my earlier discussion of familial relationships and patronage. Immigrants, especially those coming from Africa or eastern Europe, are often treated like slaves, hired as undeclared workers, and crammed into warehouses and abusive homes, particularly in the South, as many journalistic inquiries regularly show. This is the paradigm of diversity in 2011. Only Leftist parties seem to be interested in changing these xenophobic attitudes, which are rooted in the general culture of lawlessness which is widespread in every corner of the peninsula. But, the same parties seem not to care at all about the issues related to the violated rights of persons with disabilities. This claim is based on my personal experience as a person with a disability and aid to a politician for eight years. In 2007 I had a personal conversation with a so-called progressive political leader, a current governor of a region, and a possible candidate to become the next prime minister. When I asked his opinion concerning institutional discrimination based on ableism he answered, "for those issues there are the class associations or groups, it is not a matter of politics." It has to be said that this is the same "progressive" framing culture that denied and denies any association between "animals" and "rights" in my country, the same attitude I found among the local hunters where I live and the teachers at the university I attended. It is clear to me that most of the radical themes I found so interesting, the intersection of critical animal studies, disability studies, and the environment, are currently very hard to popularize in my country, and we must encourage deep, collaborative work to better understand these issues.

Environmental corruption in Italy

There is a general lack of regard for the environment in Italy. As I noted above, Italy is the second largest consumer of cement in the world, and ranks first as producer and exporter. High cement consumption is the result of high population density, due also to the Roman Catholic culture of refusing birth control. In many urban areas, among them Rome, Naples, Palermo, Florence, Genoa, Milan, Turin, and Venice, we face rates of population density higher than in China's or India's urban areas (about 60 million people live in Italy, a narrow peninsula). The lack of a serious public transportation system, the presence of heavy industries within urban areas and the lack of a waste recycling—especially in central and southern Italy—make most Italian cities high-risk environmental areas, where people face serious health problems, only even partially solved in a few cases. The notorious 17-year-long waste crisis in the Naples region testifies to the lack of attention paid to these issues, both on the part of ordinary people and politicians. Images of Naples submerged by solid waste have been seen around the world for years and could be used as a symbol of the entire environmental situation in Italy. The European Court of Human Rights recently condemned the Italian state for this never-ending emergency. The EU many times has forced Italy to pay fines for its delays and violations of the European guidelines concerning waste. It has to be acknowledged that the newest mayor of Naples is trying to end the emergency of the waste cycle in light of the chronic lack of recycling culture in the area. Structural problems still remain. The Campania region, with its capital of Naples, is also notorious for the *camorra* (mafia) connection in the illegal trade in hazardous waste. Roberto Saviano, in his book, *Gomorrah*, described how Campania became the land of (at least 6,000) illegal dumps, with thousands of tons of hazardous waste buried almost everywhere, even mixed into the concrete used to build thousands of illegal buildings. Saviano, who is often in the US to teach and whose articles are published in American national newspapers, could be considered one of the most influential witnesses of the environmental and social devastation of these Italian areas. He very clearly juxtaposes environmental and social exploitation in his work. Another consequence of the cementation of a large part of the Italian territory (it is estimated that we have already covered 1/5 of our land in concrete and asphalt), and of the factual deregulation in building procedures is the dramatic erosion of land, which causes, each rainy season, floods with hundreds of casualties. The last was in the Genoa and Liguria region in October and November, 2011, which caused almost 20 victims, dozens of injured and homeless people, and billions of euros in damage.[10] The latest, but surely not the last. Again, it is a matter of a lack of culture.

Italy is also a very seismically active area, and we build houses without paying heed to earthquake-proof construction laws and the related technical suggestions. The 2009 quake in L'Aquila, with 300 casualties and thousands of injured and homeless, showed once again the traditional lack of attention toward the environment and the land. The quake was 5 miles deep and only measured 5.9 on the Richter scale, thousands of times weaker than the last big quake in Japan. A serious quake, in Italy, would raze the entire area where it hit. Another issue connected to our way of constructing and furnishing buildings is energy related. Except for a few northern regions (Trentino Alto Adige and Valle D'Aosta), the attitude toward saving energy in heating and conditioning is very poor in my country. The result is a very low rate of solar energy diffusion, both electrical and thermal. In newly developing areas, especially in Puglia and Sardinia, the rate wind energy generation is also low. This situation must improve in the next five years.

Italy, in ancient times, was entirely covered by forests. There still are regions of Italy, such as Tuscany, where forests cover 30–40% of the land, but when we consider that 60% of the territory is mountainous, it is easy to comprehend that available arable land is going to be a serious problem in the coming decades. This will also have an impact on the energy problems we are going to face. We are too dependent on oil and natural gas energy, and the high number of private cars—concentrated in relatively small, urban areas—produces high air pollution rates in these towns, very often very much beyond regulatory limits. As is the case with many other issues, most people simply have no time or inclination to ask for a proper solution to these problems, for the reasons I described before. Environmentalism is often seen as a form of social and personal weakness or a romantic concept that is not rooted in a "practical" way of life within the Roman Catholic tradition. In other words, even though Tuscany is one of the most "green" regions in Italy, every time I try to dispose of my waste in the public receptacles, I always find plastic mixed with paper, paper mixed with plastic, compostables in the nonrecyclables, and so on. Every day. No one monitors or controls these systems, and no one pays attention. This is sad and frustrating. At a political level, the Greens have been wiped out from the national Congress because of a series of scandals, coupled with bad political alliances and choices in the last 15 years. At the moment, there is a timid attempt to rebuild the Green Party, but the generally negative political, economic, and social situation surely does not help.[11]

Lack of concern for animal welfare in Italy

Animal welfare is a very controversial issue; animal rights are more controversial still. As described before, we often have the most advanced laws in the world—for example, the one, already mentioned, about conscientious objection to vivisection—and on paper we defend the right to life for dogs and cats, even when they are strays. It is forbidden to kill healthy dogs and cats in Italy, and there is a national law to prevent straying, but, as an example of what often happens with even the best of intentions, the people who manage the dog or cat shelters often achieve a less than humane result. Very often, the media show us cases of shelters in terrible condition, but the offenders are seldom pursued by the law. Fortunately, there are more than 50,000 honest and kind people who take care of stray dogs and cats around the nation, with the best results in the North and central parts of Italy. An estimate of the total number of stray animals (dogs and cats) is very difficult: officially speaking, during 2009, almost 96,000 dogs entered the public shelters, and almost 60,000 stray cats were neutered. It is possible for individuals and families to adopt stray dogs from the shelters. Dogs who are not adopted are kept in the shelters until they die or become seriously ill, when they may be euthanized. It would be plausible to say that there are now about two million dogs under public care, and four to five million stray cats. In southern Italy shelters are not able to host all the dogs, which remain untreated or poorly treated on the roads, presenting a serious danger to themselves and traffic. In my PhD work I ethnographically examined the familial links between Italian families and their pets—dogs especially—attempting to highlight the contradictions among our attitudes toward pet animals and "useful" animals. Here in Italy, as is the case abroad, for centuries people have been speciesist (just as they are basically racist and ableist when strong institutions do not clearly oppose discrimination against people coming from abroad or people with disabilities, as will be discussed further). Speciesism could be both the result of racist attitudes and one of the causes of racism. But this is one of the most difficult things to explain to people in my personal experience. We will have to work on that issue for a long time without expecting to see major changes in the near future.

Hunting is currently a very popular practice among the lower classes in Italy, whereas, before World War II, it was the prerogative of the richest, and, in the more remote past, of the noble class. Wild animals or tamed animals reintroduced into the environment are state property, and the government gives hunters a license to hunt and kill them on the basis of "sustainability of the species," which is often decided by the European Union. Very often it happens that some Italian regions would like to hunt and shoot protected species, and in many cases the EU has condemned the Italian administration for violations of EU laws concerning migratory animals. Where I live, in Tuscany, hunters decide most of the environmental policies and also the general policies in villages, towns, and county areas. Hunting is seen not only as a "sport," but as a matter of social compensation, considering that, for a long time, only a few rich men had access to wild game. It is still the case that society considers real men (real males) to be only those who can control firearms and the lives of weak subjects (in this case, animals). The connection between such macho attitudes toward animals and the exploitation of the environment and people perceived as weak—women or immigrants coming from other countries—

could be made, but it must be said that such an argument would not easily find many Italian people to agree with it.

Vivisection is also a nationwide habit, as in most countries, and there are many groups of people who actively try to demonstrate to the public how it works. Recently, many groups have tried to have animal farming for vivisection banned by the authorities, but the battle—also being waged in the national Congress—has been very hard fought. Recently, during a session of Parliament, the proposal was rejected by the majority of congressmen because "humans are more important than animals in our society and culture." The same "gentlemen" reminded the assembly that "we still eat cows," and that "we must regulate animal experimentation but we could never abolish it, because it is necessary to medical research."[12] The day after, incidentally, a group of senators led by conservative Carlo Giovanardi, organized a public meeting at the Chamber asking "to prohibit animal rights and animal welfare campaigns during this period of economic crisis because factory farming produces 40 billion euros of GDP and must be protected at any cost." A theologian and a nutritionist were invited to speak at the meeting as well, reminding Italians of the strong connection between Roman Catholic tradition and the necessity of eating meat in order to produce healthy babies. I am absolutely serious about this quote; the news about the meeting is accessible online.[13] Another fine example of the Italian situation.

Since I do not want to be too pessimistic, it has to be pointed out that a movement for animal rights and welfare in Italy does exist, particularly among young people, and it very often fights the correct battles. But it is still a minority. Also, there are often smaller animal welfare groups that declare to the media that "10% of the Italian population is vegetarian." This is simply a lie. Probably 10% of the young population is becoming more aware of the risks of a dairy diet, but only 2% is taking any real steps toward vegetarianism and veganism. In my opinion, there is a lack of overall planning coming from the major activist groups. This could be viewed as the usual history of social fragmentation that can be found in every other aspect of our society. No common goals and plans. No common, visible results. Meat and dairy consumption are still growing, also because there are a lot of immigrants coming to Italy from some of the poorest countries who find in "cheap meat" a new dream of welfare and wealth. Sadly, history therefore repeats itself many times over, as people in the US are probably well aware.

Another problem related to our rural and medieval background concerns the exploitation of animals during popular races, festivals, and fairs, which are very widespread in Italy, as in many other Latin countries. It is a very big issue here, including for the groups that are seeking to counteract them. To me, it is very sad to see that people miss the link between the social struggle for human rights and the fight for the freedom of all living beings. As Tom Regan (1950/1987) points out in his work, humans and animals have a common origin and a common destiny.

Making the Connections Between Humans with Disabilities, Nonhuman Species, and the Environment

Since May, 2011 I have been working—and volunteering—as chairman of one of the major associations of people with disability in the Siena area. In the last few months, the sad situation of "disabled civilians" here has been quite tangible to me. The public institutions are simply trying to save money, denying or suspending economical benefits to people with disabilities as often as they can. As for myself, in 2011, after being officially recognized as a victim of a blood transfusion by a national military medical commission, I have seen my €260 per month suspended by the National Institution of Social Security for a bureaucratic issue. I am still waiting, after a 12-month trial, to get all my money back. The group I work for has no public funding. It survives only through the contributions of its members, and we actually do not know how long we will be able to continue our mission if the government does not cease to threaten people with disabilities. The economic crisis is having a very hard impact on Italian people with disabilities, who are often left alone, especially when they are older. Suicides and homicide-suicide cases have increased in the last two years.

Usually, the issues I face from day by day are not related to nonhuman species nor to the environment. For example, we are trying to explain to the local administrators that the European and national laws calling for the removal of architectural barriers are not an option but are an obligation with which every town in Italy should seek to comply. Siena is particularly backward in this regard. But this is very hard to realize because of the cultural barriers in people's minds.

My dream would be to build a local research center on disability studies and—maybe—to make the connection with animal studies and environmental studies. It will take time. In the meanwhile, we are also collaborating with Siena University regarding the universal accessibility of public places in the Siena area. It will take time. Eighty percent of stores in the area are not accessible; neither are many public offices. When you ask owners "Why?" they answer: "for all that concerns the architectural specifications and city regulations, everything was done correctly." But the existing stores and offices are not accessible, and the city hall officials responsible for this issue answer that they cannot control every project! It is a never-ending tale of "passing the buck." In my personal opinion and curriculum, respect for animals and respect for people with disabilities are not separate issues. But if you try to tell a person with disabilities that nonhuman animals are exploited just as they are marginalized by society, you will probably receive negative feedback. I remember, a few months ago, an old man coming to my office asking for information about disabilities and social welfare during retirement. He had lost a leg due to diabetes, and he was also worried about the hunting license he could lose because of the amputation, which happened a few years ago. He was still hunting. I am still bewildered.

Notes

1. Italy is the second most indebted country in the G20 group after Japan, according to the percentage of GDP criteria; the third is the US.
2. Train platforms may appear to be accessible; however, they are not.
3. The last "big" earthquake in the L'Aquila area in April 2009 (with 308 casualties, 1,600 injured and 10 billion euros of damages) revealed a country built with sand, not concrete. Consider, for example, the fact that this was a quake 30,000 times weaker than the last one in Japan. Another quake in Northern Italy killed almost 30 people in May 2012, when many new industrial buildings collapsed, killing some workers.
4. We are 51st out of 138 countries, according to the 2011 World Economic Forum report, trailing India, Malaysia, Tunisia, Oman, and Barbados, and last in Europe, alongside Greece.
5. Known as "invalid citizens" in Italian.
6. The major scandal about political corruption in European history ended the First Republic, with the resounding arrest of Bettino Craxi.
7. People who beg for money, pretending to be persons with disabilities.
8. I am not using the term, *critical animal studies*, because in Italy we have yet to develop a more widespread and shared knowledge of animal studies.
9. If you want to know more about Quasi and her project, see here: www.ilmondodimongo.blogspot.com
10. Wikipedia has a list of floods in Italy: http://it.wikipedia.org/wiki/Lista_di_alluvioni_e_inondazioni_in_Italia
11. It has to be made clear that political scandals explode almost every week in Italy, and touch all political parties, from left to right, without exception. I know that, for an American reader, this is really hard to believe, but it is our reality, and it is easily demonstrable using Google News or the following link: http://www.corriere.it/english/
12. The European Union is going to ban animal experimentation for cosmetics research, but the ban is often postponed, and it is not clear when it will be completely operative. Animal rights groups in the EU are also still working on a general system of labeling for cruelty-free products.
13. See http://www.adnkronos.com/IGN/News/Cronaca/Stop-a-campagne-animaliste-contro-carne-e-pellicce-per-difendere-il-Made-in-Italy_312929851437.html. The reader may wish to use the Google translator tool or function to translate this into English. Also see: http://www.edizionikoine.it/scheda.php?ID=175

References

(Texts, if not specified, are in Italian, with titles translated for readers.)

Banfield, E. C. (1976). *Le basi morali di una societa arretrata* [*The moral basis of a backward society*]. Bologna, Italy: Il Mulino.

Dolcetta, M. (1999). *Politica occulta : Logge, lobbies, sette e politiche trasversali nel mondo* [*Occult politics: Lodges, lobbies, sects and cross policies in the world*]. Rome, Italy: Castelvecchi.

EURISPES (2011). Retrieved from http://www.eurispes.it/index.php?option=com_content&view-article&1893:rapporto-italia-2011&catid=40:comunicati-stampa&Itemid=135

Freedom House. (2010). *Italy: Freedom in the world 2010* [In English]. Retrieved from www.freedomhouse.org/template.cfm?page=22&year=2010&country=7846

it.wikipedia.org/wiki/Bettino_Craxi#cite_ref-69.

Regan, T. (1950). *The struggle for animal rights.* (A. Arrigoni, trans.). Clark Summit, PA: International Society for Animal Rights.

Saviano, R. (2008). *Gomorrah: A personal journey into the violent international empire of Naples' organized crime system* (V. Jewiss, Trans.). New York, NY: Picador.

Schianchi, M. (2009). *La terza nazione del mondo: I disabili tra pregiudizio e realtà* [*The third nation in the world: persons with disabilities between prejudice and reality*]. Milan, Italy: Feltrinelli.

Settis, S. (2010). *Paesaggio costituzione cemento: La battaglia per l'ambiente contro il degrado civile* [*Landscape, constitution, cement*]. Torino, Italy: Einaudi.

Tullio Altan, C. (1995). I*talia: una nazione senza religione civile: Le ragioni di una democrazia incompiuta* [*Italy: A society without civil religion: Reasons for an unfulfilled democracy*]. Udine, Italy: Veneto Friulano.

Tullio Altan, C. (1997). *La coscienza civile degli italiani: Valori e disvalori nella storia nazionale: L'Italia di Tangentopoli e la crisi del sistema partitico* [*The civic consciousness of Italians: Values and disvalues: Political crimes and the crisis of the political system*]. Udine, Italy: Gaspari.

Tullio Altan, C. (1999). *Gli italiani in Europa: profilo storico comparato delle identita nazionali europee* [*The Italians in Europe: A historical comparison of European national identities*]. Bologna, Italy: Il Mulino.

Tullio Altan, C. (2000). *La nostra Italia: Clientelismo, trasformismo e ribellismo dall'unità al 2000* [*Our Italy: Patronage, political transformism and rebelliousness from unification to 2000*]. Milan, Italy: EGEA.

PART IV

Policy and Practice

CHAPTER TEN

Shocking Into Submission

Suppressive Practices and Use of Behavior Modification on Nonhuman Animals, People with Disabilities, and the Environment

DEANNA ADAMS AND KIMBERLY SOCHA

In this chapter, we consider the connection between the use of behavior modification techniques based on the works of B. F. Skinner (1938) and Ivan P. Pavlov (1927), which are used in the training of animals, and the use of such techniques on people with disabilities, such as autism, intellectual disabilities, and emotional or behavioral disorders. Further, we consider the broader implications of these control methods on the presumably insentient natural world: plants, forests, bodies of water, etc. Behavioral modification techniques used to train dogs to stop barking, stay, and roll over are the same techniques often used in the modification of behavior in students with disabilities. Although these methods may not seem directly applicable to the natural environment, we argue that the same Western, colonial mindset of controlling that which deviates from mainstream expectations and desires underpins attempts to dominate nature as well. For animals, human and nonhuman, positive reinforcement—for instance, food given for desirable behavior such as sitting in one's seat, staying, raising one's hand when called on, or speaking on command—is a basic reporter for behaviorists.

When animals and people with disabilities do not respond to the use of positive reinforcement, aversives are employed. People who do not positively react to basic behavior modification are subjected to electroshock therapies to extinguish undesirable behavior, which takes place as devices worn around the subject's waist or as intensive electroshock treatment in a medical treatment facility. The use of shock collars on animals as a training method is seen by some as extreme and cruel, yet it is still condoned by many animal trainers and veterinary specialists. In terms of the natural environment, there are tools, devices, and methodologies for keeping things "in their proper place" as well so as not to disturb the cultivated environs of industrialized Western society.

This chapter will analyze such practices from critical disability, human rights, animal liberation, and ecological perspectives, thereby linking the oppressions of groups who have been most regularly declared in need of control in Western culture. (As feminist scholars have long noted, women are one of these groups as well, but that analysis is outside the purview of this chapter.) In *Igniting a Revolution*, an anthology on radical environmental activism, Steven Best and Anthony J. Nocella II (2006), called for

> a *collective movement*... [of] multi-issue, multiracial alliances that can mount effective opposition to capitalism and other modes of domination.... Solidarity can emerge in recognition of the fact that all forms of oppression are directly or indirectly related to the values, institutions, and *system* of global capitalism and related hierarchical structures. (p. 22)

We hope that this chapter continues that conversation, with original consideration of how those with disabilities can find solidarity with the traditionally marginalized and oppressed. While we will briefly address capitalism in terms of the corporatized animal care industry, our primary focus is on distorted values and the "related hierarchical structure" of modern science and medicine, and how the culture from which they spring—one that devalues nonhuman animals and the rest of nature—sets the proverbial stage for human rights violations. We believe that by decompartmentalizing oppressions we can find practicable methods for challenging domination, and it is by expanding our critiques beyond the human condition that this objective may be reached.

Controlling the "Abnormal": Nonhuman Animals and Children

Deanna first noticed the connection between human and animal domination several years ago when she went to a pet supply chain and purchased a collar that would train her dog to stop barking. She had been getting many complaints from neighbors about his barking and was desperate to control the situation. He only barked when she was not at home, which made it difficult to train him. She knew the collar used electrical shocks to stop the barking but figured that, since the collar gradually increases in strength as the dog continues to bark, if he stopped, then he would not get a shock. Thus, his pain would be minimal, if there were any at all. Ultimately, it seemed up to her dog to decide the pain level he was willing to experience to continue the unwanted behavior.

Like Deanna once did, consumers may feel comfortable with companion animal behavioral devices, because they believe that any corporation in the animal product industry would not do anything to hurt the creatures they claim to assist. There is the further assumption that if shock collars hurt dogs, then they would be illegal. This same attitude allows for the continuation of violent animal industries such as factory farms. Some consumers cannot or will not accept that it is indeed legal to brutally exploit, torture, and slaughter nonhuman animals for consumption and profit. There is an unspoken sense that if eating animals is wrong, there would be a law to stop it from happening.

In the case of dog collars, there *are* laws preventing their use, but not in the United States. (Similarly, there are laws banning inhumane practices such as veal crates in some countries but not others.) Quite a few European countries have outlawed the use of shock collars, arguing that electronic training devices are "painful, unethical and unnecessary regardless of the severity of the training situation or problem behavior" (Salgirli, 2008, p. 2). Although some veterinary experts agree with that negative assessment, shock collars remain legal in the United States, and many "dog lovers" continue to use them without considering their ethical implications.

The shock collar controversy is not an isolated incident of "animal-friendly" corporations betraying nonhumans to make a profit. In contrast, the controversy is part of a pervasive tendency in animal "care" products. For example, Iams pet food company has notoriously farmed out inhumane experiments on dogs, while simultaneously airing advertisements that pull on the heartstrings of those with companion animals with the message that Iams loves dogs as much as so-called dog "owners." In practice, however, Iams does not love dogs, as shown by this description from 2002–2003 of how canines fare at Sinclair Research Center, the laboratory hired by Iams:

> Dogs had gone crazy because they were confined to barren steel cages and cement cells, dogs were left piled on a filthy paint-chipped floor after chunks of muscle had been hacked from their thighs, dogs were surgically debarked, and horribly sick dogs and cats were neglected and left in cages to suffer without any veterinary care. (People for the Ethical Treatment of Animals (PETA) n.d., para. 1)

Even though Iams has made progress in the animal experimentation arena over the past few years, they only did so in response to public pressure and not from any sense of obligation to canines. They now monitor dogs placed in people's homes, but they have not ceased all experiments, and they refuse to allow PETA to investigate the lab in Dayton, Ohio that continues to perform "non-invasive [canine] nutritional studies" for them (PETA, n.d., para. 6).

The Iams case is important to consider, for it showcases a routine practice of profit makers exploiting one group of nonhuman animals ("throwaway dogs" from shelters) to benefit another ("companion dogs" in loving homes). Similarly, shock collars are often marketed as training aids for hunting dogs, who will be taught to prey upon other species of animals, such as deer, ducks, rabbits, etc., for human sport. While one could argue that hunters merely allow dogs to engage in natural, instinctual behavior, the problem remains that canines are doing so at the whim of their culturally declared "masters."

Haraway (2003) coined the term "caninophiliac narcissism" to explain humans' propensity to realize themselves through their dogs in much the same way that "technophiliac narcissism" allows humans to realize themselves through their tools (p. 33). Shock collars, "wholesome" pet foods, and assorted other animal commodities give humans the power to control other species in a culture that tells humans they themselves should be controlled and obedient. This is a principal example of "caninophiliac narcissism," which views dogs as misbegotten humans who, with enough training, can mirror the ways of their "masters."

Ethics aside, electronic training devices continue to be used in the United States simply because they work—meaning that they make money. Deanna's dog's barking was greatly reduced, and she was happy with the results, although she had never actually witnessed the effects of the collar on him. However, a woman she knew used the same collar on her dog, and she reported her findings to Deanna. It was a vicious cycle. The dog barked and got a shock, and then barked because of the shock, and got another shock; this process escalated, and Deanna's friend had to chase her dog down to take the collar off because the dog was in such pain and distress. It was after this story that Deanna realized that the use of these collars to modify unwanted behavior was cruel; and she could never think of using them on her dog or encourage their use on any other animal. The thought of such devices being used on children with disabilities became even more unimaginable.

However, many parents of children with disabilities, and particularly children on the autism spectrum, or children with emotional or behavioral disorders, are sending their children to schools that use painful aversives such as skin-shock therapies to modify their children's behavior. The Judge Rotenberg Center in Canton, Massachusetts is, "a special needs school" that has been using skin-shock therapy in order to curb what they call "destructive behaviors." This school was founded by Dr. Matthew L. Israel, who studied under Skinner, and strongly believes in a behavioral approach to eliminating "behavior problems" in children and adults. Israel stated that, "a behavioral approach essentially views a treatment problem as one in which the individual has certain behaviors that need to be decreased and certain ones that need to be increased" (Israel, n.d., para. 11).

The Center claims to have a highly effective treatment program for individuals who exhibit the more extreme behavior problems that typical schools and residential facilities are unable to handle. In addition, for some parents or agencies, this is touted as the last resort. Israel believes that you cannot change behavior through medications, psychotherapy, educational approaches, or role modeling. According to Israel, "behavioral procedures that will effectively eliminate problematic behaviors and help the student improve his/her condition and live a more normal life, often have to be highly *abnormal* at first until the behavior changes sufficiently" (Israel, n.d., para. 13). These procedures may include the use of restraint and pain as children go through "abnormal" procedures to become acceptable to others.

The Judge Rotenberg Center initially used "physical aversives such as the pinch, spank, muscle squeeze, water spray, vapor spray (mixture of compressed air and water), ammonia capsule, unpleasant taste, and white noise" (Israel, n.d., para. 18). In the 1980s, they began using Self-Injurious Behavior Inhibiting System (SIBIS) machines, which produce low-level shocks to the arms and legs of individuals exhibiting "problem" behaviors. When the Center found that some residents were no longer responding to the lower-level shocks, they designed a new device that could be strapped to the back, controlled remotely, and deliver a more powerful shock (Ahern & Rosenthal, 2010). Israel, confident in his methods, boasts on his website that he "employed behavioral principles to eliminate a three-year-old girl's behavioral problems, changing her from what some considered to be extremely spoiled, demanding and annoying, into a charming presence in the house" (para. 2). The question here is: Who defines what a behavioral problem is, and in what ways were her parents responsible for her unpleasant, annoying, and demanding behavior? Those questions are not answered on the website.

It has been those in power who have influenced the social and cultural norms by which human and nonhuman animals must abide. Sociologists, psychologists, and psychiatrists have defined and medicalized what are defined as deviant or problem behaviors. Doctors and scientists have experimented on humans and nonhumans to investigate the causes of behaviors and to modify or extinguish behaviors that do not conform to social expectations. These behaviors are often ones that make humans feel physically uncomfortable and psychologically fearful, as medical professionals attempt to control *deviance*.

However, to have a concept of deviance, we must first have a vision of what constitutes *normal*, and these considerations lead back to the question of who defines normalcy (Davis, 2002). In both past and current cultural contexts, it is the Euro-American, White, hetero-normative male who holds power, and thus determines what is typical and what counts as a behavioral problem:

> Thus, all that is anomalous—that is, alive and nonpredictable—is erased or subdued in the Newtonian/Cartesian [Isaac Newton and René Descartes] epistemological paradigm. The anomalous and powerless include women and animals, both of whose subjectivities and realities are erased or converted into manipulable objects ... at the mercy of the rationalist manipulator, whose self-worth is established by the fact that he thus subdues his environment. (Donovan, 1990/2007, p. 66)

In this passage, Donovan explored the fate of women and animals under the dominion of the rationalist scientist. However, those with disabilities could easily be seen as another group whose "subjectivities and realities are erased or converted into manipulable objects" (Donovan, 1990/2007, p. 66), as they have a storied history of being used in medical experiments in the United States. Modern Western science is founded in seventeenth- and eighteenth-century epistemological paradigms, and those paradigms continue to influence contemporary medical and scientific thought. As Luke (2007) noted, modern-day medicine and science are still "hierarchically organized, male-dominated" institutions whose work is founded upon the "control and invasive manipulation of bodies" (p. 139). This manipulation continues to be true for the disabled, as much as it is for animals and nature, with behaviorism as a strong influence for its continuation.

Behaviorism and the Human/Nonhuman Animal Divide

Dr. Israel of the aforementioned Rotenberg Center credits B. F. Skinner (1938) as his mentor, the latter being a radical behaviorist whose work was based in *operant conditioning*. He claimed that all behavior is learned, and behavior that is rewarded is repeated and therefore learned. Behavior that is punished will not be repeated, so therefore it will not be learned. Rewards and punishments are the consequences that follow an animal's behavior, and they have effects on whether the animal will perform that behavior in the future or not. (By animals, we are referring to humans as well.)

Skinner's (1938), as well as Pavlov's (1927) and Watson's (1903) theories of animal learning argued that "it was scientifically improper to talk about hypothetical mental processes" in animals, and in "biology a similar trend existed in which animal behavior was seen as programs that were produced by specific environmental circumstances without cognitive involvement" (Gluck, 1998, p. 18). Pavlov's experiments with dogs on the production of saliva, on the conditioned response to a bell ringing before the presence of food, along with Watson's similar experiments with humans, led to the theory of classical conditioning. Skinner's first work was the "Pigeon Project," in which he trained pigeons using positive (rewards) and aversive (punishment, such as electric shock) reinforcements to peck on a platform and guide missiles to their intended target. This type of training was termed *operant conditioning*.

Ivar Lovaas took these theories that he had learned from Skinner (1938), and began to apply them to a variety of behavioral disorders in human animals. In 1965, Lovaas, Schaeffer, and Simmons published an article in which they had conducted experiments on twin five-year-old boys diagnosed with childhood schizophrenia (used interchangeably with autism) in order to modify their autistic-like behaviors. These behaviors included showing "no social responsiveness, speech, nor appropriate play with objects," as well as engaging in "considerable self-stimulatory behavior, and in bizarre, repetitive bodily movements" (1965, p. 99). In the experiment, electric shock, in the form of "an electrified grid on the floor upon which the children stood" was used to inflict pain immediately after a child exhibited pathological behaviors. The electric shock was not only used to extinguish "pathological" behavior but to push the child to bond with an adult. The shock would be extinguished if the child went to an adult when asked. Thus, the relief from pain was positively associated with an adult. In this scenario, the child is manipulated into establishing a "normal" relationship with another person (Lovaas et al., 1965, p. 100).

In much the same way, companion animals are forced into establishing a human-normative relationship with their legally declared owners. Shock collars are a painful tool to produce proper behavior from a being whose conduct has been deemed "abnormal"; in this case, a dog is barking too much, and that is not acceptable. In order to become the lovable companion that the dog "owner" wants, and to ensure that bonding occurs, the aversive is put in place.

Lovaas et al. (1965) explained the reasoning behind the use of pain:

> The extensive presence of pain in everyday life may suggest that it is necessary for the establishment and maintenance of normal human interactions. Despite the pervasiveness of pain in daily functioning and its possible necessity for maintaining some behaviors, psychology and related professions have shied away from and often condemned the use of pain for therapeutic purposes. We agree with Solomon (1964) that such objections to the use of pain have a moral rather than scientific basis. (p. 99)

Morality is not seen as an important factor when determining how to control behavior that disrupts mainstream expectations. Lovaas worked with these children because they had not responded to traditional psychiatric treatments and were "largely unresponsive to everyday interpersonal events" (Lovaas et al., 1965, p. 100). The children also lacked speech, and lack of speech can be interpreted as a lack of language, especially when paired with an inability to make social connections. It is the ability to make social connections with people that has been considered important in establishing membership in a moral community. To become self-aware, a person has to recognize that other people have thoughts, feelings, and desires that are separate from their own. People on the autism spectrum have been thought to lack self-awareness.

Self-awareness is the ability to recognize yourself as an individual, apart from others, with your own values, emotions, beliefs, and the ability to reflect on your actions and relationships with others (Barnbaum, 2008).

Self-awareness and self-consciousness have been tied to language, and because animals have been seen to lack language, their self-awareness and self-consciousness have been denied. Ethical theorists believed that without self-consciousness, animals were "inherently unworthy of moral concern" (Mitchell, 1998, p. 20). With this in mind, it is plausible to conclude that Lovaas et al. (1965) justified their use of shock because the children were "unworthy of moral concern," that is, at least until they successfully completed their treatment.

As to voice, animals may more properly be said to lack human voices, but they most certainly communicate. There are obvious communicative signals, such as a dog yelping in pain or a cat purring with content but also more subtle signals that may be lost on humans. Regardless of the method, and despite human beings' alleged mastery of communication, it is now accepted amongst animal behaviorists that all nonhuman animals communicate in intricate and complex ways (Hauser & Konishi, 2005). To ignore animal voices because they cannot be refigured as human language is speciesism—valuing one species over another—just as to ignore the unique communicative strategies of disabled children and adults is ableism. Consideration of these relatively new "isms" leads us to think about who gets defined as a person, as deserving of moral consideration, in contemporary culture. If people with autism are defined as not-quite-whole people, then the practice of shocking them into normality seems not all that objectionable. This is why people with disabilities have been equated with nonhuman animals, as a rhetorical tool to treat them in unethical ways, which contradict the ways our culture has come to expect human animals to be treated if we are to consider ourselves a just society.

The other justification for using shocks on people with disabilities is not just because they are equated with nonhuman animals but because they have disabilities. It seems that for Lovaas et al. (1965), Israel (n.d.), and others who support the use of aversives, these practices are morally, ethically, and scientifically acceptable because they are the last resorts in bringing the *deviant* back to something mirroring normality. But disability rights and autism self-advocates continue to ask: What is normal, and why should they be forced to comply with these standards? Why, to put it bluntly, should not neurotypicals[1] be shocked into understanding the premise and promise of biodiversity?

Temple Grandin (Grandin & Johnson, 2006), an autistic person and an animal scientist, uses examples of her own manifestations of autism to explain her understanding of animal behavior. Grandin wrote, "Autism is a kind of way station on the road from animals to humans, which puts autistic people like me in a perfect position to translate 'animal talk' into English" (p. 6). Throughout the book, Grandin made connections between animal genius and autistic genius, as well as their respective responses to pain. She addressed the topic of fear, writing:

> Autistic people have so much natural fear and anxiety—I'm almost comfortable saying it's universal—that when they're young they can be like little wild animals .... No one would call an autistic child feral today, but the word is a pretty accurate description of the way a lot of these children—not all, but quite a lot—appeared to normal people who never dealt with them before. (p. 192)

In using the phrase, "autistic people," she generalized her experiences to the broader autistic or neurodiverse community, and in doing so, reinforced the idea that people with autism are not-quite-whole people while also strengthening the human/nonhuman animal binary.

Grandin (Grandin & Johnson, 2006) is further problematic from an animal rights/liberation perspective, as she uses her supposed trans-species communicative abilities to design slaughterhouses. (We say "supposed" because the validity of Grandin's work connecting animal and autistic cognition has been questioned: see Vallortigara et al., 2008). Working with the American Meat Institute and within federal guidelines, Grandin (Grandin & Johnson, 2006) is credited with improving the way "food" animals are slaughtered, thereby peddling the paradoxical concept of "humane slaughter." Just as she reinforced the supposition that those with autism are not complete beings, her work in the slaughterhouses does the same with nonhumans who *must* be incomplete if humans have the natural right to dominate and eat them. Grandin's work is dangerous because, as an animal voice by proxy that people actually listen to, she is reinforcing the human/animal binary with the message that the issue is not so much that nonhumans dislike being killed; rather they would like to have somewhat better lives before the inevitable bullet to the brain or knife to the throat. Her work is part of a trend in welfarist animal activism that makes consumers feel better about eating animals and their by-products. However, the problem is that while Grandin is arguing that animals deserve better treatment, she is not challenging hierarchy and domination, and until those concepts are confronted, the shock and slaughter of humans and nonhumans will continue in a bid to make everyone normal, and this includes all of nature.

Controlling the *Abnormal*: Nature and Nonhuman Animals

Human history is one of subduing nature for survival, and we do not wish to cast aspersions on how one species of animal, human beings, survived through millennia of hardships and struggles for their continued existence. Rather, our focus is on the eventual gross misuse of power that developed conterminously with Western civilization, resulting in current social ills that expect the *abnormal* to assimilate or suffer. Best and Nocella (2006) effectively encapsulated the "net result of millennia of western culture":

> [After] roughly two hundred thousand years of the reign of *Homo Sapiens* as a whole, [the outcomes are] hideously visible in the current ecological crises involving dynamics such as air and water pollution, acid rain, genetic crop pollution, chemical poisoning, species extinction, rainforest destruction, coral reef deterioration, disappearance of wetlands, desertification, and global warming. (p. 8)

Environmental activist Derrick Jensen (2006) similarly summarized Western culture as one that defines success as "conquering all other cultures and conquering the planet" (p. 233). Within the conquering Euro-American cultures, even if one met the ethnic and gender criteria of being White and male, he would be subjugated if he did not appear normal. This is the story of people with disabilities, and they can similarly be seen to populate a group that dominant powers needed or need to subdue. To subdue is to control, and the authority to do so has always been in the hands of a minority of individuals with the cultural power to enforce their collective will on others.

What is the root cause of this destructive dynamic? Murray Bookchin's essay, "What Is Social Ecology?" (1993/2007), is a primer for understanding this misuse of control described above, as he incorporated the natural world into our understanding of how domination works. The mistreatment of animals and people with disabilities, from a social-ecological perspective, is underpinned by the domination of nature, and vice versa.

Of course, the differentiation of humans from the natural world is an arbitrary construct, but it was just this binary that allowed for colonial and imperialistic expansion of the Western world starting in the fifteenth century. In her comparison of human and animal slavery, Marjorie Spiegel (1996) noted the ways in which the New World could only be conquered after it had been subdued. This subjugation included both Native Americans and the wilderness of which they were a part. In diaries of that time period, nature itself was referred to as an "'enemy'" that must be "'vanquished'" (p. 16). She continued with analysis of "Christians" who "maintained that they were serving God by whipping nature, animals and black people into submission" (p. 17). When

Europeans came to the Americas and Africa, they carried with them assumptions of what is normal and abnormal, of what is to be accepted and what is to be controlled. That which did not fit the mold was cut down, beaten into submission, or slaughtered.

As arbitrary as the line may be between nature and culture, it demands continued critique as long as the binary continues to be reinforced. As Bookchin (1993/2007) defined it, nature is a dynamic "*totality*...of its evolution," including organic and inorganic life, and encompassing one- to multi-celled organisms leading to warm-blooded organisms with an "astonishing flexibility to exist in the most demanding climatic environments" (p. 24). Thus, we are all nature: the rationalist medical doctor; the adult diagnosed with schizophrenia; the energetic child who is being "shocked into submission"; the primate exploited in drug studies; the rat forced to ingest that latest carcinogen that will eventually make its way into the human food supply; and the lakes, trees, and mountains that seem to exist so far from the mechanized world.

To understand the interconnected oppressions of dominated groups, it is important to consider Bookchin's (1993/2007) concept of "second nature," or "the way in which human beings, as highly intelligent primates, inhabit and *alter* the natural world" (p. 29). More importantly, after considering "second nature," we must challenge it in all facets of our lives and look beyond the oppression of humans to understand how oppression works and from whence it comes.

When dogs will not stop barking, they are forced to wear shock collars. When children with disabilities cannot sit still, they are drugged, spanked, or shocked. This is second nature, an attempt to "alter the natural world" into a semblance of respectability based upon a set of criteria for behavior that has been determined by prevailing culture. Aside from the obvious environmental devastation that humanity now faces, there are more subtle ways that the natural environment is also "shocked into submission." However, because supposed nonsentient life does not react with sound or movement that humans can perceive, the correlations between sentient and nonsentient existence are often ignored.

In a lament against civilization, primitivist Terra Greenbrier (2006) aptly noted that humans in the industrialized world "surround [themselves] with symbolic culture" made from artificial concepts of time and history, numbing themselves via drugs and popular culture (p. 199). This world created in the name of progress "work[s] counter to any physical pattern we could observe in wild nature" (p. 200). Although the designers of this world may be unaware of their motives, consideration of the nature/culture divide leads us to believe that this *civilized* planet has been created in defiance and/or fear of "wild nature." This civilized creation eschews "wild nature," even as it attempts to subdue it within its sterile, industrial surroundings. Mechanized society is more than just steel and concrete; it is small and large "green spaces" constructed in urban and metropolitan environments; it is cultivated landscapes in suburban developments, golf courses, resorts, college campuses, etc. Each of these examples is an instance of dominating nature and bringing it under the control of those in power. These are all examples of "symbolic nature," to complement Greenbrier's idea of "symbolic culture." The "wild," as much as humans and nonhumans, is brought under command according to a predetermined plan, so that it may be seen as acceptable. This is a project begun during the conquest of the New World, and it continues to manifest today in the ways explored in this chapter.

Although shocking living beings into submission may seem relegated to animals and nonhumans, this happens with green nature, too. Weed killers prevent nature from springing up through cracks in our sidewalks, and pesticides are sprayed on plants to prevent other organisms from eating human food sources. Similarly, there are products to stop companion animals from engaging in natural behavior. Humans bring domesticated nonhumans into their homes with the expectation that they will respect social mores. Thus, there are products to prevent domesticated nonhumans from shedding, jumping on and scratching at furniture, licking windows, and chewing on home décor, and there are procedures such as removing dogs' vocal chords and cats' claws to force these beings to assimilate. All of these tools attempt to keep nature close by us while also demanding that it—meaning both greenery and nonhuman animals—conform to human standards of decorum. In effect, modern, industrialized culture sees nature as both free and unlimited natural resources, and thus exploitable, yet also as "aesthetically pleasing," but only when controlled, rendering humans dependent on nature, but also "*de*-natured," not a part of the natural world (Bookchin, 1993/2007, p. 27).

Bookchin (1993/2007) saw social ecology as something that challenges "the entire system of domination itself... and seeks to eliminate the hierarchical and class edifices that have imposed themselves on humanity and defined the relationship between nonhuman and human" (p. 46). We argue that a true understanding of eco-ability and the connected subjugation of marginalized humans, animals, and nature should have a foundation in Bookchin's philosophy, to ensure a more holistic challenge to oppressive institutions. Only then can we contend against what counts as normal, and confront the continued exploitation of, and violence against, those who have been subjugated by dominant culture. An investigation into environmental issues is the place to begin this conversation.

Conclusion

Over the past two decades, there have been many investigations by state and local agencies into the abuses at the Judge Rotenberg Center (JRC), as well as written position statements from disability rights and advocacy organizations. Yet, legislation drafted to end the use of physical restraints and painful aversives for behavior modification has been ineffective, and these practices have continued on the grounds that they are being used as a last resort for people with disabilities who pose a dangerous threat to themselves and others. Recently, Mental Disability Rights International wrote a report to the United Nations Special Rapporteur on Torture and appealed to the UN to consider the use of four-point restraint and electric shock on people with disabilities as torture and, therefore, a human rights issue which would lead to U.S. laws ending and criminalizing the use of these abusive tactics. Recently, Dr. Israel stepped down as head of JRC. However, the Center remains open, and the program has not changed, despite these judicial and activist claims. It is our contention that until we change the mindset that the environment, nonhumans, and certain humans are manipulable and disposable, such torturous practices will continue, despite growing criticisms.

For so long, mainstream culture has fought with deviance and the abnormal, failing to consider alternative perspectives. For example, when a dog is barking incessantly, the sound should be seen for what it is—a means of communication, not an attempt to disrupt the quiet neighborhood that humans have created for themselves. It is both unfair and illogical to think a canine will understand that the couch he is sitting on was expensive or that his neighbors are disturbed by his voice. As to what we commonly view as nature, those environments also need to be respected as a "*totality*" that cannot be pillaged without some consequences to those doing the pillaging. Further, we need to accept that the "green spaces" we are creating amongst the polluted environs of our cityscapes are sad attempts to mimic the real thing, and although they may look attractive, they do not counteract the destruction of nature that exists outside the city walls, nor do they negate the fact that humans, too, are a part of nature.

There is a secret battle lying within those who attempt to mold the world into a standardized image, for these are the ones who fight their own inherent connections with the autistic child, barking dog, and resilient weed. Critical theories and pedagogies such as critical animal studies and disability pedagogy (Nocella, 2008), are useful tools to expose the alliances we make in this chapter among individuals with disabilities, nonhumans, and green nature. These alliances are meant to empower our cultural conception of what social justice means, for challenges to oppression are best seen holistically, so that we can identify, problematize, and confront its source, rather than just its manifestations.

Note

1. Neurotypical is a term used by autistic self-advocates, and others, to denote those who are not labeled as having neurological "conditions." By centering autism and neurodiversity as the norm, they prefer this term to *normal*, as some people without disabilities refer to themselves.

References

Ahern, L., & Rosenthal, E. (2010). Torture not treatment: Electric shock and long-term restraint in the United States on children and adults with disabilities at the Judge Rotenberg Center. Mental Disability Rights International. Retrieved from http://www.mdri.org/PDFs/USReportandUrgentAppeal.pdf

Barnbaum, D. R. (2008). *The ethics of autism: Among them, but not of them*. Bloomington, IN: Indiana University Press.

Best, S., & Nocella II, A. J. (2006). A fire in the belly of the beast: The emergence of revolutionary environmentalism. In S. Best & A. J. Nocella II (Eds.), *Igniting a revolution: Voices in defense of the earth* (pp. 8–29). Oakland, CA: AK Press.

Bookchin, M. (2007). What is social ecology? In M. Bookchin, *Social ecology and communalism* (pp. 19–52). Oakland, CA: AK Press.

Davis, L. J. (2002). *Bending over backwards: Disability, dismodernism & other difficult positions*. New York, NY: New York University Press.

Donovan, J. (2007). Animal rights and feminist theory (1990). In J. Donovan & C. Adams (Eds.), *The feminist care tradition in animal ethics* (pp. 58–86). New York, NY: Columbia University Press.

Gluck, J. P. (1998). Animal cognition. In M. Bekoff & C. A. Meaney (Eds.), *Encyclopedia of animal rights and animal welfare* (pp. 17–19). Westport, CT: Greenwood Press.

Grandin, T. & Johnson, C. (2006). *Animals in translation: Using the mysteries of autism to decode animal behavior*. Orlando, FL: Harcourt.

Greenbrier, T. (2006). Against civilization, for reconnection to life! In S. Best & A. J. Nocella II (Eds.), *Igniting a revolution: Voices in defense of the earth* (pp. 198–203). Oakland, CA: AK Press.

Haraway, D. (2003). *The companion species manifesto: Dogs, people, and significant otherness*. Chicago, IL: Prickly Paradigm Press.

Hauser, M., & Konishi, M. (2005). *The design of animal communication*. Cambridge, MA: MIT Press.

Israel, M. L. (n.d.). History of JRC. Retrieved from http://www.judgerc.org/history.html

Jensen, D. (2006). *Endgame: The problem of civilization*. (Vol. 1). New York, NY: Seven Stories Press.

Lovaas, O. I., Schaeffer, B., & Simmons, J. Q. (1965). Building social behavior in autistic children by use of electric shock. *Journal of Experimental Research in Personality*. *1*(2), 99–109.

Luke, B. (2007). Justice, caring, and animal liberation (1992). In J. Donovan & C. Adams (Eds.), *The feminist care tradition in animal ethics* (pp. 125–152). New York, NY: Columbia University Press.

Mitchell, R. W. (1998). Self-awareness and self-recognition. In M. Bekoff & C. A. Meaney (Eds.), *Encyclopidea of animal rights and animal welfare*, (pp. 20–22). Westport, CT: Greenwood Press.

Nocella II, A. J. (2008). Emergence of disability pedagogy. *Journal for Critical Education Policy Studies*, *6*(2). Retrieved from http://www.jceps.com/?pageID=article&articleID=132 and http://www.jceps.com/index.php?pageID=article&articleID=132

Pavlov, I. P. (1927). *Conditioned reflexes: An investigation of the physiological activity of the cerebral cortex* (G. V. Anrep, Ed. & Trans.). London, UK: Oxford University Press.

People for the Ethical Treatment of Animals (PETA). (n.d.). Animals still suffer at Iams. *IamsCruelty.com*. Retrieved from http://www.iamscruelty.com/introduction.asp

Salgirli, Y. (2008). Comparison of stress and learning effects of three different training methods: Electronic training collar, pinch collar and quitting signal (Doctoral dissertation). Tierärztliche Hochshule Hannover, Institut für Tierschutz und Verhalten (University of Veterinary Medicine), Hannover, Germany. Retrieved from http://elib.tiho-hannover.de/dissertations/salgirliy_ws08.pdf

Skinner, B. F. (1938). *The behavior of organisms: An experimental analysis*. New York, NY: Appleton-Century-Crofts.

Spiegel, M. (1996). *The dreaded comparison: Human and animal slavery*. New York, NY: Mirror Books.

Vallortigara, G., Snyder, A., Kaplan, G., Bateson, P., Clayton, N. S., & Rogers, L. J. (2008). Are animals autistic savants? *PLoS Biology 6*(2): e42. doi:10.1371/journal.pbio.0060042

Watson, J. B. (1903). *Animal education: An experimental study on the psychical development of the white rat, correlated with the growth of its nervous system*. Chicago, IL: University of Chicago Press.

CHAPTER ELEVEN

Eco-Ability

Putting Theory into Action

LYNN ANDERSON, VICKI WILKINS, AND
LAURIE PENNEY MCGEE

As professionals in Recreation, Parks, and Leisure Studies, we understand the importance of people freely choosing and participating in valued activities for leisure and play. Play is a contributor to thriving as a living being, and a fundamental human right, now protected by the United Nations Convention on the Rights of Persons with Disabilities in Article 30 (United Nations, 2006). And we know that all people desire to have the opportunity to play in their communities, with their friends, neighbors, and teammates. Affiliation and social interaction are strong human needs. Historically, people with disabilities have been excluded from typical, community-based recreation programs and services or relegated to segregated offerings. As the inclusion movement gains momentum and legislation mandates accessibility for people with disabilities, recreation environments and services have needed to evolve. Yet, the systems that have been designed to monitor accessibility for public spaces have often relied on the expertise of specialists and often act in a punitive way toward the business owners and operators of such spaces. The result is a growing frustration toward bureaucrats and the "ADA Police." Consequently, the attitudes formed are based on resentment instead of acceptance toward people with disabilities.

To break away from this thinking, we have designed a public access training and reporting system, which empowers anyone of virtually any age to examine how inclusive public recreation spaces are, both physically and socially. The training model, called *Inclusion U*, is comprehensive and accessible to anyone who can participate. Inclusion U provides participants with a foundation of inclusion principles and skills in using the *Inclusivity Assessment Tool*, designed to gather descriptive information about the accessibility of recreation facilities and programs. Once trained, individuals complete an assessment, then report back to the Inclusive Recreation Resource Center to help build a web-based database of information that can be shared with anyone. We have learned from this model that when ordinary citizens have the power to critique and help make changes to recreation spaces, everyone benefits from this experience. No longer is lack of accessibility or inclusion a problem for the person with the disability to solve or avoid; rather, citizens have the ability to act directly to change a facility or program. The implications are enormous for us to consider, and in this chapter we offer theoretical insights based on our work.

The Importance of Play, Recreation, and Leisure

We start our discussion with a focus on the importance of play in our lives, regardless of ability, age, gender, or other difference. Play is an essential aspect of individual and community well-being; recreation and leisure are a part of most people's vision of a "good life." Without play in our lives, we experience a duller and less joyous existence and our communities become less vibrant (Anderson & Heyne, 2012).

Martha Nussbaum (2006) delineated play as an essential element of well-being in her capabilities approach theory. In the capabilities approach, Nussbaum and her colleagues conceptualized well-being as internal (how well one is able to be and to achieve) and external (sources of well-being, such as public action and social policy) (Nussbaum & Sen, 1993). Nussbaum (2006) stated,

> Starting from a conception of the person as a social animal, whose dignity does not derive entirely from an idealized rationality, the capabilities approach can help us to design an adequate conception of the full and equal citizenship of people with mental disabilities. (p. 92)

Nussbaum (2006) identified ten core capabilities that must be present for the good life, for respect, and for well-being. These core capabilities, described in Table 11.1, are what Nussbaum calls the bare minimum of what respect for human dignity requires. Play, or recreation, is one of the fundamental capabilities that a culture or community must support for well-being to flourish and for people to achieve.

Many scholars have provided powerful rationales for why play, leisure, and recreation are core to well-being, quality of life, and social justice (Anderson & Heyne,

Table 11.1. Nussbaum's (2006) Core Capabilities for Well-Being

1. LIFE	Is able to live to the natural end of a human life
2. BODILY HEALTH	Has good health and adequate nourishment
3. BODILY INTEGRITY	Is secure and safe, without fear of harm traveling from place to place
4. SENSES, IMAGINATION, AND THOUGHT	Can think, reason, and imagine, informed by an adequate education; has freedom of expression and freedom to have pleasurable experiences
5. EMOTIONS	Has opportunities to love and be loved and to experience a broad range of emotions
6. PRACTICAL REASON	Can form an idea about goodness and engage in critical reflection on one's life and its direction
7. AFFILIATION	Lives and engages fully with others, with self-respect and nondiscrimination
8. OTHER SPECIES	Lives in a sustainable, respectful way with the natural world
9. PLAY	Enjoys recreational activities; has opportunities to laugh and play
10. CONTROL OVER ENVIRONMENT	Participates in the political process, has material possessions, and works in respected employment

2012; Anderson & Kress, 2003; Brown, 2009; Carruthers & Hood, 2007; Hood & Carruthers, 2007; Hutchison & McGill, 1992; O'Keefe, n.d.; Sylvester, 2005; Sylvester, Voelkl, & Ellis, 2001):

- Leisure provides a context for the experience of positive emotions, which are directly linked to health and well-being.
- Leisure contributes to the development of resources and strengths in one's life, from physical to social to cognitive to environmental resources.
- Leisure directly impacts self-development and self-determination, essential to well-being.
- Leisure provides opportunities to fully engage in activity and acts as a stimulus to health.
- Leisure directly meets the creative-expressive needs of people and their drive to find meaning and purpose in their lives.
- Leisure provides a natural and sustaining vehicle to promote inclusion in community and develop friendship circles, again essential to well-being.
- Leisure can change communities, making communities healthier and more welcoming of differences, including disability and illness.

- Leisure can be pursued by everyone, everyday, everywhere—regardless of health or ability.
- People, *all* people, have a fundamental right to leisure.

Given the critical role that play, recreation, and leisure have in well-being and life quality, it is vital that all people have the opportunity to pursue their passions and interests on a daily basis in places and spaces of their choosing. Though numerous barriers continue to impede participation in inclusive recreation, we have begun to identify those actions or conditions that facilitate the participation of people of all abilities in inclusive recreation and play.

Barriers and Facilitators to Inclusive Play, Recreation, and Leisure: Barriers to Inclusive Recreation

What prevents all people from being able to play wherever they choose, regardless of ability level? What constraints must be negotiated to ensure inclusive recreation spaces? Barriers to inclusive leisure include attitudes; the pervasiveness of the medical model and the "continuum" approach to services, with a long history of segregated services persisting from that model; characteristics of the built, natural, and social environment; and lastly, an overreliance on the compliance approach.

Perhaps the most significant barrier to inclusive recreation services is that of attitudes. Research has shown that attitudes can range from negative and discriminatory, to an attitude of fear and uncertainty based on lack of skills and knowledge (Anderson & Heyne, 2000; Scholl, Smith, & Davison, 2005). George Covington, former White House adviser on disability, said it best: "The first barrier to universal design is the human mind. If we could put a ramp into the mind, the first thing down the ramp would be the understanding that all barriers are the result of narrow thinking.... You have to ramp the human mind or the rest of the ramps won't work" (Szenasy, 2010, para. 2).

The pervasiveness and overapplication of the medical model also create a barrier for people with disabilities, restricting them from experiencing full inclusion in recreation (Anderson & Heyne, 2012; Sylvester, 2011). In the medical model, people with disabilities are viewed as a diagnosis or problem, and experts are needed to help "fix" the disability. This in turn creates the need for specialists and special services, different from those offered to typical community members. Over time, our communities have created many separate, but not equal, recreation programs for people with disabilities, ranging from Special Olympics, to "Saturday Morning Gym and Swim for the Handicapped." The segregated services are often offered as "skill-building," to prepare people with disabilities for "real recreation" once they have become more acceptable for inclusion.

This "continuum" approach, though based on good intentions to help move people to the "least restrictive environment," has several pitfalls that we want to make explicit in order to truly understand the limitations of this method of providing inclusive recreation services. Taylor (2004) described one major pitfall as a "readiness" assumption, where participants get "caught in the continuum" because they are unable to earn their readiness to move to the next level of services and, consequently, the next level of control in their own lives. People with disabilities are asked to show some kind of functional or other improvement within a more specialized or segregated service environment before they can move to or "graduate" to more inclusive services. They do not graduate to the next level of control or the next less restrictive service setting until they have reached a certain level of functioning, which is determined by the expert specialist. The vicious cycle of lack of self-determination leads to further entrapment in the continuum, leading to further erosion of freedom and self-determination, essential to meaningful recreation and play experiences. Taylor (2004) emphasized the irony of this trap, as the most restrictive services meant to prepare people for a least restrictive environment do not prepare, and in fact disempower, them for self-determined community living that is needed for a high quality of life. More importantly, the continuum approach makes the false assumption that change must happen *in* the participant in order to move up the continuum toward more freedom and choice. The approach lacks attention to the environmental changes, supports, and accommodations that may need to take place in order for a participant to achieve quality of life.

The built, natural, and social environment can also present major barriers to inclusion in recreation for people with disabilities. Lack of accessibility, poor design, narrowly interpreted policies, and rigid programming practices can all prevent inclusion. The idea that "one size fits all" permeates recreation services, and disenfranchises not only people with disabilities but many citizens who do not fit into a fairly narrow *norm*.

Lastly, the "compliance approach" to moving recreation services from inaccessible to inclusive has created, at the least, a sense of disempowerment, and, perhaps worse, resentment toward making changes to be more inclusive. Disability advocates have historically needed to resort to litigation to get the changes needed to access recreation services (Lewkowicz, 2006). Under litigation, recreation providers, from businesses to public services, often see the cost of forced accessibility without seeing the benefits to a broad range of users. The compliance approach not only builds resentment, but it has been less than effective. The Americans with Disabilities Act has been in force since 1990, yet, according to a recent national survey, large gaps still exist between people without and with disabilities in many areas of life, including recreation and socialization (Kessler Foundation & National Organization on Disability, 2010; Katz & DeRose, 2010).

Though numerous barriers to inclusive recreation persist, we have learned much about what facilitates inclusion and accessibility. Focusing on facilitators has allowed us to develop a training program and a resource center that bring about positive change.

Facilitators to Inclusive Recreation

The social model of disability has helped foster inclusion in community recreation services. The social model of disability is built on a strengths-based and ecological approach. When using a strengths-based, ecological approach to recreation spaces, we must understand people in the context of the environments in which they live and play. The World Health Organization (WHO), embracing a social model of disability, recognized the importance of the environment and a strengths approach in its conceptualization of the International Classification of Functioning (ICF) (WHO, 2003). The ICF looks not only at how a person functions, it considers the "environmental factors" in which that functioning occurs. In a strengths-based approach, rather than view health and functional ability as a personal problem, the WHO regards it as a responsibility shared by society. Disability is no longer considered a minority issue; it is seen as a universal human experience. People with disabilities require more than medical care; they require social inclusion. Assistance with inclusion is designed not around deficits and diagnoses but around ability and functionality. The WHO conceptualized ability and functionality at three levels: (a) body function and structures (e.g., physical functioning related to cognition, speech, cardiovascular health, and related systems); (b) the person (e.g., age, lifestyle, education, assets); and (c) social and environmental contexts (e.g., physical environment, social attitudes, and interpersonal relationships). As such, well-being is described holistically from three perspectives: the body, the individual, and society. At the level of society and environmental contexts, the WHO acknowledges the vital role of *activities and participation* in well-being. Ultimately, the WHO recognizes that an understanding of environments and/or contexts, and the concept of inclusiveness are central to well-being at the individual level. Situating the person in the environment and focusing on strengths in both helps foster well-being and inclusion in recreation (Anderson & Heyne, 2012).

Universal design is a natural outcome from the social model of disability and a significant facilitator to inclusive recreation. Universal design is a planning concept that ensures that recreation amenities in all environments, both built and natural, are designed for access by all people, regardless of size, shape, or ability. Using principles of universal design enables participants to enter and use environments for leisure experiences (The Center for an Accessible Society, 2010; The Center for Universal Design, 1997; 2010). Universal design applies as well to programs and services, communication, and evaluation. It empowers all people to fully participate in a world designed to accommodate everyone.

An increased understanding of strategies that facilitate inclusion has also helped open up community recreation for people with disabilities. Research has helped us understand what concrete actions we can take to ensure accessible facilities, programs, and practices (Anderson & Kress, 2003; Klitzing & Wachter, 2005; Miller, Schleien, & Bowens, 2010; Miller, Schleien, & Lausier, 2009; Scholl, Smith, & Davison, 2005). With evidence-based tools at our disposal, we are able to modify normative programs, services, and environments to fully accommodate a broader range of people, including people with disabilities.

Collaboration is one of the key strategies to fostering inclusion (Anderson & Kress, 2003; Germ & Schleien, 1997; Klitzing & Wachter, 2005; Scholl, Dieser, & Davison, 2005). When partnerships are nurtured between people with disabilities, their friends, families, and recreation providers, a variety of strengths and perspectives can be used to increase inclusion. Resources, knowledge, talents, and networks are all amplified in a mutually beneficial collaboration, and inclusion becomes an easier process for everyone involved.

As inclusion in recreation becomes more the rule than the exception, a new norm is formed. Recreation providers are able to see positive outcomes from the changes made for accessibility and inclusion. Anderson (as cited in Lewkowicz, 2006), a recreation manager, stated, "We have come to realize that the changes will "improve everyone's park experience, not just for people with disabilities" (para. 19). New and modified facilities, policies, program practices, and partnerships result in inclusion of many diverse community members, shifting the "main stream" to a "wide stream" in recreation services. Deegan (1996), a self-advocate with a disability, once stated, "We say let the mainstream become a wide stream that has room for all of us and leaves no one stranded on the fringes.... The goal is not to become normal. The goal is to embrace our human vocation of becoming more deeply, more fully human. The goal is not normalization. The goal is to become the unique, awesome, never to be repeated human being that we are called to be" (p. 92). Inclusion helps us reach that goal!

Inclusion U: Helping All People Play Wherever They Choose

Inclusion U is a training program designed to capitalize on facilitators and minimize barriers to inclusive recreation services for people with disabilities and their families and friends. Using a social model of disability, a strengths or capability approach, and universal design principles, we have developed a training experience that we feel empowers everyday citizens to make changes toward a more inclusive world. Inclusion U is a major focus of the work we do at the Inclusive Recreation Resource Center.

Brief overview of the Inclusive Recreation Resource Center

The Inclusive Recreation Resource Center (IRRC) is a university-based center whose mission is to promote and sustain participation by people with disabilities in inclusive recreation activities and resources. We provide many different services, including inclusivity assessments, training, an online database for inclusive recreation, technical assistance, a recreation referral service, partnerships, and research and evaluation. Our work is guided by several principles that permeate all we do (see Table 11.2). Inclusion U is a key part of our work and trains an army of volunteers to help increase inclusion in recreation.

Table 11.2. Principles That Guide the Work of the Inclusive Recreation Resource Center

RECREATION IS IMPORTANT	Participation in recreation improves quality of life and offers numerous individual and societal benefits.
CHOICE MATTERS	Self-determination and choice are key to quality recreation experiences.
HONOR INTERESTS	People with disabilities want to participate in recreation activities based on their interests, not their disability.
STRENGTHS APPROACH	All people have potential waiting to be developed (capability-based approach).
CELEBRATE DIFFERENCES	Differences are respected and appreciated—diversity is good.
PERSON-CENTERED	The passions, interests, and dreams of the person with a disability drive the services, not the convenience of the system.
SERVICES AS SUPPORTS	Conceptualize services as individualized, person-centered supports, not programs or places.
NATURAL SUPPORTS	Natural supports are most effective to sustain inclusion.
ENVIRONMENTAL AND ACTIVITY ADAPTATION	Be ready to change environments, policies, equipment, and practices to meet a broader range of people.
COLLABORATE	Find as many diverse partners as you can.
INCLUSION IS A RIGHT…	Not a privilege. Be ready to be an advocate.

Table 11.3. Inclusion U Learning Modules

Module	Content
MODULE #1: Introduction	• The Inclusive Recreation Resource Center (mission, vision, activities) • Goals and objectives of Inclusion U • Process to complete the course and become a "Certified Inclusivity Assessor"
MODULE #2: What is Inclusion and Why Is It Important?	• Definitions and core principles • Physical accessibility–built and natural environments • Social accessibility–programs, services and events, administration • A brief note on legal mandates (ADA and other laws)
MODULE #3: What Do I Need to Know About Disability?	• Person-first language • The social model of disability • Functional abilities–physical, sensory, intellectual, emotional, social • Social model of disability
MODULE #4: Assessing Inclusivity	• Overview of the Inclusivity Assessment Tool • Tools and supplies needed • Description of each section of the Inclusivity Assessment Tool • Steps to approach a site, facility, or program (partnering, collegiality, market potential)
MODULE #5: What Is Physical Inclusion?	• Accessibility–approach, enter, use • The core Inclusivity Assessment Tool and specialty checklists • Universal design • The Access Board and other resources • The built and natural environments and inclusivity • Hands-on stations to learn how to measure physical inclusion
MODULE #6: Social Inclusion: Administrative Practices	• Mission, vision, and values • Planning and involvement of people with disabilities • Administrative and ground level support for inclusion • Staff hiring, training, and evaluation • Inclusion point of contact • Marketing and promotion, including web page design • Communication in alternative formats • Policies and procedures (policy on personal assistants, use of service animals, etc.)

MODULE #7: Social Inclusion: Program Practices	• Registration and needs assessment
	• Supports
	  • Additional staff or volunteers
	  • Peer training or orientation
	  • Positive behavioral supports
	• Accommodations
	  • Adapted equipment
	  • Activity adaptations (skills, rules, space, goal structure, team formation, etc.)
	  • Task analysis
	  • Partial participation
	• Implementation and monitoring/evaluation of supports and accommodations

MODULE #8: Putting It into Action	• Completing the assessment at the site with staff • Reporting your results to the Inclusive Recreation Resource Center for the online database

Table 11.3 cont.

MODULE #9: Networking, Partnerships, and Collaboration	• Benefits of partnerships and collaboration • How to identify potential partnerships that are win-win • How to form productive partnerships; skills needed for collaboration and partnering • Resources available to partnerships • FINAL EXAM to become a Certified Inclusivity Assessor (CIA)

Overview of Inclusion U

We have developed a simple, intuitive tool, called the *Inclusivity Assessment Tool* (see Anderson, Penney McGee, & Wilkins, 2010), to gather descriptive information about recreation spaces in terms of physical, administrative, and programmatic accessibility. The Inclusivity Assessment Tool includes a user manual, the core checklist, specialty checklists for the breadth of recreation facilities (from swimming pools to bowling alleys to museums), a 60" circle to measure wheelchair turning radius, a tape measure, and a homemade clinometer to measure slope. With the user-friendly Inclusivity Assessment Tool, trained volunteers, college students, self-advocates, professionals, and other "*Certified Inclusivity Assessors*" are able to gather information for an online recreation database that is valid, reliable, accurate, and specific. The training the volunteers complete is called *Inclusion U.*

Inclusion U is a one-day workshop that teaches one how to be a Certified Inclusivity Assessor. We have delivered Inclusion U to parks and recreation professionals, self-advocates, tourism professionals, human services professionals, families, and anyone interested in increasing opportunities for inclusive recreation. Once participants complete Inclusion U, they are able to complete accessibility surveys and submit the results to the New York State (NYS) IRRC to be included in an online recreation access database.

Inclusion U focuses on foundations of inclusion and the specific knowledge and skills needed to use the Inclusivity Assessment Tool. Table 11.3 provides an overview of the nine modules of Inclusion U. At the end of the day, participants take a "final exam" and must receive 80% or better to become certified. If a participant does not score high enough, we work individually with participants until they do understand inclusion and the tool and can become certified.

Overview of the database

The purpose of the Inclusivity Assessment Tool is to gather descriptive information about recreation opportunities to be shared on a searchable, online recreation resource database located on the IRRC website. The information on both physical access and social inclusion collected with the tool is descriptive, functional, and detailed, so that users of recreation programs, areas, and facilities can make better plans for inclusive recreation. In the database, for each recreation facility included, several tabs organize the information. Under the "physical inclusion" tab, users can learn whether they can approach, enter, and use a facility. Under the "administrative practices" tab, they can learn about policies, procedures, planning, communication, marketing, and other ways the agency accommodates people with disabilities. Under the "program practices" tab, users can learn about staffing, supports, accommodations, and the like. They can learn what adaptive equipment is available and if there are any specialized programs or services. By having this information, all people can make better decisions about the potential use of a recreational program or facility. Thousands of people have used the recreation database, as documented by web analytics we have put in place. In a user survey we complete, we found that the people with disabilities we surveyed found the database well designed and helpful to their planning. The online recreation database is located on this website: (www.nysirrc.org).

Foundations of change and Inclusion U

As we designed and field-tested Inclusion U, we found that education, empowerment, advocacy, and change were interrelated and key to the effectiveness of the training. We learned that participants needed facts and skills but also motivation and a positive attitude toward inclusion. They needed to be ready for the change process and take ownership in it. By focusing on principles and best practices and providing the theoretical foundation for inclusion, we have helped foster that readiness. We also developed a sense of trust in the IRRC with our consistent message and clearly defined and communicated values. With an enthusiasm for change, and armed with the tools, skills, and knowledge to make it, we have helped create a grassroots army of ordinary citizens widening the "mainstream" in recreation inclusion.

We also learned that participants in Inclusion U needed to have a concrete plan for action. One of the last exercises we complete during the day-long training is an "Action Plan," where participants identify a tangible change they will make based on the training, and one recreation agency they will assess for inclusivity. They also form naturally occurring partnerships that emerge throughout the day with other participants in their communities.

To date, we have trained hundreds of Certified Inclusivity Assessors who are equipped to use the Inclusivity Assessment Tool and share best practices in inclusion with recreation agencies. Our evaluation data show a significant increase in participants' knowledge about and positive attitudes toward inclusion. The online recreation database continues to grow. And we daily receive feedback that reinforces our sense that we are putting theory into practice in a powerful way. As one participant stated, "I left this training, as I am sure many did, with a renewed sense of diversity, inclusion, and cultural value.... I am glad to have received the networking, resources, foundations, and awareness for what is possible for social equality."

Conclusion

Nussbaum (2006) stated, "A society that does not guarantee these [ten core capabilities] to all its citizens, at some appropriate threshold level, falls short of being a fully just society" (p. 75). The Inclusive Recreation Resource Center, through its innovative Inclusion U training, is helping to guarantee that all people can play wherever they choose. By giving people concrete skills and a simple, intuitive tool to assess recreation spaces, we empower them to work collaboratively with business owners and administrators to make positive changes that build more inclusive parks and playgrounds, and more inclusive neighborhoods and communities.

References

Anderson, L., & Heyne, L. (2000). A statewide needs assessment using focus groups: Perceived challenges and goals in providing inclusive recreation services in rural communities. *Journal of Park and Recreation Administration, 18*(4), 17–37.

Anderson, L., & Heyne, L. (2012). *Therapeutic recreation practice: A strengths approach.* State College, PA: Venture.

Anderson, L., & Kress, C. (2003). *Inclusion: Including people with disabilities in parks and recreation opportunities.* State College, PA: Venture.

Anderson, L., Penney McGee, L., & Wilkins, V. (2010). *The inclusivity assessment tool and guide.* Cortland, NY: State University of New York at Cortland.

Carruthers, C., & Hood, C. (2007). Building a life of meaning through therapeutic recreation: The leisure and well-being model, part I. *Therapeutic Recreation Journal, 41*(4), 276–297.

The Center for an Accessible Society. (2010). Universal design. Retrieved from http://www.accessiblesociety.org/topics/universaldesign/

The Center for Universal Design. (1997). *The principles of universal design, Version 2.0.* Raleigh, NC: North Carolina State University.

The Center for Universal Design. (2010). *About UD.* Retrieved from http://www.design.ncsu.edu/cud/about_ud/about_ud.htm

Deegan, P. (1996). Recovery as a journey of the heart. *Psychiatric Rehabilitation Journal, 19*(3), 91–97.

Germ, P., & Schleien, S. (1997). Inclusive community leisure services: Responsibilities of key players. *Therapeutic Recreation Journal, 31*(1), 22–37.

Hood, C., & Carruthers, C. (2007). Enhancing leisure experience and developing resources: The leisure and well-being model, part II. *Therapeutic Recreation Journal, 41*(4), 298–325.

Hutchison, P., & McGill, J. (1992). *Leisure, integration and community.* Toronto, Canada: Leisurability.

Katz, E., & DeRose, R. (2010). The ADA 20 years later: The 2010 survey of Americans with disabilities. *Journal of Spinal Cord Medicine,* 33(4), 345. Retrieved from http://www.ncbi.nlm.nih.gov/pmc/articles/PMC2964021/

Kessler Foundation, & National Organization on Disability. (2010). The 2010 survey of Americans with disabilities. Retrieved from http://www.2010DisabilitySurveys.org

Klitzing, S., & Wachter, C. (2005). Benchmarks for the delivery of inclusive community recreation services for people with disabilities. *Therapeutic Recreation Journal, 39*(1), 63–77.

Lewkowicz, B. (2006, October 1). Opening the door to nature for people with disabilities. *Bay Nature.* Retrieved from http://baynature.org/articles/oct-dec-2006/accessible-outdoors/opening-the-door-to-nature

Miller, K., Schleien, S., & Bowens, F. (2010). Support staff as an essential component of inclusive recreation services. *Therapeutic Recreation Journal, 44*(1), 35–49.

Miller, K., Schleien, S., & Lausier, J. (2009). Search for best practices in inclusive recreation: Programmatic findings. *Therapeutic Recreation Journal, 43*(1), 27-41.

Nussbaum, M. (2006). *Frontiers of justice: Disability, nationality, species membership.* Cambridge, MA: Harvard University Press.

Nussbaum, M., & Sen, A. (1993). *The quality of life.* New York, NY: Oxford University Press.

O'Keefe, C. (n.d.). *Let's first revisit the meaning of leisure.* Handout given at the 57th Annual Metcalf Endowed Keynote Speech, Cortland Recreation Conference, SUNY Cortland, Cortland, NY, November 2, 2007.

Scholl, K., Dieser, R., & Davison, A. (2005). Together we play: An ecological approach to inclusive recreation. *Therapeutic Recreation Journal, 39*(4), 299–311.

Scholl, K., Smith, J., & Davison, A. (2005). Agency readiness to provide inclusive recreation and after-school services for children with disabilities. *Therapeutic Recreation Journal, 39*(1), 47–62.

Sylvester, C. (Ed). (2005). *Philosophy of therapeutic recreation: Ideas and issues* (Vol. III). Alexandria, VA: National Recreation and Park Association.

Sylvester, C. (2011). Therapeutic recreation, the International Classification of Functioning, Disability, and Health, and the capability approach. *Therapeutic Recreation Journal, 45*(2), 85–104.

Sylvester, C., Voelkl, J., & Ellis, G. (2001). *Therapeutic recreation programming: Theory and practice.* State College, PA: Venture.

Szenasy, S. (2010, September 15). Twenty years and counting. *Metropolis Magazine.* Retrieved from http://www.metropolismag.com/story/20100915/twenty-years-and-counting

Taylor, S. (2004). Caught in the continuum: A critical analysis of the principle of the least restrictive environment. *Research and Practice for Persons with Severe Disabilities, 29*(4), 218–230.

United Nations. (2006). *Convention on the rights of persons with disabilities and optional protocols.* New York, NY: Author.

World Health Organization (WHO). (2003). *International Classification of Functioning, Disability, and Health, Version 2.1a.* Retrieved from http://www.who.int/classifications/icf/site/checklist/icf-checklist.pdf

CHAPTER TWELVE

Private, Public, or Compassionate

Animal Rights and Disability Rights Laws

CARRIE GRIFFIN BASAS

Rights under American law can be conceived of in a variety of ways—from viewing them as individual entitlements, to the more popular notion of rights as trumps of an individual against government interference. Respect for individual and bodily autonomy and integrity is central to jurisprudence in a variety of areas that govern both these public/private dynamics and spheres, including constitutional law, criminal law, environmental law, and property law. Jurisprudence espousing privacy interests has encompassed cohabitation, religious education, surveillance, parenting, sexually intimate relationships, and reproductive choice, among other areas.

But under the law, not all *human* beings are created equal, at least in the application of the laws. As applied, the laws create a hierarchy of access to autonomy and integrity rights. Privacy is not the same for everyone, especially when viewed through the lenses of disability and animal rights paradigms. People with disabilities and animals share much in common, in that privacy, as a principle of law as applied to them, does not serve their needs; when their privacy needs are espoused, they are to mask abuses and injustices committed against them by the state or private actors. These injustices are often committed in seemingly "private" ways by happening in spaces where they are out of sight and perhaps out of mind, such as institutions, hospitals, schools, and within family spheres. Paradoxically, animals and people with disabilities share similar positions in how very public they are—they are both at once images and tools of spectacle, inquiry, subjugation, and use—and they are distanced from a system that affords them privacy in the sense of autonomy and dignity. Seen in this way, people with disabilities and animals are compelling examples of what it means to exist in the law in a state of limbo.

As I will explore in this chapter, only in narrow ways have the privacy rights of animals and people with disabilities—viewed positively—been recognized, but even when recognized, these forms of privacy are modified and lesser than those afforded nondisabled human animals. Largely, people with disabilities and nonhuman animals remain the objects of the state and other people's interests being acted upon them. Through their daily existences, they combat legal systems that try to contain them as passive, below dignity, and with limited rights subject to further review and qualification.

What Does It Mean for People with Disabilities and Nonhuman Animals to Be Private, or to Have Privacy?

Privacy can be conceived of in a number of ways, including: to be free from intervention and interference (consider issues of autonomy and independence); to belong solely to oneself (such as a property interest, ownership); to be a matter outside the public realm, for reasons of moral sensibilities (such as one's sexual proclivities, assuming they are legal and not abusive, within one's bedroom); to be hidden or secluded (such as keeping one's medical information "private") (Herzog, 2011). In all these ways, the history of people with disabilities is a private one, yet it is also very public—in the sense that people with disabilities do not often govern their own lives (e.g., guardianship, commitment, forced treatment, the Ashley X treatment). They are the objects of staring and inquiry (e.g., children's questions, job discrimination, carnival freak shows), and their bodies and impairments are seen as implicating public regulatory and policy interests that seemingly outweigh their right to privacy in their own affairs (e.g., experimentation, medical stripping, pressures for prenatal testing for Down Syndrome). In very few ways do people with disabilities occupy a positive position publically in society or under the law. When they are paraded, it is often for telethons and charitable donations, as examples of courage and heroism, and, ultimately, guilt-induced giving. They make the news for suing businesses for inaccessible entrances and restrooms, and the accompanying articles are festooned with headlines invoking the words "extortion," "shakedown," and "litigious." They become objects of pity, sometimes compassion, when stories about institutional abuse break, or children with disabilities are disciplined too severely by school systems (Langford & Stiles, 2009). Largely, however, people with disabilities are private—made private, and this is my key argument—by a society content to institutionalize (e.g., mental hospitals, nursing homes), imprison (e.g., the special education to prison pipeline, the criminalization of mental illness), and seclude them (e.g., architectural, communication, and social barriers and their replication in society). They do not fully occupy private or public spaces but, rather, exist in the kind of "betwixt" and "between" liminality that Victor Turner (1969) has described.

When dealing with the ways that they are mistreated becomes too great for those with power, the escape valve available is to return them to their prisons, group homes, special schools, and stations of poverty. Perhaps the moral failing is too great to bear, or maybe it simply is not recognized at all because it is of so little importance. In this respect, people with disabilities and nonhumans share a status of passing significance under the law. Here, it is critical to realize that the law captures and tracks societal values: without social change, legal change is difficult and untenable. Without legal change, social change is scattered and erodible.

Nonhumans share similar fates to people with disabilities, and people with disabilities share similar fates to nonhumans. While many disability rights scholars and advocates may find this comparison tenuous, even troubling, people with disabilities and animals are both subjugated beings. This is not to equate them in specific intelligence, social roles, or legal rights, but it is to shift the discussion away from those values as the most important considerations. Their common pain is one of being acted upon as if they do not possess sensing, feeling, thinking, and community-forming abilities. Surely, one might argue, people with disabilities currently are better off than animals and deserve to be better off than animals. But I present the challenge in this chapter to consider the ways in which these experiences overlap and how privacy—as a virtue—has been twisted in its application and has made both groups largely isolated and voiceless. While the expansion of notions of dominion has other manifestations, such as with the American private property system and rampant environmental abuses, the examples of nonhumans and people with disabilities are particularly telling in how power dynamics affect determinations about which lives have value.

My central thesis is that when privacy does come into play with regard to the issues facing people with disabilities or nonhumans, it is used to protect the decisions of people without disabilities acting with force toward and dominion over people with disabilities and nonhumans. All are equal, but some are more equal than others. Ironically, when people challenge this state of affairs and attempt to advocate for animals under a liberation paradigm, they are marginalized as "kooky" and "crazy," just as environmentalists are characterized as eco-terrorists. These characterizations bear witness to how disabling language colors all experiences that cause discomfort for people with power over the fates of nonhumans and disabled people (Torres, 2007). To understand the ways in which the law has or has not created a space for people with disabilities is to also understand the same issues facing animals, because both sets of experiences and rights have been largely constructed from a paradigm of degradation.

What Has the Law Done for People with Disabilities?

The Americans with Disabilities Act (ADA) (1990), and its subsequent amendments, were heralded as a civil rights act for people with disabilities, designed to end the social isolation of the community and recognize the invidious effects of disability discrimination in all realms of social and economic interaction, from shopping to job-seeking, faith-practice to theater attendance. However, the promises of the ADA remain largely unrealized, due to hostile courts, a lack in a shift of concomitant societal attitudes around disability, and general discomfort with recognizing disability as desirable diversity (Krieger, 2003). People with disabilities have a law, indeed, and the difficult fight of activists and advocates for its passage should not go unrecognized. But it is a law that remains more of a question mark than a declaration. A law without force—without belief in it, except by its drafters and its intended beneficiaries (especially when those beneficiaries are largely unemployed, underemployed, and marginalized)—is one of limited effect.

The ADA (1990) itself exemplifies the difficult position of people with disabilities vis-à-vis privacy. Its provisions, for example, in Title I, make much of an applicant or employee's right to keep his or her medical information private, subject to certain job-related inquiries at particular times in the search and employment processes. The Act also requires that employers not share information about requests for reasonable accommodations with people outside of a circle of those who need to know, such as supervisors, human resources directors, and anyone else involved in implementing the accommodation. But what does supposed confidentiality buy, and does it even exist? Even with the confidentiality provisions, studies of workplace accommodation show increasing resistance to accommodations by colleagues of workers with disabilities and the undermining of them by those coworkers who feel as if they are special benefits or perks, and not deserved and fundamental civil rights (Colella, 2001).

Disability is still treated under the law as something that should be hidden because it is an object of shame. By "hidden," I do not make reference to nonapparent disabilities but to the norms to downplay or "pass" when facing any disability experience. Many workers with disabilities feel pressure, even with a civil rights law, to make their disabilities private, even if they occupy very important, meaningful roles in their nonwork lives (Basas, 2010). A common question of applicants with disabilities is whether or not they should even disclose their disabilities, for example, because while employers may have a nondiscrimination statement copied from common EEOC (Equal Employment Opportunity Commission) language, prospective disabled workers recognize that disability is not necessarily a desired, or enforced, form of diversifying the workplace. Accordingly, many workers with disabilities may attempt to pass as less disabled or nondisabled, or self-accommodate their impairments, not desiring to flag them for employers or coworkers in order to maintain what they see as some form of privacy. But this form of *privacy* is not something that they would have selected if attitudes and protections surrounding disability were more positive. Privacy, in this example, is powerful, however, arguably undercutting any larger "coming out" effort. Public displays and disclosures of disability may encourage interactions between disabled-as-self-identified and nondisabled people that begin to erode attitudinal barriers regarding disability. The pressure to hide or to be *private* about disability stigmatizes workers with disabilities and provides a false sense of safety in the concealment of or downplaying of disability.

From these workplace dynamics, workers with disabilities may often feel as if they are alone, perhaps even first-run experiments in an office, factory, or a profession itself. This isolation is a largely unsettling feeling, professionally and financially. If they want to receive accommodations, they must make their private (medical) issues public to some extent and hope that those with this newly received information will honor its privacy implications. They, arguably, must share more about themselves and their life histories at work than other employees and all in a quiet imploration for benevolence regarding the reasonableness of their accommodations. The scale swings in both directions but never stabilizes on the side of disability justice: Employers and other social actors pressure workers with disabilities to be discreet and nondemonstrative about their disabilities, largely to provide for the comfort of nondisabled colleagues ("Keep it to yourself. It's private."). Yet, these disabled workers must reveal deeply sensitive, sometimes embarrassing or shameful information about their impairments in great detail to access their civil rights (Berg, 1999). People with disabilities are permitted to be private, but they exercise very little control over its parameters. They are made public, without much control over that process, either, even where probing or humiliating (especially if the information is not received well) levels of disclosure are expected.

A rights-based approach does not seem to be the elixir one would hope, at least when subject to review by jurists and lawyers who do not understand or relate to disability rights. Litigation under the ADA (1990) has not worked; more than 90% of Title I plaintiffs lost their cases (American Civil Liberties Union (ACLU), 2007), and too few cases exist under the new amendments of 2008 to ascertain whether this tide will change. The private issues of people with disabilities become public in this process when they are decided by fact finders, judges, and juries, who may not have the expertise to make correct or rational decisions, and who may apply their own stereotypes or biases about disability. Whatever these biases, they share common themes of both aversion and charity toward people with disabilities as inferior beings, subject to public inquiry at any time to make them "more human" than their default positions of marginalized Other (Garland-Thomson, 2009).

This kind of making public of private issues is not limited to work for people with disabilities. They routinely interact with the U.S. public benefits system, for example, that categorizes, packages, and defines them and their level of disability, and renders its translation to monetary payments (McCluskey, 2003). Even though few people can live on these benefits or abide by the rules associated with them, they must play along—and relinquish any semblance of privacy—to receive social support. If they want to be able to be "independent," they must subject themselves to inquiries beyond what most nondisabled people could ever imagine, unless they have experienced the process vicariously through family members or close friends.

The counter-argument, of course, is that if a person wants the financial support of the government, he or she must be willing to relinquish some privacy—money is traded for probing. Whether or not this process can ever be an even exchange or if it is even desirable to be constructed as one, is beyond arguing in this chapter. What is worth examining, however, are the ways in which we assume that people with disabilities are open to public inquiries, even ridicule, and how quickly that ground shifts when people with disabilities are being abused, mistreated, or acted upon by others. Then, the privileges of the private actors—the abusers, the scorners, the substituted decision-makers—are given heft and privilege, as being private and beyond the reach of society.

As a brief example: Consider states' practices of sterilizing people with disabilities up until the 1970s. Entire regimes of sterilization were funded and directed by the states to deal with the "feeble-minded," the infirm, and the genetically defective (Lombardo, 2008). While the eugenics programs of the Holocaust brought these larger ethical dilemmas to the forefront, well past that tragedy, the state-supported sterilization of people with disabilities in the United States continued—as a public good, a public health approach, or a social nightmare, depending on the critic. These programs were largely allowed to continue because the sexual intimacy issues of people with disabilities were considered to be well within the public interest as was the containment of them. Additionally, the roles of parents and physicians bolstered the longevity and veracity of these programs, where those communities were concerned about pregnancy, sex crimes, or other immoral acts and their byproducts that they thought sterilization might prevent. In essence, private actors had their fears embodied in a state/public program that carried out their wishes and more.

Even when the eugenics agenda was connected clearly with Nazi practices abroad, sterilizations continued. As the disability civil rights movement grew in the United States in the 1960s and 1970s, it directed its attention toward dismantling these programs and addressing the underlying prejudices guiding them (Longmore, 1995). The sterilization of people with disabilities remains a shameful part of American policy and history, yet is a recent one that has so quickly been forgotten by those outside the disability rights community. And arguably, it is one that lingers in discussions of genetic preconception screening, prenatal testing, and abortion counseling, and the social asexualization of people with disabilities (Meekosha, 1998). It continues in a more tangible form, at least medically, in growth attenuation treatments—as performed on Ashley X, to make the girl a child forever by removing her breast buds, performing a hysterectomy, and treating her with estrogen to prevent her physical and reproductive maturation (Hall, 2011). The goal was to make her more manageable in size for her parent caregivers.

When people with disabilities fail to own their jobs, their medical information, their bodies, they fail to own their lives. They are subjected to decision-making and inquiries in ways in which they would not be if they were people without disabilities. And this form of acting upon is a public usurpation of private interests. What makes it even more powerful is its combined effect with the privatization of what should be public concerns—such as in the sterilization example, or in the failed efficacy of the Americans with Disabilities Act. These constructions of public and private lives under the law and in society further serve to alienate and isolate people with disabilities. When they need the assistance of others in positions of power to come forward in coalition to advance their causes, their issues become private, and when they would normally—if they were nondisabled—be entitled to make private decisions, those decisions can be taken away by those in power interested in making public decisions for disabled people as a group.

This problem is further compounded by the social effect: marginalization and isolation keep injustices against people with disabilities outside of the public eye, and therefore, rallying for legal or social reform becomes more difficult. Discrimination can go unseen and unchecked, but it can also go disbelieved (Stefan, 2000). In even identifying discrimination, people with disabilities often face backlashes, having their rationality called into question and being confronted with stereotypes about people with disabilities as malingerers, welfare queens, and angry misfits that fail to appreciate all the ways in which society has already accommodated their so-framed special needs (Eskridge, 2001). While the ADA was enacted to remove the distancing barriers of architecture and communications and to give people with disabilities full access to *public* life, it has not been fully effective in closing gaps related to power, control, and attitudes.

What Has the Law Done for Nonhumans?

If people with disabilities belong to their families, medical institutions, and the state, then nonhumans belong to everyone and to no one in many of the same ways. They belong to feedlot farmers who may abuse them, with handy exceptions carved out under agricultural laws (DeCoux, 2009). They belong to circuses that may train, display, and transport them under inhumane conditions (Bryant, 2007). They belong to labs that may torture and maim them, without clear scientific needs and purposes (Regan, 2004). These activities happen largely behind closed doors, just as the abuse of people with disabilities does. It is a private matter when it is publicly too difficult, overwhelming, or uninteresting to explore. Nonhumans, like people with disabilities, belong to whoever claims them until that person or entity loses interest.

Even with animal welfare laws, the legal status of nonhumans is that of property (Francione & Charlton, 2008). Less than one hundred years ago in the United States, and many places around the world today, family members with disabilities were or are property to explore and exploit for labor and use and burdens when they seem no longer productive. This paradigm is grounded in a system of capitalism, where the worth and the corresponding dignity of humans or nonhumans is measured in terms of their relative productivity or utility (Satz, 2009). They can be profit or burden, object of exploitation or obstacle.

In this way, nonhumans and people with disabilities share much in common in terms of legal and economic status. Seen through the lenses of zoos, circuses, and piecemeal labor shops for disabled people, the relationship between the nonconforming animal (e.g., elder human, disabled human, prisoner, sick nonhuman animal) and the conforming human animal is one of master-servant, where the conforming human benefits financially. When the conforming human fails to benefit financially, the relationship often ends, and so, too, may the life of the nonconforming animal today, when it comes to nonhumans in the United States. There is less tolerance for the taking of human lives in the United States, conforming or not, but it occurs through the practices of euthanasia, withheld medical treatment, starvation, and abuse by family members, the medical system, and other caregivers (Wendell, 1996). Arguably, the devaluation of the lives of people with disabilities, and the subjection of people with disabilities to life-ending risk and violence also happen through the under-prosecution of crimes against people with disabilities and the failure to recognize those crimes as potentially driven by animus or hate (Sherry, 2010).

Further, much of what is deemed to be best for nonhumans is measured by what is best for conforming humans. Who else is to decide except the person most visible and powerful? We allow people to make decisions for animals because they cannot make decisions for themselves, but in doing so, we do not always hold those people to an ethical standard in which they must make decisions that would honor the sensate and sentient natures of those animals. People are not expected to consider the levels of pain, fear, nor communal bonding that nonhumans experience. Nonhumans are there to be acted upon, when convenient—subject to certain guardrails that are placed far apart in baseline behavior and deviance. Even with cruelty to animals laws, for example, prosecutions are rare and penalties are minimal (Rackstraw, 2003). To hurt a nonhuman animal is not the same as hurting a (nondisabled) person. Under the law, hurting an animal is more akin to damaging property. From a mainstream social perspective, the primary value in criminalizing extreme animal violence, however rare in its punishment, is because it can be a precursor to potentially violent behavior against valued humans (The Humane Society, n.d.b). And any kind of compassion towards animals that have been the victims of criminal violence is more indicative of a concern for containing violence in general, or a rejection of the display of a meager level of compassion toward living creatures, than recognizing any dignity or autonomy for nonhumans.

Further, the killing of nonhuman animals is institutionalized and industrialized and made palatable to many by happening in private places away from most people's experiences of daily life. Very few people ever venture into slaughterhouses and consider the conditions for animals and workers alike there. (Very few nondisabled people ever venture into institutions for disabled people, either.) There is little consideration of the process from living animal to dead animal. Humane meat laws, for example, go far in reinforcing the notion that transparency to the public is unnecessary and that much of what happens in the industry should be treated as private. The laws themselves fail to capture the largest issues affecting nonhumans in food production—namely, which populations are most affected, whether any kind of slaughter could be humane, and how food producers should be held more accountable for the lives and deaths of animals in their care in the United States. *The Humane Methods of Slaughter Act* (7 U.S.C. §1901–1907), for example, excludes chickens and turkeys from its definition, yet birds constitute almost all of the animals killed for meat in the United States every year—some nine billion (The Humane Society, n.d.a). "Meat"—not animals: pigs, cows, goats, chickens—simply arrives in a package to the consumer at a grocery store, clean and sterile-appearing, and people are allowed to further dissociate from any pain, suffering, and injustices incurred in its production. They praise themselves if they bought it locally, or if it is labeled with "cruelty-free" conditions, but this kind of branding is marketing toward avoidance (Taylor, 2011).

In these ways, (nondisabled) humans may make very specific demands about how their exposure to pain and suffering is regulated, and they tend, in doing so, to avoid grappling with suffering of their own creation when it comes to the treatment of people with disabilities and nonhumans. The idea that a short-lived existence of pain is somehow natural, endemic to these forms of being, is as rife as it is absurd. Even more absurd is the tendency to equate physical pain or brief lifespans among people with disabilities and nonhumans with the acceptability of inflicting further suffering and subjugation.

Perhaps, to sequester abused and mistreated beings, to make them private when the truths of their public appearances are unsettling or painful, is a way of coping—however flawed and fundamentally unjust. What could be most disturbing about nonhumans and people with disabilities is that they do live with some degree of suffering and pain, much of it socially generated, but a degree of it palpable and real. I would argue that suffering is what is inflicted by others, while pain is a physical or emotional experience. Adapting to pain and bearing witness to it and to fragility in everyday life can be troubling to others if the dominant paradigm is one of beneficence toward animals and people with disabilities, and the avoidance of public displays of difference and interdependence.

But pain made private, and suffering that goes without accountability, are as "unnatural" as any laws that exclude or marginalize the most vulnerable members of society from their protections. If there is a scale of pain that comes from the social order that nonhumans understand, it is the pecking order. Even with the pecking order, chickens are largely social creatures (Squier, 2011). They provide warmth and companionship to one another, come to one another's aid in crisis, mourn when a family member is lost, and chirp at their unborn chicks. People with disabilities and other animals understand that survivalist tendencies should not be omnipotent as well. Interdependence is a norm of nature, yet laws and the concomitant public support system fail to recognize that the way toward thriving for every being is not the triumph of one over another or the marginalization of those mistreated by society. Successful communities depend on the endurance of all in a state of balance, respect, and support.

When it comes to nonhumans and people with disabilities, injustices themselves are rationalized through a call to the natural order: "They cannot act on their own"; "They were born for these roles"; "They already have terrible lives, so this additional pain is minimal"; "Why expect much from something so different from me?" Nonhumans and people with disabilities share in being treated as lives that matter less than *normal*, human lives; this lower status allows for a range of injustices and outright atrocities to be committed in the guise of helping them, too.

Doing It for Them: A Critique of Guardianship, Charity, and Compassion

Ask anyone who has done something considered to be a good deed for a person with a disability or a nonhuman, and they are apt to tell you that they did it out of a sense of duty or compassion. They felt called to help, wanted to do something, felt like the being could not do it alone. The call to kindness, of course, is an indisputable one. But not all actions for people with disabilities or for nonhumans are based on kindness, and not all kindness is the same. Some acts veneered in the expression of kindness come from places of pity, misunderstanding, domination, control, and disrespect. They are about the person asserting herself, grasping more power over the perceived weak—even if this process is not overt, conscious, or evaluated.

In this way, the charitable paradigm of assisting nonhumans—the animal welfare approach—resembles the charitable model of helping people with disabilities. Both approaches frame disabled humans and nonhumans as only objects of care and not contributors to the larger ecological system and society itself. Most dangerous, charitable approaches have been institutionalized and legitimized through laws that make it seem as if both groups offer nothing to society and are rightfully the objects of pity and intrusion. Violations of their interests, therefore, become honored and celebrated as morally correct and functionally necessary rather than being evaluated on their terms and challenged for their assumptions.

Both charitable models revolve around notions that disabled humans and nonhumans need assistance because they can do so little for themselves and present a drain on functioning members of society. To assist is to perform a perceived social good under this model. But a helping tendency needs to be tempered with the recognition that assistance can be coupled with perceptions of the poor qualities of lives of people with disabilities and nonhumans. The action of helping, then, becomes an act of pity. To recognize suffering, segregation, isolation, deprivation, and other cruelties in society is important, and to act based on that recognition more so. But to truly act with mercy and compassion is to move forward free from a desire to laud it over another being, to expect praise and recognition, or to feel better about oneself because life could be worse—as evidenced in the experiences of the being that was helped. The practice of compassion is that of embracing interdependence.

A welfare approach to disability rights and animal rights reflects a charitable model that eschews interdependence. The same systems that "protect" animals are often used to "protect" people with disabilities, and in the act of protecting, much is done to and for both populations without recognition of their essential roles in communities. Many members of helping professions, for example, consistently undervalue the lives of people with disabilities even when they see tremendous value and fulfillment in their existences (Longmore, 1995). When asked to assist people with disabilities and their families in making medical decisions, such as about sterilization, the complexity of this devaluing can mean that paternalism and fears about disability result in the loss of reproductive capacities (Brantlinger, 1992).

In the context of nonhumans, the situation is no more optimistic. Veterinarians routinely struggle with whether or not to perform life-saving surgeries that might result in unsettling disfigurement for the animal and reactions of disgust by humans (*The Veterinary Record*, 2007). And while every state in the country requires reporting of suspected child abuse by health professionals, only eight states require the reporting of suspected animal abuse by veterinarians (Benetato, Reisman, & McCobb, 2011). If animal welfare means protecting the owners of animals, which sociolegal systems protect *animals*?

One of the dangers of the privacy inherent in actions committed *for* (but essentially, against) people with disabilities and nonhumans by nondisabled people is that charity and welfare can tidily conceal more than discomfort; they can camouflage animosity. Most people do not associate animosity with disability or with animals, largely because of a belief system informed by this model of distorted compassion and overarching dominion. The view is that people act with a sense of what is best, what is right, for those populations that cannot advocate for themselves, and that they do so out of unmitigated generosity and kindness.

This perspective, however, is largely inconsistent with research showing great animosity toward the laws protecting people with disabilities and nonhumans, as well as the environments in which they live. Whether protective laws inspire animosity or their enactment unearths and exposes existing animosity remains to be clarified, but animosity is present, whatever its source. Rather than being viewed as advocates for weak and marginalized creatures, animal rights advocates are increasingly being regarded as domestic terrorists. State enactments of eco-terrorism laws, for example, are on the rise (Lovitz, 2010). Through the Animal Enterprises Terrorism Act and the earlier Animal Enterprises Protection Act, animal liberation work carries stiff criminal penalties, beyond those for the underlying property crimes committed, such as trespassing and theft. These acts came out of the belief that the animal rights movement, specifically underground groups, presented terroristic threats to American property and businesses through revolutionary viewpoints and tactics. Drafters of the legislation and their constituents perceived animal rights advocates as greater menaces than even the White supremacy movement and other hate-based groups (Torres, 2007). Radical activism, related to honoring animals of all kinds and their environments, threatened the (im)balance of power, in which the property rights of nondisabled people took precedence and merited public and private protections.

While eco-activists and animal activists may be seen as a menace to economic and social stability, outright animal cruelty apparently is not. If animal advocacy is the enemy, then anything to expose how private actors terrorize nonhumans is doubly threatening to notions of privacy and autonomy. In the 2010 case of *U.S. v. Stevens*, the U.S. Supreme Court struck down as overly broad a federal law criminalizing the commercial creation, sale, or possession of depictions of cruelty to animals. Robert J. Stevens had been indicted under the law for selling three video tapes that included imagery of dogfights as well as a dog attacking a pig. While Stevens had not shot the footage for these films, he had added commentary and narration to them. The question before the Court was whether or not these videos could be protected under First Amendment speech rights. In its holding, an overwhelming 8–1 majority of the Court emphasized that the First Amendment of the Constitution protects "depictions" of animal cruelty, even where "prohibition of animal cruelty has a long history in American law" (*United States v. Stevens*, 2010). After the ruling, Congress passed a new bill that narrowed the language of the law, the Animal Crush Video Prohibition Act of 2010, to allow just for penalties for "animal crush" videos where one animal is killed by another or by a human. These crush videos generally are produced for the sexual gratification of the viewers (Stopcrush.org, 2012).

For animals, as well as people with disabilities, their status is one of being acted upon for the gratification of others. Abuses against them are ignored, except for perhaps the most "deviant" from a mainstream perspective, as the crush video legislation demonstrates. For example, since the U.S. Department of Justice began tracking hate crimes against people with disabilities, the agency has discovered that these crimes are on the rise, and that violence against people with disabilities is twice as likely as violence against nondisabled people (Levin, 2011). But hate crimes are largely underreported by people with disabilities and misclassified by law enforcement officers when disability is involved (Rintels & Loge, 2009). Inherent to these structural problems is the flawed assumption that no one could ever hate people with disabilities or desire to victimize them further than their existing positions in society.

Disability rights and animal rights advocates routinely confront enmity toward their legal protections. Animosity toward the Americans with Disabilities Act, and overindulgence of the business community's stereotyping of disability, fueled a series of Supreme Court cases that eroded the very definition of who counted as a person with a disability (Diller, 2003). Backlash against animal protection laws has led to their scattered enactment, social mocking, and under-enforcement (Linzey, 2009). Even when they are enacted, much of the progress comes from an animal welfare perspective that fails to confront the underlying, systemic inequalities and inequities in American society. These imbalances mark some beings as less worthy of protections and rights and reinforce the property rights of nondisabled people acting with dominion over both nonhumans and people with disabilities.

Conclusion: Pushing Toward Daily Small Victories and Long-Term Meaningful Rights

In this chapter, I have identified and criticized an American virtue—privacy—and its application to two marginalized groups—people with disabilities and nonhumans. I have questioned what it means for privacy to act in these realms and how it, as a principle, becomes deeply entangled with treating people with disabilities and nonhumans as public property and spectacle, without holding other members of society responsible and accountable for the injustices they commit against them. Challenging privacy is almost an affront to liberalism, but other scholars working on difference and oppression have recognized that privacy can be a facade behind which the state privileges certain private actors and affirms nonintervention in ways that perpetuate suffering and inequality (Olsen, 1983).

Focusing on how the law has not valued people with disabilities and nonhumans is an often frustrating project, but it should not be a directionless one, too. Animal rights and disability rights have much to offer one another in envisioning a future society in which all beings count. Anita Silvers (2003) offers a powerful tool for reimagining how society and its laws might treat disabled people and nonhuman animals. While she proposes this approach for converting archaic public policies to disability-sound practices, it could be easily applied to issues of animal rights, as well. She suggests using a test of "historically counterfactualizing," where history is rewritten in a sense—the marginalized group is assumed to hold the position of power. Would there, then, be factory farms? Buildings with only stairs as a means of accessing upper levels? Resistance on the parts of employers to accommodate? "Humane" meat laws? If the answer to those kinds of questions is "no," then those policies or laws should be rewritten.

Silvers's (2003) approach mirrors critical legal scholar Mari Matsuda's (1991) suggestion to "ask the other question" (p. 1189). If, for example, the debate is about the access of people with disabilities to adequate health care, then the "other question" might be how health care is often predicated on the exploitation of nonhumans or the environments in which they live. Or the question could simply be how we, as a society, provide for the wellness of all beings. If the conversation is about the role of factory farms in the abuse of nonhumans, then the other question could be how these factory farms also exploit people and cause disability, further marginalizing animals of all kinds. And if the policy issue is how we reenvision a prison system to be more humane toward human inmates, the other question is how the prison system closely tracks the confinement and warehousing of other animals.

With these tools and a renewed focus on the intersection of disability rights and animal rights, legal scholars, advocates, and others can begin to right some of the public and private injustices committed against people with disabilities and nonhuman animals. They can also begin to rewrite some of the dominant cultural narratives about the proper roles and abilities of these groups, which are then translated into new laws and institutions. Both movements have the strength of realizing in their visions that interdependence should be a desire and a reality of a society and legal regime that purport to advance equality and equity.

References

Aleinikoff, T. A. (1987). Constitutional law in the age of balancing. *Yale Law Journal, 96*(5), 943–1005.

American Civil Liberties Union (ACLU). (2007). ADA Restoration Act. Retrieved from http://www.aclu.org/images/asset_upload_file833_33633.pdf

Basas, C. G. (2010). The new boys: Women with disabilities and the legal profession. *Berkeley Women's Law Journal, 25*(1), 32–124.

Benetato, M. A., Reisman, R., & McCobb, E. (2011). The veterinarian's role in animal cruelty cases. *Journal of the American Veterinary Medical Association, 238*(1), 31–34.

Berg, P. E. (1999). Ill/legal: Interrogating the meaning and function of the category of disability in antidiscrimination law. *Yale Law and Policy Review, 18*(1), 1–51.

Bhagwat, A. A. (2010). *The myth of rights: The purposes and limits of constitutional rights*. New York, NY: Oxford University Press.

Brantlinger, E. (1992). Professionals' attitudes toward the sterilization of people with disabilities. *Journal of the Association for Persons with Severe Handicaps, 17*(1), 4–18.

Bryant, T. L. (2007). Similarity or difference as a basis for justice: Must animals be like humans to be legally protected from humans? *Law and Contemporary Problems*, 70(1), 207–254.

Colella, A. (2001). Coworker distributive fairness judgments of the workplace accommodation of employees with disabilities. *The Academy of Management Review, 26*(1), 100–116.

DeCoux, E. (2009). Speaking for the modern Prometheus: The significance of animal suffering to the abolition movement. *Animal Law, 16*, 9–64.

Diller, M. (2003). Judicial backlash, the ADA, and the civil rights model of disability. In L. H. Krieger (Ed.), *Backlash against the ADA: Reinterpreting disability rights* (pp. 62–97). Ann Arbor, MI: University of Michigan Press.

Dworkin, R. M. (1977). *Taking rights seriously*. Cambridge, MA: Harvard University Press.

Eskridge Jr., W. N. (2001). Channeling: Identity-based social movements and public law. *University of Pennsylvania Law Review, 150*(1), 419–525.

Francione, G. L., & Charlton, A. E. (2008). Animal advocacy in the 21st century: The abolition of the property status of nonhumans. In T. L. Bryant, R. J. Huss, & D. N. Cassuto (Eds.), *Animal law and the courts: A reader* (pp. 7–35). St. Paul, MN: Thomson West.

Garland-Thomson, R. (2009). *Staring: How we look*. New York, NY: Oxford University Press.

Hall, K. Q. (2011). *Feminist disability studies*. Bloomington, IN: Indiana University Press.

Herzog, D. (2011). Public man, private woman (working paper).

The Humane Society of the United States. (n.d.a). Cruel slaughter practices. Retrieved from http://www.humanesociety.org/issues/slaughter/

The Humane Society of the United States. (n.d.b). First Strike: The violence connection. Retrieved from http://www.humanesociety.org/assets/pdfs/abuse/first_strike.pdf

Krieger, L. H. (2003). Sociolegal backlash. In L. H. Krieger (Ed.), *Backlash against the ADA: Reinterpreting disability rights* (pp. 340–393). Ann Arbor, MI: University of Michigan Press.

Langford, T., & Stiles, M. (2009, March 11). Schools for disabled see statewide spike in complaints. *Houston Chronicle Online*. Retrieved from http://www.chron.com/disp/story.mpl/metropolitan/6306442.html

Levin, J. (2011, March 1). The invisible hate crime. *Miller-McCune*. Retrieved from http://www.miller-mccune.com/legal-affairs/the-invisible-hate-crime-27984/#

Linzey, A. (2009). *Why animal suffering matters: Philosophy, theology, and practical ethics.* New York, NY: Oxford University Press.

Lombardo, P. A. (2008). *Three generations, no imbeciles: Eugenics, the Supreme Court, and Buck v. Bell.* Baltimore, MD: Johns Hopkins University Press.

Longmore, P. K. (1995). Medical decision making and people with disabilities: A clash of cultures. *Journal of Law, Medicine, and Ethics, 23*(1), 82–87.

Lovitz, D. (2010). *Muzzling a movement: The effects of anti-terrorism law, money, and politics on animal activism.* Brooklyn, NY: Lantern Books.

Matsuda, M. J. (1991). Beside my sister, facing the enemy: Legal theory out of coalition. *Stanford Law Review, 43*(6), 1183–1192.

McCluskey, M. T. (2003). Efficiency and social citizenship: Challenging the neoliberal attack on the welfare state. *Indiana Law Journal, 78*(2), 783–876.

Meekosha, H. (1998). Body battles: Bodies, gender and disability. In T. Shakespeare (Ed.), *The disability reader: Social science perspectives* (pp. 163–180). New York, NY: Continuum.

Meyer, L. R. (2000). Unruly rights. *Cardozo Law Review, 22*(1), 1–50.

Olsen, F. E. (1983). The family and the market: A study of ideology and legal reform. *Harvard Law Review, 96*(7), 1497–1578.

Rackstraw, J. H. (2003). Reaching for justice: An analysis of self-help prosecution for animal crime. *Animal Law, 9*, 243–266.

Regan, T. (2004). *The case for animal rights.* Berkeley, CA: University of California Press.

Rintels, J., & Loge, P. (2009). *Confronting the new faces of hate: Hate crimes in America.* Washington, DC: Leadership Conference on Civil Rights Education Fund. Retrieved from http://www.protectcivilrights.org/pdf/reports/hatecrimes/lccref_hate_crimes_report.pdf

Satz, A. B. (2009). Animals as vulnerable subjects: Beyond interest-convergence, hierarchy and property. *Animal Law, 16*, 65–122.

Sherry, M. (2010). *Disability hate crimes: Does anyone really hate disabled people?* London, UK: Ashgate.

Silvers, A. (2003). People with disabilities. In H. LaFollette (Ed.), *The Oxford handbook of practical ethics* (pp. 311–313). New York, NY: Oxford University Press.

Squier, S. M. (2011). *Poultry science, chicken culture: A partial alphabet.* New Brunswick, NJ: Rutgers University Press.

Stefan, S. (2000). Delusions of rights: Americans with psychiatric disabilities, employment discrimination and the Americans with Disabilities Act. *Alabama Law Review, 52*(1), 271–320.

Stopcrush,org (2012). Retrieved from http://www.stopcrush.org/.

Taylor, S. (2011). Beasts of burden: Disability studies and animal rights. *Qui Parle: Critical Humanities and Social Sciences, 19*(2), 191–222.

Torres, B. (2007). *Making a killing: The political economy of animal rights.* Oakland, CA: AK Press.

Turner, V. (1969). *The ritual process: Structure and anti-structure.* New York, NY: Aldine de Gruyter.

United States v. Stevens (No. 08-769). (2010). Retrieved from http://www.law.cornell.edu/supct/html/08-769.ZS.html

The Veterinary Record. (2007). Ethical dilemmas and quality of life. *Veterinary Record,* 160(17), 568.

Wendell, S. (1996). *The rejected body: Feminist philosophical reflections on disability.* London, UK: Routledge.

PART V

Inclusive World

CHAPTER THIRTEEN

Infinite Ethics

An Inclusive Vision for a Diverse World

Norm Phelps

Ethics is infinite responsibility toward all that lives.

—*Albert Schweitzer*

Pretty much any textbook you pick up for Ethics 101 will tell you that there are four primary ethical systems competing in the marketplace of ideas: utilitarianism, natural rights philosophy, social contract theory, and—with the recent revival of an old favorite from classical Greece—virtue ethics. This is not wrong, at least in the sense that it accurately reports what is being taught in classrooms and discussed in journals. But there is, I want to suggest, a way of looking at ethics that is simpler, more profound, and less dependent upon cultural or intellectual context than these hyper-rationalized outcroppings of Western academic philosophy. In terms of both theory and praxis, I believe that a more useful way to think about ethics is to posit two broad ethical orientations: *exclusive* and *inclusive*.

The Ethics of Exclusion

The oldest, and still the most widespread, form of ethics divides the world into "Us and Them," into those who are entitled to the protections and benefits of society and those who are not. Exclusionists draw a circle around "Us," and say, "The only people who matter are those inside this circle, and the well-being of outsiders may be—indeed, ought to be—sacrificed for their benefit."

This is exclusionary ethics in its most elementary form. In its more sophisticated (and more frequently encountered) formulations, we find it broken out into two categories: one that we might picture as horizontal, the other vertical. The first draws a series of concentric circles around an inner core that includes oneself and says, "Only those who inhabit the innermost circle are entitled to full protection and benefit; and as we move outward, the inhabitants of each successive ring are entitled to progressively less." This concentric circle approach to ethics is neatly captured in the ancient Bedouin saying, "I against my brother; my brothers and I against my cousins; my cousins and I against the strangers" (n.d.).

Vertical exclusionary ethics are hierarchical, rather than concentric. Instead of assessing moral value on the basis of closeness to oneself, they equate moral value with status and power in society. Vertical exclusionary ethics create a moral hierarchy identical to an economic, social, and/or political hierarchy—most often the actually existing order, but sometimes an idealized hierarchy that incorporates changes the authors wish to bring about in the social order. In the first instance, the existing social order is endowed with moral value; while in the second, moral values shape the desired social order.

In either case, those who occupy the highest level of the hierarchy are seen as most deserving. At these rarified heights, they enjoy the fullest measure of society's protections and benefits. As we descend the hierarchy, we find that the inhabitants of each level enjoy fewer protections and benefits than their neighbors in the next higher level and are expected to serve the interests of those above them.

Western philosophy's most famous example of a vertical ethical system is that of Aristotle (n.d.). Alexander the Great's tutor recognized a moral hierarchy that mimicked the actual social order in ancient Greece. Plants existed for the benefit of humans and nonhuman animals; nonhuman animals existed for the benefit of humans and/or other nonhuman animals (Aristotle, I: 8); "barbarians" existed for the benefit of Greeks; slaves existed for the benefit of free men and women (Aristotle, I: 2; III: 6); women existed for the benefit of men (Aristotle, I:12; I:13); and so on up the ladder.

Although Aristotle never explicitly assigned individuals with disabilities to a specific location in his moral hierarchy, Wilson (2006) has noted that in the *Nicomachean Ethics*, Aristotle argued that virtue resided in the normal, and vice in the abnormal. "Thus, physical 'deformity' becomes moral flaw, exposing Aristotle's binary configuration for what it really is—a social hierarchy" (p. 74).

Under the exclusionary ethical systems that prevailed throughout the ancient world, individuals with disabilities occupied an ambiguous and precarious position in society, in large part because there was no sense that the society as a whole had any obligation to maintain the welfare of individuals. In times of widespread calamity, like drought or famine, the government would typically step in to the extent that it had the resources to do so, and in some ancient cities—most notably Rome—government officials might pass out free or highly subsidized grain to the poor in order to forestall rioting and revolution or to advance their own political careers. But in most places and times this was the extent of social welfare programs. With only the rarest of exceptions, there was no "social safety net" in the ancient world.

In the Greco-Roman world, babies born with physical abnormalities were commonly "exposed"—taken to a designated spot in or near the city (or, in rural areas, simply taken into the woods) and left to die of thirst, hunger, predation, and the elements. (Newborns were also exposed for reasons other than disability. Girls were often exposed because of their gender, and poor families might expose babies because they could not afford to raise them.)

Due to the primitive state of medical knowledge, children with physical disabilities who were not exposed often died before they grew up. Boys who did reach maturity, but whose disability prevented them from earning a living, were dependent on their families to support them, something few families could do. The instances of ancients with disabilities who made their mark in the world—such as Alexander the Great and Julius Caesar (epilepsy); the Roman emperor Claudius (probably cerebral palsy); and Kautilya, prime minister to the Indian Emperor, Chandragupta Maurya (possibly birth injuries caused by a postmortem Caesarian section)—are exceptions to the rule made possible only because their families were wealthy and powerful. If their families could not support them, and there was no private charity consistently available (which was most often the case), men with disabilities were forced to beg for their food. Crippled, blind, deaf, chronically ill, or mentally ill, beggars were a common sight in ancient cities and towns and along the sides of well-travelled roads.

For women, the situation was worse yet, since the economic well-being of almost all women in the ancient world was dependent upon male relatives: most often fathers, husbands, brothers, and uncles. If her disability made a woman "unmarriageable," and her family was either unable or unwilling to support her, she had few options. The work that was considered "suitable" for women was mostly performed by slaves rather than paid workers, although a woman who could spin or weave could often earn a meager living, and a woman who had the ability to tell fortunes or cast spells could also get by, at the cost of being a social outcast. Begging was generally considered even more shameful for women than men, but there were women beggars.

Romans had particularly cruel tastes in entertainment. Individuals with physical abnormalities—who were called *monstra* in Latin (singular, *monstrum*), a word that meant precisely what it sounds like—were sometimes sold into slavery for the wealthy to display at banquets for the amusement of their guests.

Exacerbating this already grim situation was the fact that disability was widely considered a punishment by God (or the gods) for some sin committed by either the person with the disability or that person's parents. And so, even people with compassionate proclivities might be reluctant to help the disabled, for fear of incurring guilt and bringing misfortune on themselves by interfering in the working of the divine will—although, somewhat paradoxically, giving alms to beggars, including beggars with disabilities, was generally considered virtuous.

The best-known example of a moral hierarchy based on an ideal, rather than an actually existing, social order is Marxism. Marxism upends the existing order by placing the proletariat at the top of the moral hierarchy, entitled to the full benefits and protections of society. Various categories of the bourgeoisie and other "social parasites" are arranged beneath the working class. (It is important to note here that Marxist theory regards its proletariat-dominated hierarchy as a temporary expedient, an instrument to be employed in creating an egalitarian society based on the ethics of inclusion.) Thus "the dictatorship of the proletariat" (Marx, Part IV, 1875, n.d.) is to be a transitional phase between a society based on exclusionary ethics—bourgeois-capitalist society—and an egalitarian society based on inclusionary ethics—the genuinely communist society that would emerge from the "withering away of the state." (Engels, Part III, 1880, n.d.). (The German phrase, *Der Staat stirbt ab*, is rendered more literally as "The state will die out." But "wither away" has been standard for over a century.) In the Soviet empire, what actually occurred was not the withering away of the state, but its ossification, the establishment of a conservative, hierarchical society with the *nomenklatura* permanently enthroned at its highest level.

Exclusionary ethical systems are the earliest systems that we know. They are so ancient that their beginnings are lost in the opaque depths of prehistory. It seems likely that their origins are to be found deep in our evolutionary past and that we had been living by them in one form or another for millions of years before we began strutting around on our hind legs and thinking we were better than everyone else. The pecking order of chickens and the pack structure of canids, for example, in which the social order depends on the creation and maintenance of a complex hierarchy, would appear to be early (although quite sophisticated) instances of vertical ethical systems (Barber, 1993; Bekoff & Pierce, 2009; Peterson, 2011). By the same token, chimpanzees form kinship communities that stake out territories and go to war against neighboring communities, evidencing a form of horizontal ethics (Peterson, 2011).

By contrast, inclusionary ethical systems have a visible and comparatively recent origin. They date back no more than three thousand years, to the most creative period in human history.

When Ethics Burst Its Bounds: The Ethics of Universal Inclusion

Gore Vidal wrote a novel about this era, which he called *Creation* (2002). Karen Armstrong wrote a history of it, which she called *The Great Transformation* (2007). Karl Jaspers (1953), who first recognized its importance, named it *das Achsenzeitalter*, "the pivotal era" (p. 153), the time when our understanding of humanity's place in the world swung about, as if rotating on an axis 180°, and began moving in an altogether new direction. In English, we call it the Axial Age.

This unique period in history, which lasted roughly from 800–200 BCE, saw the appearance of remarkable thinkers and teachers: Confucius (551–479 BCE) and his older contemporary, LaoZi (dates are uncertain, and current estimates range from 600–200 BCE) in China; Mahavira (599–527 BCE); the Buddha (566–486 BCE) and the anonymous sixth- and fifth-century Hindu sages who created the Upanishads and the Bhagavad-Gita in India; Zoroaster in Persia (*fl.* *c.*588 BCE); Judaism's Latter Prophets (*fl. c.*750–*c.*400 BCE); and Pythagoras (*fl.* *c.*530 BCE), Socrates (469–399 BCE), Plato (428–348 BCE), Aristotle (384–322 BCE), and others in Greece. The most visionary among these teachers brought about the most radical revolution in ethical thought that the world has ever undergone. They rejected exclusionary ethics and created, in its place, the ethics of universal inclusion.

Before the Axial Age, exclusionary ethics, both horizontal and vertical, reigned unchallenged. Not because human nature was different in those days; it was not. Human nature has not changed, either for better or worse, during the entire span of recorded history. We are the same shifting, unstable amalgam of selfishness and altruism, love and hate, rage and forgiveness, hope and fear that we have always been, with the same potential for both good and evil that we have always possessed. Empathy and compassion, the qualities on which the ethics of inclusion are based, were present in the world as individual traits, just as they are now. What has changed are the intellectual and social systems within which we have to function. Before the Axial Age, these systems were almost wholly shaped either by tribalism (horizontal exclusionary ethics), elitism (vertical exclusionary ethics), or some combination of the two. Horizontal and vertical ethics are not mutually exclusive; a group, up to and including an entire society, can practice a horizontal ethic toward their neighbors, for example, while maintaining a vertical ethic within the group. Prior to the Axial Age, empathy and compassion outside the boundaries of the exclusionary ethical system received little, if any, support from religion, law, or custom. Instead, they were viewed as weakness and vulnerability. They were dangerous, and those who indulged in these traits put themselves, their families, and their societies at risk.

The Infinite Ethic

Rather than base ethics on the closeness of family and tribal connections or on an existing or idealized social hierarchy, the greatest sages of the Axial Age—Mahavira, the Buddha, the authors of the Upanishads, the Latter Prophets, and Pythagoras—based their ethics on something far more fundamental: individual consciousness. These revolutionary teachers created an ethic that recognized no moral distance among individuals and held group identity to be morally insignificant. They observed that good and evil were entirely functions of life and death, happiness and suffering. That is to say, they experienced their own continued lives as good, and their deaths as evil, their own happiness as good, and their suffering as evil. They experienced this as an integral part of their own consciousness, inseparable temporally, epistemologically, and ontologically from the raw, unmediated experience itself.

From this they concluded that all conscious beings experienced good and evil with the same immediacy and intensity that they did. Therefore, they concluded, since every conscious being's life and death, happiness and suffering were equally urgent to the being experiencing it, there could be no justification for assigning any conscious being greater or lesser moral value than any other conscious being.

In reaching this conclusion, the sages of the Axial Age arrived at an infinite ethic in place of the finite ethics that had prevailed until then. Infinity has two primary characteristics. First, it has no boundaries. And second, it has no center point, because every point within infinity has an equal claim to being its center. Likewise, the inclusionary ethic of the Axial Age had no boundaries because it excluded no conscious being from the fullness of its protection. And every conscious being was its moral center.

Furthermore, within infinity, no point can be considered higher or lower than any other point. Nothing is closer to the top or bottom than anything else, because *there is no top or bottom. In their fundamental character, infinite ethics, like infinity itself, are absolutely egalitarian.*

The great sages of the Axial Age who created infinite ethics were not academic philosophers; they were practical, down-to-earth teachers who taught in specifics. When asked, the Buddha explicitly declined to enter the realm of theory on the grounds that theory was a useless waste of time. Like Mahavira, the authors of the Upanishads, Pythagoras, and the Latter Prophets, the Buddha taught nothing that was not based upon his personal experience. Even his ontology, known as "interdependent origination," which has been the subject of much metaphysical speculation since his death, was a description of specific, concrete meditational experiences. Hence, we have to extrapolate the Axial Age's radical ethical theory from the specific precepts of its teachers. A few examples will serve to illustrate.

Mahavira, the Buddha, and their contemporary, the radical Hindu teacher Makkhali Gosala, rejected India's caste system outright in favor of universal social and spiritual equality, as at least some of the authors of the Upanishads also seem to have done, thus rejecting the vertical ethic that dominated Hindu society. Some introductory verses of the Axial Age poem, *Bhagavad Gita*, defend the caste system, but these would seem to have originally been part of the ancient Hindu epic, *Mahabbharata*, in which the Gita was later embedded, rather than a part of the original Gita. (*Mahabbharata* is an amalgam of archaic material dating back as far as 1500 BCE and more recent material; it was not edited into its final form until late in the Axial Age.)

The Latter Prophets attacked the vertical ethic of ancient Israel and Judah by denouncing the unholy alliance between the royal court and the wealthy priests who controlled the Jerusalem Temple. The prophets' condemnations of this power elite were so pointed, that "prophetic religion" has come to mean calling the powerful to account for their abuses in language that owes everything to truth and clarity and nothing to politeness. Most notable were their attacks on the political and religious establishment for using their position to expropriate the meager property of widows and orphans, who, in a rigidly patriarchal society, were among the most vulnerable members of the community.

When the Latter Prophets spoke of disabilities, it was to use them as metaphors for moral failings or foolish government policies. Kings who failed to foresee a coming foreign invasion, for example, were "blind." This led Schipper (n.d.) to observe that, "Such passages may tell us what a particular prophet thought about how the Israelites conducted themselves. They tell us very little, however, about the actual living conditions or everyday experiences of disabled people in ancient Israel (although it may indicate that the disabled suffered a social stigma)."

Breaking Down the Species Barrier

If individuals with disabilities have been consigned to the lower levels of the social and moral hierarchy throughout history, the lowest level has always been reserved for nonhuman animals. Among the pioneers of the Axial Age, Lord Mahavira, the Buddha, the Hindu sages, the Latter Prophets, and Pythagoras made their new ethic truly infinite by including all conscious beings, regardless of species. In the *Akaranga Sutra*, a primary Jain scripture, Lord Mahavira instructed that, "All sorts of living beings should not be slain, nor treated with violence, nor abused, nor tormented, nor driven away" (*Akaranga Sutra*, I: 4: 2: 4).

In *The Dhammapada* (1973), the most widely known and beloved scripture in the Buddhist canon, the Buddha said, "All beings tremble before danger; all fear death. When a man considers this, he does not kill or cause others to kill. All beings fear before danger; life is dear to all. When a man considers this, he does not kill or cause others to kill" (pp. 129–131). The *Thirukural* (n.d.), a scripture somewhat more recent than the Axial Age, but firmly in the tradition of Axial Age Hinduism, tells us that, "When a man realizes that meat is the butchered flesh of another creature, he must abstain from eating it," or, expressed more poetically: "From eating flesh men must abstain / If they but feel the being's pain" (verse 257).

Although we have no actual teachings of Pythagoras in the form that he gave them, he was credited in the classical world with condemning animal sacrifice and meat eating out of compassion for the suffering of animals and concern that the animals one slaughtered might be reincarnated family members or friends. The Roman poet, Ovid, calling Pythagoras "the first to ban the serving of animal food at our tables," put the following words into his mouth, which undoubtedly reflect the substance of his teaching about meat as preserved by the religious order that he had founded, "The earth offers a lavish supply ... of innocent foods .... What wickedness ... to have one living creature fed by the death of another" (Ovid, 1955, Bk. XV). Pythagoras's views regarding individuals with disabilities are not known.

The Latter Prophets are not reported to have spoken explicitly on the subject of meat eating, but several of them condemned animal sacrifice. Since Jews of this period were only allowed to eat meat so long as sacrifice continued at the Temple, condemnations of sacrifice were implicit condemnations of meat eating (Phelps, 2002, p. 94).

Among the Latter Prophets, for example, Isaiah not only condemned sacrifice, he denied that God had ever commanded it. These are God's words as reported by the prophet:

> I take no pleasure in the blood of bulls, lambs or goats. When you come to appear before Me [in the Temple], Who requires of you this trampling of My courts? ... So when you spread out your hands in prayer, I will hide My eyes from you; Yes, even though you multiply prayers, I will not listen. Your hands are covered with blood. (*New American Standard Bible* (NASB), Isaiah 1: 11–12, 15)

Other prophetic condemnations of sacrifice are found in Isaiah 66: 3–4, Jeremiah 7: 21–23,[1] Hosea 6: 6, Amos 5: 21–25, and Micah 6: 6–8.

Tragically, the infinite ethic of the great Axial Age sages has never been implemented in any society anywhere. In India, the Buddhist king, Ashoka (reigned *c.* 269–232 BCE), made a valiant effort to create a society organized around an infinite ethic, issuing prohibitions against the killing of animals for any reason except self-defense, and orders for the establishment of a network of hospitals where both human and nonhuman animals could receive free health care (Phelps, 2004; Rich, 2010). Little is known about these hospitals beyond the fact that they were chartered and funded by the government and that they brought health care to those who had the most need of it and the least opportunity to receive it—nonhuman animals and poor human beings, including those with disabilities. Quite possibly, they were co-located with Jain and Buddhist monasteries and run by renunciates, but be that as it may, these facilities are the only functioning legacy that has survived of Ashoka's effort to govern his empire according to the infinite ethic; such hospitals still exist in India, maintained by Jain communities.

Apart from the hospitals, Ashoka's reforms were scrapped shortly after his death, and things reverted to "normal." The ideal remained alive in the ancient world, however, and became deeply engrained in Jainism, Buddhism, Hinduism, and Judaism. The Pythagorean ethic hung on in the Hellenic, Hellenistic, and Roman worlds as the teaching of a tiny religious sect—albeit a teaching that influenced such mainstream thinkers as Plutarch and Plotinus—until the fourth century when Christianity became the state religion of the Roman Empire and systematically eradicated all competing schools of thought.

Given this latter circumstance, it is ironic that the teachings of Jesus of Nazareth, on which the Christian church claims to be founded (although that claim is vulnerable to rebuttal on a number of fronts), are the primary form in which the infinite ethic of the Axial Age was preserved and transmitted in the West. Jesus was not—as he is often portrayed, even by non-Christians—a particularly original ethical thinker although he was certainly a charismatic personality and a teacher of considerable insight and power. Jesus was the inheritor, through his mentor John the Baptist, of the infinite ethic of the Latter Prophets, whose teachings had remained alive as a minority tradition within Judaism, whose adherents referred to themselves variously as *ha-ebionim* ("the Poor") and "The New Covenant." (This minority tradition also profoundly influenced the school of Hillel the Great within Pharisaic Judaism, and hence, modern Judaism.) Jesus's remarkable ability to capture profound principles in deceptively simple sayings is perhaps best exemplified in his one-sentence statement of the infinite ethic: "Do unto others as you would have them do unto you." That is the infinite ethic in a nutshell.

Despite the clear instruction of Jesus, Christian Europe did not even make a serious attempt to create a society governed by the Golden Rule. Instead, Christian Europe paid lip service to the infinite ethic while organizing society along strictly hierarchical lines and defending this bizarre arrangement with an oxymoronic blend of Christian theology and Greek philosophy. Jesus and the infinite ethic were lost in the shuffle.

The Enlightenment

Finally, around the 18th century, a group of thinkers in Europe, primarily France, Germany, England, and Scotland, looked around and realized that the infinite ethic was as far from being made a reality as it had ever been. Despite centuries of pious preaching, the Word was no nearer being made Flesh than when Jesus had enunciated the Golden Rule. The many who were poor still lived and died in hopeless misery. Widows and orphans were as destitute as they had been in the days of the Latter Prophets, while individuals with disabilities were still relegated to the lower margins of society. The few who were rich still hoarded their riches; and the few who were powerful still hoarded their power. And the coercive instruments of society—from the churches to the armies—still defended the rich against the poor and the powerful against the weak, while placing only the mildest of restraints upon their selfish and callous exploitation of the less fortunate. Nonhuman animals, of course, remained at the bottom of the social and moral hierarchy—where they had been all along.

Reliance on individual conscience and personal goodwill had utterly failed to create a society governed by the infinite ethic. And so these European thinkers of the era that has come to be known as the Enlightenment cast about for some other way to assure that the rich treated the poor and the powerful treated the weak at least in some rough measure according to the Golden Rule. The greatest accomplishment of the Enlightenment was not, as is often claimed, the supremacy of reason and the birth of the scientific method. It was the creation of political principles and institutions that would enable the state to enforce the Golden Rule—principles like government by the consent of the governed, equality before the law, and the supremacy of the rule of laws to which even the rulers are subject. The institutions they advocated (some of which had made their first, tentative appearances earlier as progressions of English common law) included universal (or at least greatly expanded) suffrage, parliamentary democracy, trial by a jury of one's peers, and *habeas corpus*. The Enlightenment was the greatest step toward the realization of the infinite ethic since the sages of the Axial Age created it.

Although the Enlightenment articulated the fundamental ethical principles on which the modern animal liberation movement would eventually be founded (utilitarianism, deontology, contractarianism, etc.), Enlightenment thinkers applied these principles only to the *treatment* of nonhuman animals and not to their *use*. They argued that nonhuman animals could be enslaved and even slaughtered for human benefit but that they should be spared any suffering that was not intrinsic to their use (Phelps, 2007). In other words, although they laid the philosophical groundwork for animal rights, they actually taught and practiced animal welfare, arguing that since animals have no understanding of death and no sense of the future, killing them painlessly does not harm them (Bentham, 1789/1948).

Inclusive Ethics in the Modern World

Since the Enlightenment, the approach to implementing the infinite ethic has generally been to hold it out as an ideal to be attained in some indefinite future era, while taking small, incremental steps in the here and now to shorten the moral distance between the highest and the lowest and reduce the number of concentric circles by including more and more groups within the innermost core. Historically, this has not been a consistent process, and progress has been achieved only in a zigzag manner. Sometimes it looks like two steps forward and one step back, while at other times it looks more like one step forward and two steps back. In the United States, for example, the era of the New Deal was a period of rapid, incremental progress toward the infinite ethic, as were the Civil Rights era and Lyndon Johnson's Great Society. For the last three decades we have been living in an age of resurgence for the old hierarchical ethic, ushered in by the election of Ronald Reagan, an age that has witnessed the progressive dismantling of the incremental steps that had been taken during the Great Society, the Civil Rights Era, and the New Deal. Watching the social and economic regression that characterizes the Reagan-Bush era is like watching a film of the social and economic progress of the Roosevelt-Johnson era being run through the projector backwards. Like advocates for African Americans, women, and Lesbian Gay Bisexual Transgendered (LGBT) people, advocates for animals and individuals with disabilities have found themselves scrambling just to hold onto gains made earlier as the country's political and financial leadership act to reimpose the old, hierarchical structure.

Conservatism is the modern political and economic form of the ancient hierarchical ethic. It is the enemy of the infinite ethic, as testified to by the popular conservative motto, "Equal opportunities, not equal outcomes." The practice of the infinite ethic is the pursuit of equal outcomes. This principle is reflected in the motto of the earliest followers of Jesus, "From each according to his abilities and to each according to his needs" (see, for example, Acts 2: 44–45, 4: 32–35), a principle appropriated in 1839 by French socialist, Louis Blanc, in his seminal work, *The Organization of Labor*, and, more famously, in 1875 by Karl Marx in his *Critique of the Gotha Programme*. This motto describes the societal application of the infinite ethic, just as the Golden Rule describes its individual application.

The Infinite Ethic: Individuality Versus Group Identity

There are several traits of the infinite ethic that should be emphasized: First, the infinite ethic is based upon consciousness—specifically, the experience of happiness and suffering, and the love of life and dread of death—and the locus of consciousness is the individual. Therefore, the concern of the infinite ethic is the individual, not the collective. Strategically, for reasons usually having to do with focusing public awareness and marshaling the political will to act, it is often advantageous to conduct single-issue campaigns on behalf of specific identity groups, but we should never lose sight of the fact that morally (as opposed to strategically), groups and group identity are meaningless. Membership in a race, gender, nationality, species, or other identity group does not affect moral standing, neither positively or negatively.

Second, since consciousness is entirely subjective, there can be no "objective" scale of sentience according to which the level of consciousness of one individual can be compared to that of another. A being's consciousness is her whole life. It is all she has, the totality of her existence. It is her universe entire and complete.

The suffering of a lobster in a tank is as urgent to the lobster as the suffering of a chicken in a battery cage is to the chicken; while the suffering of the battery hen is as urgent to her as the sufferings of Martin Niemoeller, Nelson Mandela, and Aung San Suu Kyi were to them. The fact that human beings may (or may not, we really do not know) have a wider scope of consciousness, or a more complex and intellectualized form of consciousness than lobsters, is of no ethical significance, because *the urgency of the suffering, and the urgency of the love of life to the being actually experiencing them, are the only factors that are morally relevant.* To quote Barley Scott Blair in Tom Stoppard's screenplay of John le Carré's *The Russia House*, "All victims are equal, and none is more equal than others" (le Carré, 1989, as cited in Maslansky & Schepisi, 1990).

Third, the infinite ethic is to be practiced by individuals, organizations, businesses, institutions, governments, and entire societies. As I noted earlier, its individual formulation is, "Do unto others as you would have them do unto you," and its group, governmental, and societal formulation is, "From each according to his abilities, to each according to his needs." In this regard, *governments must protect and nurture all conscious beings who live within the ambit of their power, not merely those who wield power.*

Fourth, beings that are not conscious—plants and minerals—are aware of nothing and, therefore, experience neither suffering nor the fear of death. They can and should be treated as resources for conscious beings. We need to protect the environment, not for its own sake—because it has no sake—but for the sake of all of the conscious beings who depend upon it. The Earth is as essential to the maintenance of our consciousness as our own bodies are. Every conscious being, which is to say, every locus of moral value, exists only because our planet sustains us. It is for this reason that we have an urgent moral obligation to preserve and protect the Earth as a functioning system. To put it in Kantian language, we have direct moral duties to every sentient being and only to sentient beings. Our duties to the insentient environment are indirect duties only—and their focus is species and systems rather than individuals—*but they are absolute duties nonetheless.*

Fifth, the infinite ethic does not distinguish between positive and negative obligations. As the anonymous saying widely, but wrongly, attributed to St. Francis of Assisi expresses it: "Not to harm our fellow creatures is our first duty to them. But to stop there is not enough. We must be of service to them whenever they are in need." If I see a blind man having trouble crossing a busy street, it is not enough for me to refrain from pushing him under a bus. If I am sighted and able to walk steadily, I must help him cross the street safely.

On the societal level, the government, as the instrument of the society's will, must not simply refrain from actively and directly disadvantaging any individual or class, it must actively provide assistance to everyone who is disadvantaged, and the cost must be distributed equitably across the society through a system of progressive taxation: "From each according to his abilities, to each according to his needs." Government must create programs to lift the poor out of poverty—and not relent until those programs are successful. It must make comprehensive, state-of-the-art health care easily available to everyone, urban and rural, rich and poor, while paying special attention to the needs of all who need special attention. Thus, a society organized according to the infinite ethic does not treat everyone identically. Identical treatment gives a comforting illusion of fairness while promoting starkly unequal outcomes. Other things being equal, a blind person who is treated identically to a sighted person and provided no adaptive assistance will be unable to match the achievements of a sighted person. The infinite ethic treats everyone in such a way as to achieve, as nearly as possible, equal outcomes.

Hierarchical societies are organized for the convenience of those with power. In regard to physical and mental prowess, this means they are organized to meet the needs and accommodate the abilities of persons who have the range of physical and mental characteristics that are typical of human beings. Thus, human societies organized according to vertical ethics are structured for the convenience of people who can walk, who can see, who can absorb and utilize an education, who can interact with others in accordance with patterns of behavior that are common to most people in the society, and so on. Thus, *disabled* is a comparative, rather than an absolute term. It refers to individuals who lack a physical or mental ability that human beings typically possess (sometimes known as the "medical" aspect of disability), when and only when that ability is important for success in the society (sometimes known as the "socially constructed" aspect of disability), or for satisfying what is generally considered a major life function. Humans who cannot walk unaided, for example, are considered disabled, while humans who cannot flap their arms and fly are not. Humans who cannot hear are considered disabled, while humans who cannot curl their tongues are not. Men who are sexually impotent are considered disabled today, because our society considers sex to be an important life function, although in societies that are less driven by sexuality than ours, impotence might not be considered a disability.

Persons with disabilities (i.e., persons who lack a physical or mental ability that is typical of adult human beings and is important for success in the society) cannot achieve outcomes equal to those that can be achieved by persons without disabilities unless the society attacks both the medical and the socially constructed aspects of disability. That is to say, society must assure that persons with physical, intellectual, and emotional disabilities receive the best treatment available while adequately funding research to prevent, ameliorate, and, if possible, cure the condition from which they suffer. But at the same time, the society must work energetically to tear down the socially imposed barriers that impede their full enjoyment of the protections and benefits of the society. This would encompass both changes to the physical environment (wheelchair accessibility, traffic signals that are audible as well as visible, to cite just two simple examples) and to the social environment (an end to discrimination in employment, public education, awareness campaigns to break down old patterns of prejudice, and so on). It is this focus on equality of outcome (insofar as this is possible in a structurally imperfect world), as opposed to equality of treatment or equality of opportunity, that distinguishes a society organized according to the infinite ethic.

Although there are certain relevant similarities between individuals with disabilities and nonhuman animals (both have physical and/or mental characteristics that interfere with their ability to fully participate in the life of human society), it would be misleading to conceptualize nonhuman animals as if they were human individuals with disabilities. While both have been victimized throughout history by being relegated to the lowest levels of hierarchical ethical systems, the antidote to this for nonhuman animals is radically different from the solution for humans with disabilities. The latter need medical and social interventions to empower them to participate more fully and comfortably in the life of human society.

But nonhuman animals need just the opposite. They are not suited by nature to participate in human society, any more than humans are suited to participate in canid or avian societies. Left to their own devices, nonhuman animals organize their own societies quite skillfully. These societies—which, in our ignorance of their workings, we dismiss with terms like "flocks," "herds," "packs," and "schools"—are sophisticated responses to their needs and natures, just as human societies are responses to human needs and human nature. It is in their own societies that nonhuman animals, like their human cousins, can lead the most fulfilled and satisfying lives, simply because these societies are suited to the imperatives of their being. Thus, while human individuals with disabilities need for human society to adapt itself to their range of abilities, nonhuman animals need to be left alone by human society.

There are, however, at least two exceptions to this general rule. First, individual nonhuman animals who have disabilities by the standards of what is necessary for members of their species to survive and participate in the lives of their communities (birds who have been injured and cannot fly, for example), are the most desperate of the desperate. Left alone, they will die. If we can help them, either through rehabilitative care or by giving them permanent homes when this is necessary, the infinite ethic calls upon us to do so.

Companion animals are the second exception. We have bred into them an unnatural dependency on us, and in so doing assumed an obligation for their well-being. Thus, we have a duty to integrate them into our families and our society in ways that look to the satisfaction of *their* needs and the fulfillment of *their* natures as much as our own. A starting point here would be a permanent ban on all breeding and—for as long as there are animals being killed in our "shelters"—the sterilization of all companion animals. These simple steps would, in and of themselves, end a system that commodifies sentient beings and put in its place a system that treats them as genuine companions.

Once again, a direct comparison between nonhuman animals and human individuals with disabilities would be misleading. The forced sterilization of human beings with disabilities violates their rights, and is not necessary in order to prevent a greater harm. The forced sterilization of dogs and cats also violates their rights but is justified, even required, on consequentialist grounds, to prevent a greater harm *to dogs and cats* (although not necessarily the same individuals). The best estimate is that four million healthy, "adoptable" dogs and cats are put to death every year in shelters simply because no homes are found for them (The Humane Society, 2012). This unconscionable mass killing will not end as long as breeders and puppy mills are offering millions of animals for sale every year. Albert Schweitzer noted that practicing the infinite ethic sometimes requires us to commit a lesser harm for a greater good (Phelps, 2009). This is such an instance.

It goes without saying (but I will say it anyway) that the infinite ethic would not countenance the breeding, enslaving, and slaughtering of animals for food, fiber, scientific knowledge, and other human purposes. To paraphrase Friedrich Engels, as the demand for meat, eggs, and dairy dwindles under the influence of the infinite ethic, our herds and flocks of farmed animals should be allowed to simply "wither away." Some, no doubt, will escape or be released into the wild, where they will form their own societies and live as their ancestors did. In the southeastern United States, there are already populations of wild pigs descended from domesticated pigs who escaped from farms.

Finally, the infinite ethic is not a single, precisely defined system like utilitarianism or social contract theory. It is an orientation toward ethics that allows for the existence of differing theories and strategies. The five most influential proponents of infinite ethics in the modern world—Henry Salt, Mohandas Gandhi, Leo Tolstoy, Albert Schweitzer, and Donald Watson—all approached the infinite ethic in different ways and pursued different strategies as they tried to bring it to reality in the world. There is room for difference of opinion and debate—even robust debate—within the context of the infinite ethic.

Seen from afar (our present perspective), a society governed by the infinite ethic appears as an indivisible monad bound together by its unifying ethical principle. But as we approach it, this society will reveal itself to be a mosaic composed of many small pieces, all of which must be made to fit together in a precise order. Carving and sanding the pieces and fitting them into a coherent whole will prove to be a complex and difficult undertaking, requiring humility, perseverance, open-mindedness, and patience with ourselves and with one another.

As a corollary to this, we must not expect even the most insightful advocates to grasp all of the practical implications of the infinite ethic. The prejudices that we absorb from our families and societies, and the insidious inroads that our own appetites can make upon our principles—often without us even being aware of their presence—can create moral blind spots in the best of us. Jesus regarded gentiles as inferior to Jews (Mark 7: 25–30; Matthew 15: 22–28), and some aspects of Albert Schweitzer's attitude toward Africans can most kindly be described as paternalistic (Phelps, 2009). We must not turn a blind eye to these personal failings. But neither should we allow them to discredit the vision that these great teachers articulated. The infinite ethic first conceived by the spiritual pioneers of the Axial Age remains the best hope for humanity, nonhuman animals, and the planet on which we all depend. Human fulfillment, animal liberation, and environmental regeneration are all contained within the single enterprise of erasing the boundaries that create moral distance between us, so that the infinite ethic may flourish in its place.

Note

1. The first sentence of this passage, "Add your burnt offerings to your sacrifices and eat flesh," may give the superficial appearance of commanding animal sacrifice and meat eating. In fact, however, it does the opposite. God is using irony to express contempt for animal sacrifice and flesh eating. As Samuel Sandmel (1911–1979) of Hebrew Union College, one of the twentieth century's premier authorities on Biblical Judaism, puts it, "Jeremiah . . . represents Yahve [God] as speaking in a sarcastic vein.," (136).

References

Akaranga Sutra. (n.d.). *The Internet Sacred Text Archive*. Retrieved from www.sacred-texts.com/jai/akaranga.htm

Aristotle. (n.d.). *Politics* (B. Jowett, Trans.). Retrieved from http://classics.mit.edu/Aristotle/politics.html

Armstrong, K. (2007). *The great transformation: The beginning of our religious traditions*. New York, NY: Anchor Books.

Barber, T. X. (1993). *The human nature of birds: A scientific discovery with startling implications*. New York, NY: St. Martin's Press.

Bedouin. (n.d.). Retrieved from http://wikipedia.org/wiki/Bedouin

Bekoff, M., & Pierce, J. (2009). *Wild justice: The moral lives of animals*. Chicago, IL: University of Chicago Press.

Bentham, J. (1948). *An introduction to the principles of morals and legislation*. New York, NY: Hafner.

The Dhammapada: The path of perfection (J. Mascaro, Trans.). (1973). London, UK: Penguin.

Engels, F. (n.d.). *Socialism: Utopian and scientific*. (original work published 1880). Retrieved from http://www.marxists.org/archive/marx/works/1880/soc-utop/index.htm and http://www.marxists.org/archive/marx/works/1880/soc-utop/ch03.htm

The Humane Society of the United States. (2012). *Pet overpopulation*. Retrieved from www.humanesociety.org/issues/pet_overpopulation/

Jaspers, K. (1953). *The origin and goal of history*. New Haven, CT: Yale University Press.

Marx, K. (n.d.). *Critique of the Gotha programme*. Retrieved from www.marxists.org/archive/marx/works/1875/gotha/ch04.htm

Maslansky, P. (Producer), & Schepisi, F. (Producer/Director). (1990). *The Russia house* [Motion picture]. United States: Pathé Entertainment.

New American standard Bible (NASB). (1995). La Habra, CA: The Lockman Foundation.

Ovid. (1955). *The metamorphoses of Ovid* (M. M. Innes, Trans.). London, UK: Penguin.

Peterson, D. (2011). *The moral lives of animals*. New York, NY: Bloomsbury Press.

Phelps, N. (2009). The quest for a boundless ethic: A reassessment of Albert Schweitzer. *Journal of Critical Animal Studies*, *VII*(I), 172–193.

Phelps, N. (2007). *The longest struggle: Animal advocacy from Pythagoras to PETA*. New York, NY: Lantern Books.

Phelps, N. (2004). *The great compassion: Buddhism and animal rights*. New York, NY: Lantern Books.

Phelps, N. (2002). *The dominion of love: Animal rights according to the Bible*. New York. NY: Lantern Books.

Rich, B. (2010). *To uphold the world: A call for a new global ethic from ancient India*. Boston, MA: Beacon Press.

Sandmel, S. (1963). *The Hebrew scriptures: An introduction to their literature and religious ideas*. New York, NY: Alfred A. Knopf.

Schipper, J. (n.d.). *Disability in the Hebrew bible*. Retrieved from http://www.sbl-site.org/assets/pdfs/TBv2i8_SchipperDisability.pdf

Thirukural (K. Y. S. Bharatiar, Trans.). (n.d.). Retrieved from www.tamilnation.org/literature/kural/E1.htm (no longer accessible), and http://www.projectmadurai.org.vt.edu/pm_etexts/tscii/pmtsc0017.html

Vidal, G. (2002). *Creation: A novel.* New York, NY: Vintage Books.

Wilson, J. C. (2006). (Re)Writing the genetic body-text: Disability, textuality, and the human genome project. In L. J. Davis (Ed.), *The disability studies reader* (2nd ed., pp. 67–75). New York, NY: Routledge.

CHAPTER FOURTEEN

Developmental Disability, Animal Oppression, and the Environment

DAVID NIBERT

An investigative report in *The New York Times Magazine* (Jones, 2008) disclosed rampant abuse of animals raised and killed to be sold as food by U.S. agribusiness and food retail corporations. The report featured the treatment of cows at the Westland/Hallmark "meat"[1] company in California, where employees had been videotaped kicking cows in the head, shocking them in their rectums with electric prods, and dragging them by their necks and legs with forklifts. Comparably, in 2011 *The New York Times* (Hakima, 2011) reported on hundreds of instances of employees at state facilities for people with developmental disabilities sexually abusing, beating, and taunting residents.

The capitalist quest for profits in the 21st century imperils the earth and the majority of its inhabitants. The most devalued groups are the most at risk—and none more so than other animals and people with developmental disabilities. Each group experiences terrible treatment throughout most of the world. Although their fates have been entangled for centuries, their oppression still is a relatively recent historical practice.

Animal Oppression and the Degeneration of Human Society

For most of the 200,000 years that *Homo sapiens* have inhabited the planet, foraging was the primary mode of production. Foraging generally produced abundant resources, and societal members were able to meet their subsistence needs while leaving time for leisure, play, and social activities. This mode of production was conducive to egalitarianism and thus was accommodating to people with milder developmental disabilities. As long as they were capable of keeping up with group movement, most such individuals survived relatively well in foraging communities (Scheerenberger, 1983). Similarly, throughout most of human history our relationship with the other animals on the planet was largely one of cohabitation, although increasingly, other animals were harmed with the start of organized hunts begun roughly 20,000 years ago (Nibert, 2002). For many millennia, the experiences of most other animals and people with developmental disabilities were qualitatively better than what they would be when human societies became more "civilized." This change began 10,000 years ago when humans in Eurasia began capturing cows, sheep, goats, horses, pigs, and other animals and raising and exploiting them as sources of food and as laborers. Their oppression made possible the development of a new mode of production—agriculture. However, "devastation came with agriculture" (Sernau, 2009, p. 332).

In comparison with the lifestyles of foragers, early agriculturalists faced hard physical labor and increased risks to their welfare. While the diets of foragers were varied and complete, agriculturalists were limited to a few crops and the flesh and milk derived from other animals—food sources constantly threatened by drought, crop failure, and parasitic infection. Moreover, the growing practice of confining animals in crowded conditions facilitated the mutation and spread of infectious, multiple-host-species microbes. These mutating pathogens not only killed countless other animals but also were deadly for humans, whose permanent settlements and increasing population density furthered the transmission of infectious diseases like smallpox and tuberculosis.

Over time, priests and warriors began to take control of surplus food and resources; egalitarianism declined, and caste-like systems of social stratification emerged (Heilbroner, 1993; Mayer, 1955). These agrarian-based economies increasingly were driven by war and conquest and by the expropriated wealth produced by people relegated to the positions of "slaves" and "peasants."

With food supplies much more precarious—and the social order routinely threatened by infectious disease and continual warfare—food shortages, malnutrition, and famine-plagued agricultural communities. Since nutritional deficiencies are one of the primary factors causally linked to the occurrence of developmental disability (see, for example, Institute of Medicine [U.S.] Committee on Nervous System Disorders in Developing Countries, 2001; Miller & Spoolman, 2009), it reasonably can be assumed that the percentage of societal members with developmental disabilities grew under agriculturalism.

In agricultural societies, systems deeply dependent on the oppression of other animals, the perceived value of these sentient beings largely was reduced to their utility in the production or expropriation of wealth. In this context, animals that could not be exploited and were a perceived threat to the accumulation of wealth were exterminated. Humans with developmental disabilities were treated similarly. In the militaristic Spartan society, for example, infants deemed unfit for the rigors of Spartan life and a drain on economic resources were thrown from cliffs to their deaths (Scheerenberger, 1983). In other societies, infants believed to be "defective" were abandoned and left to die from exposure (Macklin & Gaylin, 1981).

While many other animals and people with developmental disabilities were killed due to their lack of economic worth, some were exploited for their entertainment value. During the years of the Roman Empire, for example, masses of people were distracted from their deprivations by the spectacle of deadly combat and mass killings in the Coliseum; sometimes large numbers of exotic animals were massacred for public amusement. Increasingly, other animals were displayed in early zoos or maintained for the pleasure of elites in their personal menageries. Similarly, some people with developmental disabilities also were used to entertain. In Rome in the 4th century BCE, for example, wealthy families kept people with developmental disabilities for the amusement of their guests, and by the 2nd century viewing people with disabilities became a source of public entertainment (Evans, 1983; Scheerenberger, 1983). During the Middle Ages, a "Ship of Fools" sailed from port to port displaying its cargo to the curious (Foucault, 1965), and elites commonly kept jesters, or "fools." One 17th-century Spanish monarch, Philip IV, was reported to have maintained a sizable collection of people with disabilities (Evans, 1983), while a French dutchess had two neck irons specially made—one for a girl with a disability and one for her other "pet," a monkey (Evans, 1983). Throughout this history, the flesh of animals was disproportionately consumed by social elites, frequently produced at the expense of generating enough plant-based food for all. This practice led to periodic "grievous and unwonted famines" (Helleiner, 1967, p. 69)—and no doubt further increased the prevalence of developmental disability.

While the value of other animals and people with developmental disabilities in elite-controlled agricultural society was based on their economic worth, their oppression was legitimated by religious doctrine. For example, in the 16th century, Martin Luther took the position that people with developmental disabilities "were merely a mass of flesh" with no soul (Kanner, 1949, p. 7). Similarly, 17th-century philosopher René Descartes maintained that other animals did not possess souls and were mindless and unfeeling.

Nonetheless, people with less severe disabilities were reasonably integrated into the highly stratified agrarian society. Marie Crissey (1975) wrote: "In an almost wholly illiterate population, functioning at the simplest vocational level . . . [people with developmental disabilities . . . no doubt were indistinguishable" (p. 800).

Industrial Capitalism and Deepening Oppression

The emergence of a new economic system—capitalism—and a new mode of production, industrialization, brought additional problems for other animals and people with disabilities, due in part to the slow but steady reorganization of labor and the onset of European global imperialism. Increasingly, people who tilled the soil in Europe were displaced, as elites expropriated common lands to raise growing numbers of sheep and cows, who were exploited for profits derived from the sale of their hair, skin, and flesh. Masses of displaced people were forced to migrate to urban areas in an effort to survive by selling their labor. Marx (1867/1967) commented upon this historical process in *Capital*:

> The proletariat created by the breaking-up of the bands of feudal retainers and by the forcible expropriation of people from the soil, this free and rightless proletariat could not possibly be absorbed by the nascent manufacturers as fast as it was thrown upon the world. On the other hand, these men, suddenly dragged from their accustomed mode of life, could not immediately adapt themselves to the discipline of their new condition. They were turned in massive quantities into beggars, robbers and vagabonds, partly from inclination, in most cases under the force of circumstances. (p. 896)

While many persons with developmental disabilities could assist in providing for a "peasant" household, their ability to contribute economically lessened as more were forced into the ranks of the urban proletariat. The emergence of a disenfranchised and destitute population in the developing cities led to efforts to isolate the varieties of urban "deviants" in prisons, almshouses, and asylums (Crissey & Rosen, 1986). The incarceration of people with developmental and other forms of disabilities created new opportunities for exhibition and profit-making. For instance, a popular amusement destination in London was one of the first "lunatic asylums" in Europe, the Bethlehem Royal Hospital, popularly known as Bedlam. Evans (1983) noted:

> In Bethlehem (Bedlam), "idiots" and "lunatics" were exhibited for the price of about a penny every Sunday. The annual revenue for these shows at Bethlehem in 1815 was £400, indicating an audience of approximately 96,000 people that year. The visitors' curiosity was evoked, in part, by certain attendants who were particularly adept at getting the inmates to perform dances and acrobatics with a few flicks of the whip. (p. 37)

There were some efforts to train people with developmental disabilities in the mid-19th century, to make them "obedient and productive" (see, for example,

Trent, 1994, Chapter One, "Idiots in America"). However, they remained largely marginalized and devalued, even by some professed advocates—one of whom described people with disabilities as "passionate, filthy...and animal-like" (Trent, 1994, 17). Other animals were at the bottom of a hegemonically created hierarchy of worth from which other oppressed and devalued groups were ranked. Their disparagement and objectification legitimated the expanding practice of vivisection as well as their use as laborers, instruments of warfare and rations as Britain, France, the Netherlands, Germany, Spain, and the United States pursued imperialist practices globally. Countless indigenous people and other animals were displaced or killed and their land expropriated—disproportionately for the expansion of profitable ranching operations. People who were enslaved in the United States were fed salted "meat," purchased from as far away as Argentina, while U.S. wars against Mexico and Native Americans allowed the expropriation of Western lands for the expansion of ranching enterprises. Methods of mass production were pioneered in slaughterhouse enterprises as animals increasingly were treated in brutal ways while workers—mainly exploited immigrants and people of color—were driven to kill and dismember growing numbers of animals in shorter amounts of time.

Long hours of labor in unsafe factories and mines in the United States and Europe during the 19th century ruined the health and stunted the mental and physical development of children, women, and men alike. The physical conditions of the industrial towns and cities as a whole were no better than the factories. Housing units were small, often just a windowless room. The poor, malnourished and without clean water, were highly vulnerable to epidemics of tuberculosis and typhoid fever. Lacking sewage systems, public lighting, parks, and other amenities, the industrial cities were miserable places (Engels, 1892; Thompson, 1963).

In the United States these conditions were exacerbated by the growth in population from 31 million in 1860 to 92 million in 1910 (with most of the increase occurring in urban areas) and by the increasing economic concentration and centralization characteristic of the late 19th and early 20th centuries (Gold, 1982). In the 1890s, one study found that the wealthiest one percent of the U.S. population held more wealth than the remaining 99 percent (Spahr, 1896).

Social critics and reformers of the period increasingly placed responsibility for social problems on the capitalist system. Books such as Henry George's *Progress and Poverty* (1879/2005), Edward Bellamy's *Looking Backward* (1887/2009) and Henry Demarest Lloyd's *Wealth Against Commonwealth* (1894/2005) were among the most widely read of the period. They suggested that the problems of the United States and similar societies were largely due to the private ownership of economic resources. Successful efforts to organize workers occurred in the late 19th and early 20th centuries, including the formation of the National Labor Union, the Knights of Labor, the American Federation of Labor, the American Railway Union and the Industrial Workers of the World. Labor leader, Eugene Debs, ran for President and convinced thousands of voters to support the Socialist Party of America, while Populists attracted the votes of American farmers.

Confronted with continual calls for economic and social justice in the late 19th and early 20th centuries, the privileged took refuge in the moral philosophy of reactionary writers like Herbert Spencer (1884) and William Graham Sumner, 1992), whose social-Darwinist perspective largely blamed the disenfranchised for their own plight. This victim-blaming perspective was furthered by a late-19th-century book by Richard Dugdale (1877/1969) about a "criminal" and "degenerate" family, the Jukes. Although Dugdale emphasized environmental factors that hindered the Jukes, and his book uncovered only one case of "idiocy" out of 709 subjects, capitalist elites concluded that crime, pauperism, and disease were genetically based (as cited in Macklin & Gaylin, 1981). Accordingly, a class of scapegoats was found for the economic and social ills of the United States—"mental defectives."

Alleged Mental Deficiency of the Poor

At the beginning of the 20th century people who had immigrated to the United States from Ireland and eastern and southern Europe faced significant prejudice, due in part to the increasing competition for jobs. Although their disproportionate rate of impoverishment was caused by their exclusion and exploitation, elites asserted that urban poverty resulted from growing populations of people with mental deficiencies. The presence of immigrants was claimed to be the cause of rising levels of developmental disability in the country (Burlingame, 1940; Popenoe & Johnson, 1927). In an 1896 speech to the U.S. Senate calling for restrictive immigration legislation, Senator Henry Cabot Lodge (1896/1968) stated:

> If a *lower race* [emphasis added] mixes with a higher in sufficient numbers, history teaches us that the *lower race* [emphasis added] will prevail. The *lower race* [emphasis added] will absorb the higher, not the higher the lower, when the two strains approach equality in numbers. In other words, there is a limit to the capacity of any race for assimilating and elevating an *inferior capacity race* [emphasis added], and when you begin to pour in unlimited numbers of people of alien or *lower races* [emphasis added] of less social efficiency and less moral force, you are running the most frightful risk that any people can run. (p. 91)

In 1907, Congress passed an immigration law that excluded the following people:

> *Idiots, imbeciles, feeble-minded persons,* [emphasis added] epileptics, *insane* [emphasis added] persons who have been *insane* [emphasis added] within five years previously; persons who have had two or more attacks of insanity at any time previously or who are affected by constitutional *psychopathic inferiority* [emphasis added] or chronic alcoholism; *paupers, vagrants* [emphasis added], persons likely to become public charges, professional beggars, persons afflicted with tuberculosis or with a loathsome or contagious disease; persons who have been convicted of a crime involving moral turpitude; polygamists, anarchists, contract laborers, prostitutes, persons not comprehended within any one of the foregoing excluded cases who are found to be and are certified by the examining surgeon as being mentally or physically defective, such mental or physical defect being of such a nature as to affect the ability of the alien to earn a living. (as cited in Popenoe & Johnson, 1927, p. 303)

Many scientists and professionals supported the popular labeling of immigrants as defective and their scapegoating for the increasing social disorganization and crime. In 1912, Walter E. Fernald shared the following view with the Massachusetts Medical Society:

> The social and economic burdens of uncomplicated *feeble-mindedness* [emphasis added] are only too well known. The *feeble-minded* [emphasis added] are a parasitic, predatory class, never capable of self support or of managing their own affairs .... They cause unutterable sorrow at home and are a menace and danger to the community. We have only begun to understand the importance of *feeble-mindedness* [emphasis added] as a factor in the causation of pauperism, crime and other social problems .... Every *feeble-minded* [emphasis added] person, especially the high-grade *imbecile* [emphasis added], is a potential criminal, needing only the proper environment and opportunity for the development and expression of his criminal tendencies. (as cited in Evans, 1983, p. 43)

Writing in 1918, Paul Popenoe and Roswell Hill Johnson, the latter a professor at the University of Pittsburgh, commented: "In amount of inherent ability these immigrants are not only less highly endowed than is desirable, but they furnish, despite weeding out, altogether too large a proportion of the "three D's"—defectives, delinquents and dependents" (Popenoe & Johnson, 1927, p. 303).

The problem of the "legions of the ill-born" in the United States demanded action. Apologists for capitalism found support in the "science which deals with all influences that improve the inborn qualities of the race"—eugenics (Evans, 1983).

Fearing that "mental defectives" were reproducing themselves, many began to call for their sterilization. Popenoe and Johnson (1927) supported sterilization, while arguing against the release of sterilized persons who were institutionalized. They suggested profitable use be made of the people they called "waste humanity."

> *Feeble-minded* [emphasis added] men are capable of much rough labor. Most of the cost of segregating the *mentally defective* [emphasis added] can be met by properly organizing their labor, so as to make them as nearly self-supporting as possible. It has been found that they perform excellently such work as clearing forest land, or reforesting cleared land, and great gangs of them might profitably be put at such work, in most states.... [Thus] these unskilled fellows find happy and useful occupation, *waste humanity* [emphasis added] taking waste land and thus not only contributing to their own support, but also making over land that would otherwise be useless....Nor need this be confined to the males alone. The *girl-women* [emphasis added] raise *poultry* [emphasis added], small fruits and vegetables very successfully....No manufacturer of today has let the product of his plant go to waste as society has wasted the energies of this by-product of humanity. (Popenoe & Johnson, 1927, p. 192)

Many states developed dual policies of sterilization and segregation. By 1926, 23 states had mandatory sterilization laws; in 1927, the Supreme Court upheld the constitutionality of such legislation. Justice Holmes wrote in *Buck v. Bell*:

> It is better for all the world, if instead of waiting to execute their degenerate offspring for crime, or to let them starve for their *imbecility* [emphasis added], society can prevent those who are manifestly unfit from continuing their kind....Three generations of *imbeciles* [emphasis added] are enough. (*Buck v. Bell*, 1927, p. 207)

Such scapegoating of people with developmental disabilities—and their profound devaluation and stigmatization—became deeply imbedded in U.S. culture. For example, prejudice against people with developmental disabilities was reflected in the form of commonly used insults. The lexicon of such terms is vast: stupid, dumb, nitwit, half-wit, dimwit, blockhead, bonehead, numskull, lamebrain, pea brain, fool, dope, and on and on. Stereotypes of people with developmental disabilities as dangerous also saturated the culture. For example, a popular novel by one of America's foremost writers, John Steinbeck, *Of Mice and Men* (1937/1993), featured a character with a developmental disability named Lennie, who unintentionally kills a young woman. While Steinbeck's portrayal of Lennie was sympathetic, the popular and widely read novel reinforced the perceived need for policies of sterilization and institutionalization.

Pseudoscientific "proof" that genetic defects cause social problems continued into the mid-20th century. For example, in 1940, L. L. Burlingame, professor of biology at Stanford University, wrote:

> From what we have already learned about the phenotypic distribution of intelligence in populations and the genetic basis thereof, it would be expected that the immigrant groups that have low averages and few gifted children and eminent men would be the ones to contribute most heavily to the *feeble-minded* [emphasis added] group of dependents. (1940, pp. 232–233)

The "dysgenic problem"—dysgenic being the opposite of eugenic and meaning "bad origin"—was not believed to be confined only to European immigrants. African Americans and people from Mexico were also viewed as a threat to American society. Burlingame (1940) wrote:

> In proportion to their number, Negroes contribute far too few persons of high ability and far too many who are low normal or deficient in ability.... Mexicans are the second most serious race problem. They are apparently of distinctly low mental caliber, have not yet produced eminence and do contribute heavily to various dependent classes. (pp. 256–257)

It is estimated that more than 50,000 people labeled as "defective" were sterilized in the United States between 1925 and 1955 (Evans, 1983). Many of these and countless others were confined to state institutions and endured torturous conditions (Blatt, 1970; Blatt & Kaplan, 1974; Vail, 1966). All the while, the growing oppression of other animals by vivisectionists and agribusiness was supported by behaviorism, a pseudoscientific theory similar to social Darwinism that maintained that animals were unconscious and unfeeling (Balcombe, 2007).

U.S. Food Policy and Third World Malnutrition

While social Darwinism helped to stave off effective challenges to capitalism in the early 20th century, machinations by Wall Street moguls and similar elites throughout the world led to the Great Depression of the 1930s. As part of its response to the crisis, the U.S. government attempted to cope with a grain surplus and falling grain prices by implementing agricultural price supports for farmers. The policy, however, only served to generate further surpluses. The difficulty was compounded by the advent of "green revolution" agricultural practices that increased yields through the use of chemical products and monocropping. Organizations representing large farming enterprises and grain merchants persuaded the government to solve the problem of grain surpluses in two ways. First, an initiative would be undertaken to increase public consumption of products derived from other animals, which would create greater demand for feed grains (Winders & Nibert, 2004). Second, government policies worked to increase Third World dependence on U.S. grain.

In 1954 Congress enacted Public Law 480 (P.L. 480) with the purpose of "disposing of agricultural surpluses and developing future markets for American agricultural products" (Nelson, 1980, p. 20). Initially, the policy permitted Third World nations to buy grain at discounted prices and to pay using their own currencies. Proceeds from these sales were used in part to provide low-interest loans to large U.S. corporations to support the expansion of their operations and control of resources in poorer nations. As cheap U.S. grains poured into the Third World, many small and medium-sized producers there were driven out of business. P. L. 480 substantially undermined food production in the Third World—leading to food dependency.

The promotion of "meat"-eating in the United States—part of the strategy to reduce grain surpluses—effectively increased the practice to record levels (Winders & Nibert, 2004). As U.S. "meat" producers disproportionately used ranched cows for the production of more expensive "cuts of meat," the growing fast-food industry sought to acquire cheaper, "industrial-grade" cow flesh from Latin America—especially Central America. As the demand for ranched cows in Central America grew, local elites used hundreds of millions of dollars in U.S. loans to expand their ranching operations and began displacing large numbers of subsistence farmers. While many people left the land in the face of threats from state-supported ranching elites, others resisted their displacement. Revenues created by P. L. 480 therefore, also were used to fund aggressive and deadly counterinsurgency programs (Nelson, 1980).

While Third World nations initially bought U.S. grain at below-market prices using their currencies, once their dependence was established, they were required to pay full market prices using dollars. As people in the U.S. were being strongly encouraged to eat increasing amounts of "hamburgers" and other products derived from animals, people in the Third World saw their system of food production undermined while problems of landlessness and poverty increased.

After Third World reliance on U.S. grain was established, a second surplus presented problems for U.S. capitalism. The green revolution spurred the production of numerous products—farm machinery, seeds, pesticides, fertilizers, herbicides, and so forth—that largely had saturated the domestic market. In the 1960s manufacturers sought to stimulate sales of these products in the Third World (Nelson, 1980). Agricultural concentration then was exacerbated further in many poor nations because only wealthy landowners could afford the products and equipment that produced higher yields. More food was created, but more hunger followed because of high levels of poverty and the inability of the poor to purchase food produced for the global market.

When global grain prices increased in the 1970s, people in poor countries forced to purchase U.S. grain at market cost experienced increasing hunger and malnutrition. Malnutrition, a primary cause of developmental disability, disproportionately became a Third World problem (Desjarlais, Eisenberg, Good, & Kleinman, 1996). At the same time, people in the U.S. and other affluent nations were strongly persuaded by ubiquitous advertisements to consume record levels of "meat," "dairy," and "eggs." The increased consumption was made possible by "meat" imports from Latin America and by the growing numbers of animals intensively confined on factory farms.

Continued Cultural Devaluation and Oppression

The hegemonically created culture in the United States promoted the view that most other animals were unworthy of moral consideration and were merely resources for profit taking. As hundreds of millions were exploited by the food industry, others were used in growing numbers by vivisectionists in experiments by universities, corporations, and the military. For example, in 1946 the U.S. military loaded 4,000 animals on a ship in the South Pacific and exposed them to an atomic blast to record the effects of the radiation (Goldstein & Goldstein, 2001). Devalued humans similarly were treated as subjects for experimentation. Between 1946 and 1953 boys with developmental disabilities at the Fernald School in Massachusetts were given radiated iron and calcium supplements in their breakfast cereal by researchers from Harvard and M.I.T. who wanted to study the effects (Welsome, 2000). Not surprisingly, since people of color were viewed as disproportionately contributing to the ranks of "mental defectives" and also positioned low on the hierarchy of worth, they too were subjected to harmful experimentation. The U.S. Public Health Service between 1932 and 1972 conducted an experiment on 600 African American men in Tuskegee, Alabama to study the effects of untreated syphilis (Reverby, 2009). Between 1946 and 1948 U.S. public health researchers infected nearly 700 people in Guatemala with syphilis or gonorrhea to test the efficacy of penicillin (Editorial, 2010; McNeil, 2010).

The profound devaluation of people with developmental disabilities, coupled with the disproportionate control of income and wealth by U.S. elites in the 20th century, left resource-strapped institutions for people with disabilities overcrowded and understaffed, and residents often were subjected to terrible treatment. Increasingly, explicit institutional abuse and neglect of people with disabilities became a political issue, brought to public attention by the publication of *Christmas in Purgatory* (Blatt & Kaplan, 1974) and scandals such as the gross neglect of residents at the Willowbrook facility in New York in the 1970s.

Advocates for people with developmental disabilities pressed for reform (Rothman & Rothman, 2005), and Congress responded by enacting the Developmental Disabilities Act of 1975. This law set forth a bill of rights for persons with developmental disabilities, and established minimum standards for state habilitation programs. That same year, Congress also enacted the Education for All Handicapped Children Act, which allocated federal funds and established standards for the education of young people with disabilities, including developmental disabilities. In 1980 Congress enacted the Civil Rights of Institutionalized Persons Act. Court decisions established the rights of people with developmental disabilities in institutions to receive active treatment (*Wyatt v. Stickney*, 1971) and to be cared for in the least restrictive environment (*Pennsylvania Association for* Retarded [italics removed] *Children v. Commonwealth of Pennsylvania*, 1971).

Cumulatively, these and other such efforts formed the legal basis for improving the quality of life for individuals with developmental disabilities. However, realization of this goal has been undermined by persistent cultural devaluation and a shortage of public resources resulting from disparities in the distribution of wealth under capitalism. For example, although the state of Ohio was widely praised in 1971 for state legislation that established protection and advocacy programs for people with developmental disabilities, more than a decade later investigative reporting revealed "savage abuse" in several state institutions there (Long & Neff, 1985), including unexplained deaths, physical and sexual abuse, neglect, and falsification of client records. Reflecting on the failure of federal legislative efforts to improve the quality of life for people with disabilities in state institutions around the country, Senator Lowell Weicker observed:

> Protection for these frailest of our society exists largely on paper.... When we passed the Civil Rights of Institutionalized Persons Act in 1980 we expected that these persons would, at last, live and be helped in conditions that meet tests of constitutional certainty and human decency. When we provided for federal audits of institutional care as part of Medicaid funding, we expected that federal tax money would be linked directly to quality care. However, neither the U.S. Justice Department nor the Department of Health and Human Services has lived up to these expectations....
>
> If 1/100 of [the abuses documented in] this Senate report ever related to these hospitals and institutions which serve us and our family members we would all be on the ceiling. But let us face that, as a nation ... we do not in-

> clude treatment of the mentally ill and . . . [people with developmental disabilities] in that category. (U.S. Senate Committee on Labor and Human Resources, 1985: 1–3)

Advocate Burton Blatt (1987) wrote:

> More and more, the legislatures of our country are reluctant to either pass progressive legislation or to fully implement current legislation that would cost the taxpayers money—money which the states say they do not have, and money which the taxpayers say they do not want to give for such purposes as providing for the fullest educational opportunities for handicapped individuals. . . . It is not inconceivable that historians will characterize the eighties as the time when society broke faith with its earlier promises, as a time of reaction, a time of return to the dark days before the people were enlightened. (pp. 230–231)

As has been observed regarding other legal efforts to promote civil rights and social justice, long-standing norms, values, and beliefs frequently can undermine, if not negate, the spirit of the law (Kidder, 1983). Cultural stereotypes of people with developmental disabilities as dangerous continued, notwithstanding Congressional acts and judicial decisions ostensibly intended to improve their lives. Lennie—the John Steinbeck character discussed earlier—was recreated countless times in television programs, movies, and even cartoons, and the novel itself has been made into a movie several times. One 1992 version emphasized Lennie's dangerousness by opening with an image of a terror-stricken woman in torn clothing running from an encounter with Lennie, even though the novel does not begin this way. And stereotypic portrayals of people with developmental disabilities continued as amusement. For example, on the popular 1990s television comedy, *Roseanne* (Williams, 1988–1997), the Conners often performed caricatures of defective "hillbillies." On an episode of *Seinfeld* (Castle Rock Entertainment, 1990–1998), a shot of Novocain by the dentist left Kramer with a contorted face and slurred speech; the running gag was based on his treatment by strangers who took him for a person with a developmental disability. In 2008 a popular Ben Stiller film, *Tropic Thunder* (2008), made frequent use of the word, *retard*, for the amusement of moviegoers while devaluing children with developmental disabilities.

The violence directed at people with developmental disabilities is seen as a normal response when someone does something "dumb." Audiences laughed—and still do, with the popularity of classic movie channels—as Oliver Hardy hit a "dim-witted" Stan Laurel for doing something "stupid," as Moe hit Curly and as Bud Abbott hit Lou Costello. In a cartoon take-off on *Of Mice and Men* (Steinbeck,

1937/1993), the small but smart mouse repeatedly slaps the large but "dumb" Lennie mouse; in Disney's *Beauty and the Beast* (Hahn, 1991), the character, Gaston, repeatedly punches his "dim-witted" sidekick, and on and on. This form of entertainment can be seen as a modern version of the ancient practice of "displaying" people with disabilities. These images reflect and promote a strong cultural intimation of a hierarchy of worth promoted by social Darwinism—and other animals and people with developmental disabilities continue to be at the bottom.

Legislation in the latter part of the 20th century, ostensibly intended to ameliorate the terrible treatment of other animals by agribusiness, vivisectionists, and other industries, and to provide for their "humane treatment," similarly has been compromised by insufficient funding (Nibert, 2002). These efforts also have been undermined by continued media portrayals of other animals as dangerous and lacking in intelligence. From television programs such as *When Animals Attack* (Darnell & Mathis, 1996), to David Letterman's "stupid pet tricks" (Markoe, 1982–1993), other animals—largely invisible on television or in film except as food and clothing for humans—mostly were stigmatized and devalued when they were represented (Nibert, 2002). Within this hierarchy of worth, people seek to distance themselves from the most devalued in order to receive social approval. No one wants to be treated "like an animal" or like an "idiot."

At the beginning of the 21st century, elite capitalists and giant corporations tightened their global control by pushing governments to acquiesce to free-trade agreements and the corporate priorities established by the World Trade Organization. Disparities in the distribution of wealth in the United States increased as precious public resources were appropriated for the "War on Terror." The funding of two invasions in the Middle East, coupled with further tax cuts for the affluent, left scant resources available for effecting policies to improve conditions for those most devalued.

New reports emerged about the abuse and neglect of people with developmental disabilities under state care. For instance, an investigative report by the *Cincinnati Enquirer* revealed violence against and abuse of people with developmental disabilities in group homes across Ohio (Hunt & Jasper, 2002). In Texas, investigators reported that people with developmental disabilities in state institutions were neglected, beaten, sexually abused, and even killed by staff members (Associated Press, 2008). As mentioned earlier, *The New York Times* reported on the existence of hundreds of cases in 2010 involving "employees who sexually abused, beat or taunted residents" (Hakima, 2011, para. 2) in facilities for people with developmental disabilities. Similarly, despite laws stipulating "humane treatment" of animals by agribusiness and other industries, there have been continual reports—frequently videotaped—of the horrific treatment of other animals. The predictable, corporate-friendly response has sought to stop not the violence but the *complaints.* In the spring of 2011 lawmakers in Florida, Iowa, and Minnesota introduced legislation to make videotaping of abuse of animals by agribusiness firms a criminal offense and to label the whistleblowers as "eco-terrorists" (Peterka, 2011).

Finite Resources and Entangled Fates

In the 21st century, not only does the cultural devaluation of both groups continue, but the exigencies of global capitalism, with its imperative for continual growth and profit taking, are profoundly affecting the future of both groups. For years giant agribusiness corporations in the United States and abroad have boosted profits by promoting increased consumption of animal products. Countless people in the Third World have been driven from their land for the expansion of large ranching and feed crop operations and made dependent on U.S. grain imports. Seventy percent of the world's agricultural land now is used in the production of food products derived from animals (Food and Agriculture Organization of the United Nations (FAO), 2006). Approximately 2.25 billion people around the world—largely in affluent societies—are consuming diets consisting primarily of animal products, while 4.5 billion live primarily on plant-based diets, and one billion are hungry and malnourished (Pimentel & Pimentel, 2008).

Most powerful capitalist nations are unwilling to allocate the resources necessary to provide people with developmental disabilities a decent quality of life, and poorer countries cannot afford to. In a vicious cycle, contemporary global food production and distribution based on the miserable oppression of tens of billions of other animals on factory farms are contributing to hunger and malnutrition—and, in turn, to growing numbers of people with developmental disabilities.

The human population of the world is projected to reach nine billion by 2050, and it is estimated that the consumption of products derived from exploited animals will double by that date. Even more of the world's agricultural land necessarily will be expropriated for the production of animal products (ScienceDaily, 2010). Malnutrition resulting from this continued maldistribution of global food resources will be compounded by the exhaustion of finite resources—including fresh water, topsoil, and oil—disproportionately used for the creation of "meat," "dairy," and "eggs" (Nibert, 2002). Moreover, environmental destruction caused by the exploitation of other animals as food, including global warming, water and air pollution, and desertification, will increase as the number of other animals exploited for food rises.

As important, finite resources become scarce and environmental destruction continues, powerful nations like the United States unquestionably will use military force to obtain control of water sources, arable land, and other valuable resources—

as presaged in the invasion of oil-rich Iraq. Indeed, contemplating the environmental, social, economic, and political effects of global warming, a panel of military leaders urged that the threat should be fully integrated into national security and national defense strategies (Revkin & Williams, 2007). The prevalence of developmental disability is certain to increase, as the drive by global agribusiness and food retailers to increase the consumption of products derived from oppressed animals will lead to resource scarcity, international conflict, and growing levels of malnutrition. Already, rates of developmental disability are two to eight times greater in poor countries than in wealthy ones (Desjarlais et al., 1996, p. 164). According to the United Nations, an increase in the number of people with developmental disabilities, particularly in poor countries, is linked to poverty and malnutrition, problems exacerbated by war and violence (United Nations Enable, 2011).

In sum, the fates of other animals and people with developmental disabilities have been closely entangled for the past 10,000 years, beginning when egalitarian, foraging societies were eclipsed by agriculturists. The numbers of people with developmental disabilities increased—and their oppression began—as human societies incorporated the systemic oppression of other animals. The oppression of other animals as food and sources of transport and labor made possible thousands of years of elite-driven warfare and violence. People with disabilities were even more devalued, and the emergence of capitalism did relatively little to ameliorate the oppression and disparities. As the unequal distribution of wealth and power grew, by the early 20th century, resistance from workers and reformers threatened capitalism; people with developmental disabilities were scapegoated and further disparaged.

U.S. grain producers and their government supporters further harmed other animals and contributed to the numbers of people with developmental disabilities by promoting increased consumption of products derived from animals, and by fostering Third World dependence on U.S. grain. As growing numbers of other animals were intensively confined on factory farms, mothers and children in poor nations suffered hunger and malnourishment.

Today, U.S. and global capitalists are promoting a doubling of the consumption of products derived from animals in the next 40 years. Increasing numbers of other animals and people around the world will suffer. People in poor nations not only will face food shortages but also will be highly vulnerable to international conflict and violence from the struggle to control finite resources in an era of climate change, drought, and increasingly severe weather. Unless activists and workers around the world unite and cooperate to transcend the capitalist system and promote a transition to sustainable, plant-based diets, the 21st century will be the worst yet for other animals, people with developmental disabilities, and all devalued groups.

Note

1. Words and expressions that are disparaging to devalued groups, and euphemisms that tend to disguise the reality of oppression (such as the term "meat," which disguises the reality that other animals' dead bodies are used for food) are placed in quotation marks. If such language is used in quoted material, the devaluative terms are placed in italics. While this may make the text somewhat awkward at times, it is much preferable to using smoother language that implicitly supports oppressive arrangements.

References

Associated Press. (2008, December 3). Texas lambasted over care of mentally disabled. Retrieved from http://www.msnbc.msn.com/id/28036793/ns/health-health_care/t/texas-lambasted-over-care-mentally-disabled/

Balcombe, J. (2007). *Pleasurable kingdom: Animals and the nature of feeling good.* New York, NY: Macmillan.

Bellamy, E. (2009). *Looking backward: 2000–1887.* Retrieved from www.gutenberg.org

Blatt, B. (1970). *Exodus from pandemonium: Human abuse and a reformation of public policy.* Boston, MA: Allyn & Bacon.

Blatt, B. (1987). *The conquest of mental retardation.* Austin, TX: Pro-Ed.

Blatt, B., & Kaplan, F. (1974). *Christmas in purgatory: A photographic essay on mental retardation.* Syracuse, NY: Human Policy Press.

Buck v. Bell. (1927). *United States Supreme Court Reports,* 274: 200–208.

Burlingame, L. L. (1940). *Heredity and social problems.* New York, NY: McGraw-Hill.

Castle Rock Entertainment (Producer). (1990–1998). *Seinfeld* [Television series]. United States: National Broadcasting Company (NBC).

Crissey, M. (1975). Mental retardation: Past, present and future. *American Psychologist, 30*(8), 800–808.

Crissey, M., & Rosen, M. (1986). *Institutions for the mentally retarded: A changing role in changing times.* Austin, TX: Pro-Ed.

Darnell, M. (Producer), & Mathis, M. (Director). (1996). *When animals attack!* [Television special]. United States: A. Smith & Co..

Desjarlais, R., Eisenberg, L., Good, B., & Kleinman, A. (1996). *World mental health: Problems and priorities in low-income countries.* London, UK: Oxford University Press.

Dugdale, R. (1969). *The Jukes: A study in crime, pauperism, disease and heredity.* Atlanta, GA: Georgia State University Digital Archive.

Editorial: The experiments in Guatemala. (2010, October 7). *The New York Times.* Retrieved from http://www.nytimes.com/2010/10/08/opinion/08fri3.html

Engels, F. (1892). *The condition of the working class in England.* London, UK: George Allen & Unwin.

Evans, D. P. (1983). *The lives of mentally retarded people.* Boulder, CO: Westview Press.

Food and Agriculture Organization of the United Nations (FAO). (2006). *Livestock's long shadow: Environmental issues and options.* Retrieved from http://www.fao.org/docrep/010/a0701e/a0701e00.HTM

Foucault, M. (1965). *Madness and civilization: A history of insanity in the age of reason*. New York, NY: Pantheon Books.

George, H. (2005). *Progress and poverty: An inquiry into the course of industrial depressions and of increase of want with increase of wealth: The remedy*. New York, NY: Cosimo.

Gold, H. (1982). *The sociology of urban life*. Englewood Cliffs, NJ: Prentice-Hall.

Goldstein, M. C., & Goldstein, M. A. (2001). *Controversies in the practice of medicine*. Westport, CT: Greenwood Press.

Hahn, D. (Producer), Trousdale, G. (Director), & Wise, K. (Director). (1991). *Beauty and the beast*. United States: Disney.

Hakima, D. (2011, March 12). At state-run homes, abuse and impunity. *The New York Times*. Retrieved from http://www.nytimes.com/2011/03/13/nyregion/13homes.html?_r=1

Heilbroner, R. (1993). *The making of economic society* (9th ed.). Englewood Cliffs, NJ: Prentice-Hall.

Helleiner, K. F. (1967). The population of Europe from the black death to the eve of the vital revolution. In E. E. Rich & C. H. Wilson (Eds.), *The Cambridge economic history of Europe, Vol. IV: The economy of expanding Europe in the 16th and 17th centuries*, pp. 1–95). Cambridge, UK: Cambridge University Press.

Hunt, S., & Jasper, D. (2002, April). Abuse, neglect go unpunished. *The Cincinnati Enquirer*. Retrieved from http://www.enquirer.com/mrdd/abuse_neglect.html

Institute of Medicine (U.S.), Committee on Nervous System Disorders in Developing Countries. (2001). *Neurological, psychiatric, and developmental disorders: Meeting the challenge in the developing world*. Washington, DC: National Academy Press.

Jones, M. (2008, October 24). The barnyard strategist. *The New York Times*. Retrieved from http://www.nytimes.com/2008/10/26/magazine/26animal-t.html

Kanner, L. (1949). *A miniature textbook of feeblemindedness*. New York, NY: Child Care.

Kidder, R. L. (1983). *Connecting law and society: An introduction to research and theory*. Englewood Cliffs, NJ: Prentice-Hall.

Lloyd, H. D. (2005). *Wealth against commonwealth*. New York, NY: Elibron Classics.

Lodge, H. C. (1968). For immigration restrictions. In *The annals of America* (Vol. 12). Chicago, IL: Encyclopaedia Britannica.

Long, J. S., & Neff, J. (1985, September 24). Retarded are raped in state homes. *The Plain Dealer* (Cleveland, OH).

Macklin, R., & Gaylin, W. (1981). *Mental retardation and sterilization: A problem of competency and paternalism*. New York, NY: Plenum.

Markoe, M., Morton. R., Sand, B. (Executive Producers), & Gurnee, H. (Director). (1982–1993). Stupid pet tricks. *Late night with David Letterman*. [Television program].United States: National Broadcasting Company (NBC).

Marx, K. (1967). *Capital* (Vol. 1). New York, NY: Penguin.

Mayer, K. (1955). *Class and society*. New York, NY: Random House.

McNeil Jr., D. G. (2010, October 1). U.S. apologizes for syphilis tests in Guatemala. *The New York Times*. Retrieved from www.nytimes.com/2010/10/02/health/research/02infect.html

Miller, G. T., & Spoolman, S. (2009). *Environmental science* (13th ed.). Belmont, CA: Brooks/Cole.

Nelson, J. A. (1980). *Hunger for justice: The politics of food and faith*. Maryknoll, NY: Orbis Books.

Nibert, D. (2002). *Animal rights/human rights: Entanglements of oppression and liberation*. Lanham, MD: Rowman & Littlefield.

Pennsylvania Association for Retarded Children v. Commonwealth of Pennsylvania, 1971, 344 F. Supp. 1275, E. D. Pa.

Peterka, A. (2011, May 5). State legislatures take up bills barring undercover videos of confined animal feeding operations. *The New York Times.* Retrieved from http://www.nytimes.com/gwire/2011/05/05/05greenwire-state-legislatures-take-up-bills-barring-under-88103.html

Pimentel, D., & Pimentel, M. (2008). *Food, energy and society* (3rd ed.). Boca Raton, FL: CRC Press.

Popenoe, P., & Johnson, R. H. (1927). *Applied eugenics.* New York, NY: MacMillan.

Reverby, S. (2009). *Examining Tuskegee: The infamous syphilis study and its legacy.* Chapel Hill, NC : University of North Carolina Press.

Revkin, A. C., & Williams, T. (2007, April 15). Global warming called security threat. *The New York Times.* Retrieved from http://www.nytimes.com/2007/04/15/us/15warm.html

Rothman, D. J., & Rothman, S. M. (2005). *The Willowbrook wars: Bringing the mentally disabled into the community.* New Brunswick, NJ: Transaction.

Scheerenberger, R. C. (1983). *A history of mental retardation.* Baltimore, MD: Brookes.

ScienceDaily. (2010, March 16). Environmental and social impact of the 'Livestock Revolution.' Retrieved from .http://www.sciencedaily.com/releases/2010/03/100316101703.htm

Sernau, S. (2009). *Global problems: The search for equity, peace, and sustainability* (2nd ed.). Boston, MA: Pearson Education.

Spahr, C. B. (1896). "The present distribution of wealth in the United States." Cited in H. Faulkner, *The quest for social justice*, 1898-1914, Chicago: Quadrangle 1971 [1931], 21.

Spencer, H. (1884). *The principles of biology.* London, UK: William and Norgate.

Steinbeck, J. (1993). *Of mice and men.* New York, NY: Penguin.

Stiller, B. (Producer/Director). (2008). *Tropic thunder* [Motion picture]. United States: Dream Works in association with Red Hour Films & Goldcrest Pictures.

Sumner, W. G. (1992). *On liberty, society, and politics: The essential essays of William Graham Sumner* (R. C. Bannister, Ed.). Indianapolis, IN: Liberty Fund.

Thompson, E.P. (1963). *The making of the English working class.* New York: Pantheon –Random House.

Trent, J. W. (1994). *Inventing the feeble mind: A history of mental retardation in the United States.* Berkeley, CA: University of California Press.

United Nations Enable. (2011). *World programme of action concerning disabled persons.* Retrieved from http://www.un.org/disabilities/default.asp?id=23

U.S. Senate Committee on Labor and Human Resources. (1985). *Care of institutionalized mentally disabled persons* (Parts 1 & 2). Washington, DC: U.S. Government Printing Office.

Vail, D. (1966). *Dehumanization and the institutional career.* Springfield, IL: Charles C. Thomas.

Welsome, E. (2000). *The plutonium files: America's secret medical experiments in the Cold War.* New York, NY: Random House.

Williams, M. (Creator). (1988–1997). *Roseanne.* [Television series]. United States: Wind Dancer Productions in association with Carsey-Werner Company & Paramount Television.

Winders, W., & Nibert, D. (2004). Expanding the surplus: Expanding 'meat' consumption and animal oppression. *International Journal of Sociology and Social Policy, 24*(9), 76–92.

Wyatt v. Stickney, Civil Action No. 3195-N, U.S. District Court, Alabama, North Division, 1972.

CHAPTER FIFTEEN

Eco-Ability Theory in Action

A Challenge to Ableism in the Environmental Movement

ANTHONY J. NOCELLA II

For as long as the environmental movement has existed, emerging out of the Western, colonial, Euro-American-centric paradigm, it has been dominated and founded by white, heterosexual, able-bodied, wealthy, Christian males, who ate nonhuman meat and exploited others. The environmental movement has been challenged by many for its romanticization, construction, and destruction of nature. Indigenous and First Peoples argue against a Christian global conquest (Churchill, 2002); eco-feminists challenge patriarchal domination (Mies & Shiva, 1993), exploitation, and the domestication of nature, nonhuman animals, and women; green anarchists shed light on the commodification of nature and nonhuman animals by capitalism and authoritarianism (Zerzan, 2005); environmental justice activists address the intersectional connection of the destruction of the planet to the destruction of communities of color, both being polluted and exploited for labor and resources (Pellow, 2002).

This book is the first to make an intersectional connection between nonhuman animals, the ecological world, those with disabilities, and the philosophical interconnections of the three. We hope that eco-ability will grow and be taken as seriously as those critical perspectives noted above. Eco-ability is not welfarist, reformist, or conservationist. Rather, it is a philosophy that argues against all domination and notions of *normalcy* while championing an interwoven, interdependent, collaborative relationship with all and respect for difference. Eco-ability, therefore, is not about paving pathways through the forest for those with wheelchairs; nor is it for establishing paths for walkers to enjoy nature; nor is it about exploiting dolphins, horses, dogs, or any other nonhuman animal in the name of service, rehabilitation, testing, entertainment, protection, or food.

Eco-ability praises the different abilities one has, whether flying, crawling, swimming, rolling, or walking, and promotes a locally grown, nonpackaged, nonprocessed, organic, vegan-based diet. Eco-ability acknowledges the limits and destructive possibilities when using technology to assist individuals, while being against animal testing (human or nonhuman) and ecological destruction. Eco-ability argues that if one is to use technology, it must be to help others and the planet. Technology should not be used as merely fun, convenient gadgets around our offices and homes as we partake in capitalist society. Technology is not apolitical or natural. Educators should not be promoting digital equity as a way to end poverty and classism, where everyone has a laptop and cellular phone to end the digital divide, but whoever uses digital technology should use it to promote social justice and peace, not merely as entertainment or for the use of economic profit and exploitation.

Philosophically, we must understand how disability is sociopolitical and economically constructed to benefit normalcy, sameness, equality, and average, not difference. Traditionally, everything that is not serving the elite, dominant concept of what is *normal*—i.e., the white, heterosexual, wealthy, able-bodied, formally educated, Christian, Euro-American male who eats meat—is categorized as dysfunctional, damaged, deviant, demonic, delinquent, and distorted. Similar to the environmental justice movement, eco-ability also calls for a new path to protect and live in the world, arguing that the environmental movement and environmental studies are rooted in domination, purification, and so-called normalcy of the ecological world. Through their images and narratives, environmentalists have traditionally constructed the idea of nature as perfect. Their stories construct the perfect snake, perfect shark, perfect ladybug, perfect hummingbird, perfect lion, perfect tree, etc. The images are perpetuated in art, tattoos, logos, mascots, books, magazines, cartoons, and movies, and they "freakify" those that deviate from these socially constructed images of what is natural and, consequently, normal.

Environmental Studies and Environmentalism: A Critical Analysis[1]

Environmental studies, which emerged out of the environmental movement, is an interdisciplinary field of study dedicated to examining the relationship between humans and the *natural* environment (Best & Nocella, 2006). Its foundations are attached to a colonialist worldview. While many environmental studies programs are committed to protection and preservation of the ecological global community, of which humans are an integral part, other programs are dedicated to conservation of natural resources, which humans are not part of but still use. Many of the top environmental studies programs were established in the 1970s within natural resource and/or forestry colleges or departments. Today, much of environmental studies is rooted in a white, *patriarchal*, colonial relationship to *nature* (i.e., man versus nature), along with being entrenched in and based on environmental science and natural resources, rather than the liberal arts and humanities. The field of environmental studies has become an increasingly popular marketing tool for the greening of college campuses for students and government grants.

While much of the environmental movement in the colonial world is highly problematic because of its patriarchal, racist, ableist, and homophobic philosophical foundations (Best & Nocella, 2006), I want to speak to one particular, current subenvironmental movement that has received attention not only for its brilliant critiques of colonialism, technology, and civilization but for its problematic ableist perspectives as well. Among the modern U.S. environmental movement, there is a radical, leftist subculture known as green anarchism, or primitivism (Zerzan, 2008).

Based on Do-It-Yourself (DIY) values—with DIY being an anarcho-punk reference to self-reliance (Malott & Peña, 2004)—some green anarchists and primitivists are independent and grounded in an antitechnology and anticivilization "back to nature" philosophy. Concepts such as interdependency, mutual aid, and respect for difference are the antithesis of green anarchism, because the ideology promotes individualistic, able-bodied, competitive beliefs. Antitechnology, antisociety green anarchists argue for humans being dominant over nonhuman animals. This logic fails to meet the needs of those in the dis-ability and transgender communities, because it excludes technologized medical operations, such as prosthetic limbs and sex changes and promotes hunting and gathering.

Hunting and gathering takes a great amount of energy and time in the wilderness, including picking things up, walking, running, and climbing in order to find food and water. These are activities that many people with physical disabilities cannot accomplish on their own or without technology. Further, green anarchism promotes not only the able-bodied as integral to survival but condones the corporate, industrialized consumption of nonhuman animals (i.e., wearing them for shoes, clothing, and eating them). The green anarchist philosophy has been critiqued by animal liberation anarchists for still being dominators of nonhuman animals and speciesist, even if the killing of nonhuman animals is through nonindustrial means such as road kill, hunting, and trapping (Best & Nocella, 2004, 2006).

The process of moving to a primitive lifestyle would utilize more energy than striving to move forward with technology in a sustainable manner for two reasons: first, because of the destruction of urban areas and use of nonmaintained contaminates; and second, because with the current population of the planet, spreading people out, rather than condensing human areas of mass impact, would damage more areas of the planet. While there are those in green anarchism who promote a vegan or animal liberation philosophy, as well as an ecological or green technology, they are few and far between (Best & Nocella, 2006). In addressing an audience question about painful deaths and difficult childbirth in a primitivist society, John Zerzan, one of the leading voices of the green anarchist movement, noted:

> Are we supposed to keep this whole industrialized suicide going for the sake of the people that you don't want to pull the plug on? I don't want to pull the plug either. I'm not comfortable with that answer but to some degree ... I don't think it's a full answer. If you discover what it is that creates the problem and the problem just keeps on being created, whatever it is, like more people with all kinds of conditions, all kinds of problematic things including [dangerous or risky] child birth, including autism, including health threatening obesity.... These are creations of mass society so ... where is the healthy direction? I don't know what to do about disabled people .... I don't want to pull the plug on people, but we have a reality to ... where do we go with that? You tell me, I don't know. (Miltsov.org, 2008)

Dis-Ability Anarchists and Green Anarchists: At a Crossroads

Rather than aiding and supporting their needs through technology and interdependence, green anarchists and primitivists argue that those who have disabilities, identified as the weak of society, will die off because of their lack of ability to survive in nature independent of technology and other people. While Zerzan might feel uncomfortable about excluding people with dis-abilities at best and accept them being killed or dying off at worst, by supporting green anarchism's antitechnology position, it appears that he and other green anarchists are advocating for a survival-of-the-fittest approach. They promote a society that would fail to meet the needs of people with disabilities.

Some green anarchists may not understand that disability is a social construct, created through the arbitrary idea of normalcy, and that the goal of taking down civilization and colonialism also includes taking down the notion of normalcy in which we are all socialized. Everyone is dis-abled by capitalism, colonialism, civilization, and industrialization throughout their lives. These systems of domination promote standardization, normalcy, *equality*, and sameness, disrespecting different abilities and identities. Computers, cars, doorways, homes, books, clothes, and pencils are all designed with a particular type of person in mind. Concurrent with primitivism, dis-ability anarchism is a rising movement that agrees with the notion that we should be wary of technological innovation. For example, green anarchists and dis-ability anarchists are critical of the medical and pharmaceutical industrial complexes because of the human, nonhuman, plant, and ecological exploitation they cause. However, dis-ability anarchists support technological innovation that will aid in human freedom and inclusion but not at the expense of plants, nonhuman animals, human and global ecological exploitation and destruction, much of it due to capitalism (Kovel, 2002).

Conclusion

To challenge any system or institution of domination, all life must coexist collaboratively in a respectful and harmonious relationship. We maintain the hope of global transformation toward a peaceful world community devoid of the violence that affects all elements and life both on and off this planet. This will demand changing one's diet to an organic, local, polyculture or permaculture, plant-based, vegan diet, to embrace difference and dismantle normalcy and to end the valuing of the natural worlds as mere, and unlimited, resources. Begin a mutually respectful relationship with *all* life. For the day may come when, as oft envisioned by Hollywood, Earthlings will create a socially constructed, dominating divide between ourselves and those from another planet (Msnbc.com, 2010), defining them as abnormal, freakish, or dangerous, as beings that must be tested, imprisoned, and destroyed.

Let it be that the day we meet other non-Earth life forms we come together in a peaceful, welcoming manner, rather than mimic a scene from the film, *The Day the Earth Stood Still* (Derrickson, 2008), where guns were pointed at aliens that came to Earth. In the film, Klaatu (played by Keanu Reeves) expresses what dis-ability advocates and environmentalists have been saying all along, "The universe grows smaller every day, and the threat of aggression by any group, anywhere, can no longer be tolerated. There must be security for all, or no one is secure." Through the colonial mentality, humans have attempted to deny that they, too, are part of nature, which includes seeing themselves as animals. Those who promote civilization as such deny their interdependence with fellow members of the ecological world. The colonial mindset is one of ruthless expansion and conquering, but little do its adherents know that they are only dominating and conquering themselves. Once the oppression caused by economic, social, and political factors is overcome, the values of intradependent or interdependent life, global inclusion, respect for difference, and biodiversity can flourish. A movement away from domination, marginalization, manipulation, and control can be used to bring about a world of peace, love, and respect for others' beliefs, abilities, and identities. We must acknowledge and transform our relationships with fellow Earthlings and elements into a respectful, inclusive, interdependent, peaceful community, or else we will find ourselves traveling down the road of destruction.

Note

1. Some sentences in this section come from the "Introduction" to *Igniting a Revolution: Voices in Defense of the Earth*, which I coedited with Steve Best (2006).

Bibliography

Best, S., & Nocella II, A. J. (2004). *Terrorists or freedom fighters? Reflections on the liberation of animals.* New York, NY: Lantern Books.

Best, S., & Nocella II, A. J. (2006). *Igniting a revolution: Voices in defense of the earth.* Oakland, CA: AK Press.

Churchill, W. (2002). *Struggle for the land: Native North American resistance to genocide, ecocide, and colonization.* San Francisco, CA: City Lights.

Derrickson, S. (Director). (2008). *The day the earth stood still* [Motion picture]. United States: 20th Century Fox.

Kovel, J. (2002). *The enemy of nature: The end of capitalism or the end of the world?* Halifax, Nova Scotia, Canada: Fernwood.

Malott, C., & Peña, M.. (2004). *Punk rockers' revolution.* New York, NY: Peter Lang.

Mies, M. & Shiva, V. (1993). *Ecofeminism.* London, UK: Zed Books.

Miltsov.org. (2008, June 18). Anarcho-primitivism, archeology and anthropology 8/10. Retrieved from http://www.youtube.com/watch?v=FomlQHwqlpk&feature=related

Msnbc.com. (2010, April 25). Hawking: Aliens may pose risks to earth. Retrieved from http://www.msnbc.msn.com/id/36769422/ns/technology_and_science-space/t/hawking-aliens-may-pose-risks-earth/#.T1uBF3koFIE

Pellow, D. N. (2002). *Garbage wars: The struggle for environmental justice in Chicago.* Cambridge, MA: MIT Press.

Zerzan, J. (2005). *Against civilization: Readings and reflections.* Los Angeles, CA: Feral House.

Zerzan, J. (2008). *Running on emptiness: The pathology of civilization.* Los Angeles, CA: Feral House.

Contributors

Deanna Adams is a Ph.D. candidate in Special Education, Disability Studies, and Women and Gender Studies at Syracuse University in New York. She is currently an Instructor in Special Education at National-Louis University in Chicago, as well as Syracuse University. Her interests are in the critical study of special education, as well as school-to-prison pipeline, the over-representation of kids of color in special education, and supporting LGBTQ students in schools. She is currently doing research on school-wide behavior management. Deanna has been a teacher in special education in both public schools as well as correctional facilities for boys in New York State.

Lynn Anderson, Ph.D., CTRS, CPRP, is Distinguished Service Professor and Chair in the department of Recreation, Parks and Leisure Studies at the State University of New York College at Cortland and project director for the New York State Inclusive Recreation Resource Center. Dr. Anderson has been active in the field of therapeutic recreation and inclusion for over 25 years. She has worked in both outdoor recreation and therapeutic recreation settings and has conducted research on inclusive outdoor recreation opportunities. She received her master's degree in outdoor recreation and park management from the University of Oregon and her Ph.D. in therapeutic recreation from the University of Minnesota.

Julie Andrzejewski, Ph.D., is a professor, activist scholar, and co-director of the master's degree program in Social Responsibility at St. Cloud State University in

Minnesota and the editor of *Oppression and Social Justice: Critical Frameworks*, and co-author of *Why Can't Sharon Kowalski Come Home?*, which was nominated for the Minnesota Book Award and received the national Lambda Literary Award. Dr. Andrzejewski has a long history of social action including founding a women's center, organizing nationally on GLBT, feminist, and disability issues, supporting legal actions against discriminatory institutions, serving as union president, initiating program development and curriculum transformation for global social responsibility, and directing grants to foster global peace and justice. She is passionate about teaching animal rights and the important connections between animal rights and global social and environmental justice. She is currently writing about animal rights and humane education.

ALESSANDRO (ALEX) ARRIGONI, PH.D., was born in 1971 in northern Italy. Three days after his birth he had a terrible accident. Alex spent his first ten years of life in and out of Italian and German hospitals, enduring 18 surgeries in the first five years. Thanks to his family's never-ending support, in 1997 he graduated in Philosophy at Siena University. His paper on animal rights philosophy, was published in 1998 (and 2004) as *Animal Rights: Toward a Civilization Without Blood*. In May 2006 he finished his Ph.D. studies in Methodologies of Ethno-Anthropological Research at Siena University. He applies cultural anthropology methodologies to a theoretical-practical research base in zooanthropology, concerning the human & dog partnership. Dr. Arrigoni felt himself to be a slaughtered animal since what happened in 1971. He represents the National Association of Mutilated and Disabled Civilians in Siena district, Italy.

CARRIE GRIFFIN BASAS, J.D., is an assistant law professor at the University of Tulsa, teaching disability rights, constitutional law, and ethics. Before coming to Tulsa, she was a visiting assistant professor at Penn State University and a visiting researcher at the University of Virginia. Her research interests include the intersection of disability law, animal rights, bioethics, and feminist legal theory. She has published her work in *Disability Studies Quarterly, The Review of Disability Studies, The Berkeley Journal of Employment and Labor Law,* and *The Food and Drug Law Journal.* She is one of the first women in the U.S. with a visible disability to hold a tenure-track position teaching law. Before becoming a law professor, Professor Basas was a disability rights advocate in nonprofit settings. Today, she serves on the Advisory Board of the Mitsubishi Electric America Foundation and the American Bar Association's Commission on Physical and Mental Disability Law. Professor Basas is a graduate of Swarthmore College and Harvard Law School. In 2001, the Ethel Louise Armstrong Foundation recognized her for "changing the face of disability," and in 2002, the American Association of People with Disabilities named her as an emerging leader in disability rights.

JUDY K. C. BENTLEY, PH.D., is an Associate Professor in the Department of Foundations and Social Advocacy at the State University of New York College at Cortland, and the founding Editor-in-Chief of *Social Advocacy and Systems Change,* a peer-reviewed social justice journal. She has published nationally and internationally on the topics of Symbolic Inclusion and Critical Animal Studies. Her research interests include youth transition, inclusive education, disability studies, and critical animal studies. Dr. Bentley serves on the Board of Directors of Access to Independence of Cortland County, Inc. and is the recent recipient of the SUNY Cortland President's Award for Excellence in Research, Service and Outreach, and the Civic Engagement Leadership Award.

SARAT COLLING grew up on Hornby Island, a small island off the west coast of British Columbia, where the wilderness surroundings inspired her passion to advocate for animal rights and environmentalism, a focus which continues to this day. She is currently completing a degree in Writing, Rhetoric and Discourse Studies and will be pursuing a masters in Critical Sociology at Brock University. Ms. Colling serves on the board of directors of the Institute for Critical Animal Studies and is the founder of Political Media Review, a reviewing clearinghouse for social justice media. Her research interests include critical media studies, critical animal studies, disability studies, postcolonialism, anarchist studies and transnational feminism. Much of her time is spent organizing and volunteering with activist organizations. Most recently she co-authored with (Anthony J. Nocella II) *Love and Liberation: An Animal Liberation Front Story* (Williamstown, MI: Piraeus, 2012).

JANET DUNCAN, PH.D., is the Director of the Institute for Disability Studies at SUNY Cortland. She is a founding member and the first Chair of the Foundations and Social Advocacy Deptartment of Education at SUNY Cortland. The department is committed to teaching pre-service teachers and graduate students about issues related to disability and the social construction of identities. Her research interests include international human rights for persons with disabilities, Education for All, and inclusive international development. She has written articles concerning communication rights for persons with disabilities and is currently working on a book about Michael Kennedy, self-advocate.

AMBER E. GEORGE, PH.D., is an educator, social activist, and artist currently teaching courses in ethical and social philosophy at SUNY Cortland, Le Moyne College, and Misericordia University. She received her doctorate in philosophy from Binghamton University in 2007. Her dissertation, "Interpreting Dislocation: Gathering a Sense of Belonging," employs various visual and poetic metaphors to analyze oppression based on race, gender, and disability. Themes of her work center on challenging the systemic nature of oppression as it materializes in various cultural situations such as in films and television. For many years she worked as an advocate, counselor, and community educator at the Southern Tier Independence Center in Binghamton, New York, where she assisted in fostering independent living for individuals with a broad range of disabilities.

ANNA GRIMM received her master's degree in 2005 from Bethel Seminary. She currently practices as a licensed marriage and family therapist in Lake Ann, Michigan. She has spent the last year immersing herself in the area of equine therapies and has recently become certified to practice by the EAGALA (Equine Growth and Learning Association) and model equine-assisted psychotherapy and learning. In addition to her private practice as a home-based marriage and family therapist, she has been working with Jacquelyn Kaschel and PEACE Ranch as the EAGALA mental health specialist team member. PEACE Ranch is a nonprofit, faith-based organization offering equine-assisted therapies and learning opportunities.

BILL LINDQUIST, PH.D., is an Assistant Professor and Associate Department Chair in the department of Teacher Education at Hamline University. Bill grew up camping and canoeing in the Boundary Waters Canoe Area. This led to guiding canoe trips and completion of an internship at Wolf Ridge Environmental Learning Center. He has led annual 3-day trips with urban elementary students to the Audubon Center of the North Woods. His passion for the environment included serving as environmental education specialist with the School Nature Area Project (St. Olaf College) and assisting schools in the establishment of nature areas on their grounds for use in the curriculum. Bill's expertise is in elementary science education with a particular emphasis on the use of inquiry to engage the learner.

JACK P. MANNO, PH.D., is an Associate Professor of Environmental Studies at SUNY College of Environmental Science and Forestry. His research interests include environmental studies, the practical application of ecological wisdom to governance and policy, ecosystem-based management, protection and restoration of the Great Lakes, and the relationship between indigenous environmental knowledge and western scientific knowledge.

LAURIE PENNEY MCGEE, CTRS, is the full-time project coordinator for the New York State Inclusive Recreation Resource Center at SUNY Cortland. In addition, she teaches for the Recreation and Leisure Studies Department and supervises student internships. Laurie has extensive experience in the area of recreation and inclusion and has worked in the inclusive recreation field since 1999. Laurie's work focuses on advocacy, systems change, and inclusive recreation in general. Laurie received her bachelor's degree in political science from Glassboro State College and her masters degree from SUNY Cortland in therapeutic recreation. Laurie is a certified therapeutic recreation specialist.

DAVID NIBERT, PH.D., is Professor of Sociology at Wittenberg University, where he teaches Animals & Society, Global Change, Social Stratification and Law and Society. His published works include *Domesecration: Animal Oppression and Human Violence* (Columbia University Press, forthcoming) and *Animal Rights/Human Rights: Entanglements of Oppression and Liberation* (Rowman & Littlefield, 2002). He co-organized the section on Animals and Society of the American Sociological Association and serves as a member of the section council. His research interests include the historical and contemporary entanglement of the oppression of humans and other animals.

ANTHONY J. NOCELLA II, PH.D., a scholar-activist, is a Visiting Professor at Hamline University in the School of Education. Nocella received his doctoral degree from Syracuse University's Maxwell School. Nocella focuses his attention on urban education, peace and conflict studies, inclusive social justice education, environmental education, disability pedagogy, queer studies, transformative justice, critical criminology, critical pedagogy, anarchist studies, critical animal studies, and hip-hop pedagogy. He has taught workshops in mediation, negotiation, strategic social movement building, and has assisted in a number of legal committees in North and South America. He has provided expressive and experiential education workshops with Alternative to Violence Program, Save the Kids, and American Friends Service Committee (AFSC) in hopes of increasing the peace and providing skills to revert violent conflicts to nonviolent transformation. He is on more than a dozen boards including the Arissa Media Group, Center for Gender and Intercultural Studies (CGIS), Institute for Critical Animal Studies (ICAS), and the Central New York Peace Studies Consortium. Nocella has written scholarly articles in more than two dozen publications, co-founded more than twenty active socio-political organizations, four academic journals, and is working on his sixteenth book, "Animals and War: Confronting the Military-Animal Industrial Complex," co-edited with Judy K. C. Bentley and Colin Salter.

NORM PHELPS has been an animal rights activist for 25 years and is the former spiritual outreach director of The Fund for Animals as well as a founding member of the Society of Ethical and Religious Vegetarians (SERV). He is the author of

The Dominion of Love: Animal Rights According to the Bible (Lantern, 2002), *The Great Compassion: Buddhism and Animal Rights* (Lantern, 2004), *and The Longest Struggle: Animal Advocacy from Pythagoras to PETA* (Lantern, 2007). A frequent speaker at animal rights conferences, his primary areas of interest are animal rights and religion, the moral foundations of animal rights, and the strategy of the animal rights movement.

ROBIN M. SMITH, PH.D., is an Associate Professor of Special Education at the State University of New York at New Paltz in the Department of Educational Studies/Special Education Program. Her research and teaching interests are in the areas of disability studies, inclusion, assuming competence, and social justice, and how meridian therapies support these issues. Dr. Smith is the author of numerous papers on disability studies, behavioral and cultural diversity, and inclusive education. Her current research explores teacher understanding and implementation of strength-based, person-centered positive behavioral support and broader concepts of motivational assessment to include quality of life values. She is a member of The American Education Association, The Association for the Severely Handicapped, and the Council on Exceptional Children as well as being an active member of the Association for Comprehensive Energy Psychology (ACEP)'s research committee.

KIM SOCHA, PH.D., is an activist from the Twin Cities, Minnesota. She sits on the board of the Animal Rights Coalition in Minneapolis and has certification in assisting survivors and perpetrators of domestic violence and sexual abuse in their recoveries. She holds a Ph.D. in Hispanic literature, with scholarship on topics such as surrealism and Latino/a literature and pedagogy. Her book *Women, Destruction, and the Avant-Garde: A Paradigm for Animal Liberation* (2012)—a study of intersectionality among radical feminist, animal liberation and arts movements—was published through the Institute for Critical Animal Studies' Rodopi book series. She is also co-editing and contributing to *Animal Liberation: Essays from the Grassroots* [tentative title] (McFarland, 2012), a collection of articles by Twin Cities activists.

VICKI WILKINS, PH.D., is a professor and international coordinator for the Recreation, Parks and Leisure Studies Department at SUNY Cortland. Dr. Wilkins serves as project faculty for the New York State Inclusive Recreation Resource Center. Dr. Wilkins' work focuses on diversity, inclusion, and recreation. She has been active in the field of recreation and therapeutic recreation for over 30 years and has won numerous teaching awards as a professor at SUNY Cortland. Dr. Wilkins received her master's degree in therapeutic recreation at Florida State University, and her Ph.D. in therapeutic recreation/family development from Penn State University.

A.J. WITHERS is an anti-poverty and radical disability organizer in Toronto and a co-founder of DAMN 2025, a radical cross disability organization that does political education and direct action on the issues of public transit, social assistance and globalization among others. A.J. came to radical organizing through the environmental movement on the Canadian West Coast.

Index

A

B

C

D

E

F

G

H

I

J

L

M

N

P

R

S

T

U

W

Z